COMMERCIAL DISPUTE RESOLUTION

Edited by

A Martin Odams
Research Assistant
King's College London

Joanna Higgins
Solicitor
Ashurst Morris Crisp

Construction Law Press
London
1996

Construction Law Press ® is the imprint of the Centre of Construction Law and Management, King's College London.

Published in Great Britain by
Centre of Construction Law and Management,
King's College London,
The Old Watch House,
Strand,
London WC2R 2LS
44 (0) 171 873 24 46
44 (0) 171 872 02 10
Email m.odams@kcl.ac.uk

ISBN 0-9514866-6-7

A copy of the CIP entry for this book is available from the British Library

Printed in Great Britain by Redwood Books Limited, Trowbridge, Wilts.

Acknowledgments

The editors wish to take this opportunity to express thanks to all who have contributed to this collection, without whose co-operation coverage of the subject area would neither have achieved such depth nor breadth. Special thanks are due to Art McInnis who produced his paper at very short notice towards the end of his sabbatical period in London.

The publishers and ourselves wish to thank Ted Pons of the American Arbitration Association for his kind permission in allowing us to reprint the new Construction Industry Arbitration Rules

Martin Odams
King's College London

Joanna Higgins
Ashurst Morris Crisp
July 1996

Contents

Part I
Adversarialism in Construction

Part II
Comparative Arbitration Issues

Part II (Contd)

Part III
ADR and Fast Track Procedures

Part IV
The Role of the Court

Appendix

Contributors

Ian H Bailey BArch, ARAIA, Barrister.

Andrew Baird PrEng, CEng, BSc(Hons), FICE, MSAICE, MAPM. Corporate Consultant, ESKOM, South Africa.

Andrew Berkeley, BSc, MSc.(LOND), FCIArb, Barrister and Registered Arbitrator.

Philip Davenport LLB, MIAA, Solicitor of Supreme Court of NSW, Lecturer, School of Building, New South Wales.

Richard Fernyhough, QC, LLB(LOND), FCIArb, Barrister.

Joanna Higgins, BA, MA(Cantab), MSc, ACIArb, Solicitor

Pamela Kirby-Johnson, Co Sec. IGPA, Sec FCA, Director-General GAFTA.

Edward Lightburn Development Director CEDR.

J Arthur McInnis, BA, BCL, LLB, LLM, FCIArb, Lecturer, The University of Hong Kong, Solicitor Hong Kong Consultant Baker and McKenzie.

Carole Malinvaud, LLM (HARV), Paris Bar, New York Bar, Gide Loyrette Nouel, Paris.

Charles B Molineaux, JD, Wickwire Gavin, P.C., Vienna, Virginia.

Sir Alastair Morton, Co-Chairman, Eurotunnel.

A Martin Odams, BSc.(Hons) MSc.(LOND), FRICS, ACIArb, King's College London.

Claude Reymond FCIArb., Prof Hon Lausanne University, Senior Partner, Reymond, Bonnard, Maire, Freymond, Tschum, Lausanne.

Richard B Potter, QC, BA LLB, Partner, Fasken Martineau, Toronto.

Professor Simon Roberts, London School of Economics and
Political Science

Peter Towson BE, LLM, PhD MIEAust, Chartered Professional
Engineer, Solicitor.

Professor John Uff, QC, Ph.D, FEng., FICE, FCIArb, Nash
Professor of Engineering Law, Director, Centre of Construction Law,
Kings College London.

Caselist

Legislation

Australia

Capital Territory

New South Wales

Australia (Contd)

New South Wales (Contd)

Australia (Contd)

Australia (Contd)

Western Australia

Canada

France

United Kingdom

United Kingdom (Contd)

United States

Statutory Instruments

New York Convention on the Recognition and Enforcement of Foreign Arbitral Awards

UNCITRAL Model Law on International Commercial Arbitration 1985

General Introduction

The title of this volume, and its contents, are intended to convey a particular approach to dispute resolution, focusing not on any particular procedure but on the commercial interests of the user, ie the potential parties to disputes. The work represents the edited, collated and expanded proceedings of the 8th Annual Conference of the Centre of Construction Law and Management at King's College London, held in September 1995. Both the conference and these papers have intentionally avoided the current but fast developing topic of the new English Arbitration Bill, now the Arbitration Act 1996. Mature consideration and reflection on that major legislative step will follow at a later date. It will remain important, however, to see the new Act in its proper context as part of the spectrum of commercial dispute resolution procedures, which must justify its own place. It is particularly appropriate, therefore, that the alternative processes and indeed the place of disputes within the construction industry should be considered at this time.

No conference or collection of writings on construction disputes or contracts can currently avoid the shadow of the Latham Report. Sir Michael Latham himself contributed the keynote paper to the 7th Annual Conference of the CCLM[1] where extensive consideration was given to risk issues, including the new Engineering Contract. Part I of the present volume addresses the approach of the construction industry towards disputes and is to be seen in the context of Latham's proposals for the avoidance of conflict. The first paper in this section is a frank and robust account of the Channel Tunnel project and its disputes contributed by Sir Alastair Morton, the Co-Chairman of Eurotunnel. The editors have, wisely, left Sir Alastair's contribution substantially in the characteristic form in which it was delivered. Many will recall that, on the day preceding the conference, 14 September 1995, Eurotunnel announced the suspension of interest payments to their banks. The organisers were particularly grateful to Sir Alastair for the contribution which he gave. It was followed by Ted Lightburn's paper taking a broader view of disputes and their commercial background, written after a long career in the

---

[1] *Risk, Management and Procurement in Construction*, Uff, J. & Odams, A.M. Centre of Construction Law and Management, King's College London, 1995.

construction industry leading to eventual conversion to the doctrine of conciliation. Ted Lightburn is now commercial direction of CEDR, the centre for promoting conciliated settlement. Next, Andrew Baird's paper gives an original view on use of the NEC (now the New Engineering and Construction Contract) within the special confines of the South African electricity supply industry. Their extensive use of NEC is often quoted. Mr Baird explains the merits of the form as seen in practice. Finally in Part I Joanna Higgins of Ashurst Morris Crisp discusses the particular needs of major infrastructure projects in terms of risk and dispute resolution procedures.

The remaining parts of the volume are divided between the three estates of dispute resolution—arbitration, conciliation and litigation. Each topic is treated comparatively, within the necessary limitations imposed by the papers. Part II has six papers on arbitration subjects, commencing with Andrew Berkeley's paper which draws a comparison between England and the US on the courts' policy in support of the arbitration process[2]. Peter Towson's paper then considers the Australian view of confidentiality following the recent decision of the High Court in *Esso v Plowman*[3] and the wider topic of the courts' powers to intervene in arbitration proceedings. By contrast, the paper by Richard Potter QC discusses the strong commitment to the arbitration process in Canada, following the adoption of the Model Law in each of the provinces and territories. The paper by Art McInnis (who is based in Hong Kong) charts the progress in England and elsewhere towards recognition of equity clauses, now fully integrated into English law as a result of the Arbitration Act 1996. The final two papers in this section discuss procedural aspects of arbitration: Pamela Kirby Johnson describes the use of user-specific procedures in the field of commodity arbitration; and my own paper develops the theme of predictability, conspicuously absent in most international arbitrations despite the apparent prominence of institutional rules and procedural laws.

Part III presents a number of different approaches to ADR and fast track procedures. In a new paper by Martin Odams, the links between

---

[2]   The paper is based on the author's dissertation submitted for the CCLM MSc in Construction Law and Arbitration.

[3]   (1995) 128 ALR 391

ADR and the desires of commece are examined in the context of progress towards achieving a workable regime. Philip Davenport discusses the working of the Building Disputes Tribunal of New South Wales which, despite its limited jurisdiction, has achieved substantial success. Ian Bailey describes an alternative approach to ADR developed through the courts of New South Wales. Charles Molineaux describes the full panoply of ADR processes (including arbitration) which are now available in the US, including construction specific procedures; and offers some timely comments on the Latham Report from an American viewpoint. Finally, Simon Roberts gives an alternative and radical view of the Woolf Report in which he questions the basic premises of the enquiry and its conclusions.

Part IV presents three papers with a range of current views on the use of court procedures. Richard Fernyhough QC discusses English litigation, including Official Referee's practice, in the context of other dispute resolution procedures; Carole Malinvaud discusses the role of the French court in relation to arbitration proceedings; and finally, Professor Claude Reymond considers the civil law approach to procedure both in terms of litigation and arbitration.

This collection of papers is launched by a stimulating keynote address delivered by Lord Mustill, Lord of Appeal in Ordinary and current President of the Chartered Institute of Arbitrators, who addresses the whole gamut of dispute resolution and avoidance issues. The conference as a whole was steered by the firm and able Chairmanship of Lady Justice Elizabeth Butler-Sloss whose valuable contribution to the proceedings must be acknowledged. The conference was sponsored and supported by Ashurst Morris Crisp, solicitors, whose senior partner, Andrew Soundy, also addressed the conference. This volume has appropriately been edited by Martin Odams, research assistant at CCLM and Joanna Higgins, solicitor with Ashurst Morris Crisp, to both of whom the Centre expresses its grateful thanks.

Professor John Uff QC
July 1996

Keynote Address

Lord Mustill

Our lives are dictated by custom, which changes from time to time and occasion to occasion. A present custom of conferences, colloquia, workshops, seminars and the like is to begin with a keynote speech. Although I have given more than one, I have never known what they are meant to be. The allusion sounds musical, but this is not convincing for the keynote is the lowest note, which can hardly be what the organisers intend. The keynote is also called the tonic, a word not apt to describe all keynote speeches which I have heard. Most often it seems to be an opportunity for a speaker to begin the proceedings by reflecting, often at considerable length, and in quite general terms, on a topic which interests him or her, and which has at least a distance connection with the subject matter of the meeting. It may contain much of value, but rarely serves to launch an interchange on practical matters.

I do not believe that the organisers of this conference can have intended me to speak in this vein, and I am glad of it. The timetable shows that I detain the audience for only a short time in advance of a series of carefully chosen interchanges on specific topics of contemporary concern. This is not the time for expatiation or generalities. I will therefore take the opportunity to make only four quite brief points, under the headings of fragmentation; the user; transparency; and spirit.

First, as to fragmentation. I use this term to emphasise what it is damaging to overlook, that the various methods of dispute resolution now in use, even where superficially similar, are not the same, and that these methods are not in a continuous spectrum, with formal litigation at one end and the most informal and non-binding types of mediation at the other, but are at distinct points on a spectrum which exhibits sharp discontinuities. This is the case, not only for the different main genera of dispute resolution, but also for individual species within each genus.

As examples we may take the two traditional methods, litigation and arbitration; other methods existed, but were not systematically discussed. These two differed in every respect, and were meant to differ. In medieval times the royal courts were quite incapable of handling contractual disputes between merchants, both through procedural inadequacies and the absence of a generalised law of contract. Around the Mediterranean littoral and to a lesser extent in trading centres elsewhere, private tribunals sprang up designed to provide a practical service, difference in form and substance from central justice, and owing no allegiance to it. These methods were, however, dependant for efficacy on the moral force of the agreement to submit to arbitration, and on the practical impact of peer pressure on defaulters. They were not proof against the cynical obligor for whom honour and disapproval did not outweigh the direct advantage of not being forced to perform. In many countries the problem was not solved for centuries, but almost exactly three hundred years ago in England some unknown genius devised the trick of making a voluntary arbitration what was called a "rule of court", so that in a sense it became an offshoot of legal proceedings and was reinforced by legal sanctions, so that the contract to submit future disputes to arbitration and to co-operate in the arbitration once begun, could much less readily be frustrated. This movement, which was two centuries ahead of anything which existed elsewhere in the world, was to give birth to a relationship between the court and the arbitral process which can properly be called a partnership. The term has become something of a cliché, but it remains apposite, and after a very rocky time some twenty or so years ago is now recognised as one of the cornerstones of an effective arbitration regime.

In much more recent times, the temptation to regard arbitration and litigation as opposite sides of the same coin has been reinforced by, in the first place, the movement for the liberalisation of commercial court procedures from the excessive orality and procedural straitjacket of the Rules of Court and of traditional adversarial methods. This began fifteen years ago, and to my personal knowledge was directly inspired by the example of procedures in international commercial arbitration. A few years later a counterflow began, when increasing dissatisfaction with the cost and duration of elephantine arbitration made the Commercial Court seem an attractive form of ADR, with its capacity to act with great speed and decisiveness, once convinced that this is what the situation really demands. Numerous other pressures, some born of exasperation and others drawing on the example of the trade arbitration tribunals which, entirely untrumpeted in the grand doctrinal texts and journals, have been quietly getting on with the determination of disputes with relative speed and economy, have spawned the strange concept of the "fast-track" arbitration. It is strange, or at any rate depressing, because one of the prime factors which has made arbitration seem attractive in the past is its capacity for speed, whereas the identification of a special category of fast-track procedure seems to acknowledge that arbitration in general is intrinsically "slow-track". We should not, I think, allow ourselves to fall into this way of thinking.

This vision of a convergence of litigation and arbitration is attractive, but misleading. There is a fundamental distinction between the two which has nothing to do with salaried tribunals, wigs and gowns and limitless cross-examination, and everything to do with the availability to the court but not to the arbitrator f the means to make the contestants do what he says. One of the recent buzz-words of arbitration, a world in which fashion often rules, is "party-autonomy". This embodies a simple truth, that the parties have agreed for their disputes to be resolved in a particular way and for the arbitrator to resolve them accordingly. This is not at all the case with the court. If you choose the court as a medium or if your opponent chooses it for you, the choice carries with it the entire package. Compute buffs of three or four years ago—a generation in this culture—will recall the acronym "WYSIWYG": What you See is What You Get. In court it is "WYGIWIS" : What You Get is What I Say. Consumer choice may come into the question at the most general and long-term level, but scarcely at all in relation to the individual dispute. The more the world of arbitration comes to emphasise that the power to choose the modes of procedure resides ultimately with the disputants, and thereby diminishes the arbitrator's room to impose his own ideas on the structure of the reference, the idea that litigation and arbitration inhabit the same world, albeit in different continents, becomes less and less tenable.

So also with the interface (another buzz-word) between arbitration and ADR. For a time it was possible to believe that arbitration was a form of ADR, but inevitably this idea has died away. Arbitration and litigation have this aspect in common, that the process is aimed at a hard-edged resolution of the dispute, in accordance with the best that the tribunal can make of the contract, the law and the facts. This resolution is imposed on the parties, whether they like it or not. The whole point of ADR, in all its manifold shapes, is that the solution is agreed, not imposed, and that it may engage a reconciled, if grudging, departure from an outcome which is strictly accurate in terms of law and fact. This makes the discontinuity between ADR and the essentially adjudicatory procedures of arbitration just as marked as that which exists between arbitration and litigation.

This leads to another aspect of fragmentation, which is internal rather than external. The use of the word "arbitration" in the singular disguises the fact that unlike the case of proceedings in court, where within a given legal system there will usually be one, or at most a very few, ways of conducting a dispute, so that litigation may properly be treated as a single institution, about which reliable generalisations can be made, this is not so for arbitration which has always existed in many different varieties, ranging from those which resemble litigation in every respect apart from being more costly, to those which are so informal and abbreviated that there is no resemblance at all. For the writers of texts and statutes, and for the organisers of and participants in conferences, it is convenient to describe all of these by the single word arbitration; and indeed this is harmless enough provided those concerned have always in mind that arbitration is not a single institution, and that the procedures grouped under its title are not monolithic. In recent years a failure to observe this has been a source of theoretical misconception, spilling over into the practical. Thus, for example, it was only by considerable effort and almost at the last minute that it was possible to divert the otherwise excellent discussions at UNCITRAL on the Model Law of Arbitration from treating as a paradigm that type of macro-arbitration with which most of the participants were familiar, and thus clamping the informal trade arbitrations which were and are the bulk of English international arbitrations into an inappropriate and restrictive mould.

This error is, I believe, well on the way to a remedy. That other buzz-word which has gained currency, "party-autonomy", emphasises that arbitrations are the creatures of consent; that there can be no arbitration in preference to litigation unless that is what the parties have agreed; no arbitrator in preference to a judge unless that is what the parties have agreed; and no procedures which do not conform with what the parties have expressly or impliedly agreed. Some arbitrators are uneasy about this, fearing that they may become, not the agents or even the servants of the parties, but their prisoners. For myself, whilst I sympathise, I believe this view to be mistaken. This is however no occasion to debate it, but simply to recognise that notwithstanding the use of the singular noun "arbitration"—a usage which it is impossible to avoid—there is not one procedure with one procedural philosophy, but many and various, all of which must be accommodated within any statutory, institutional and theoretical frameworks which may be put in place.

This reference to "party-autonomy" leads me to my second subject, namely the user. Now that this person is firmly back in the saddle, where he (or she) belongs, it is out of date to regard him as an absent friend, as the passive recipient of a benevolent prescription by others of what they conceive to be his best interests. Without the users there can be no arbitrations; without the user's true interests being accommodated, the procedure fails in its purpose. it is true that those wishes differ from user to user, and shift broadly with the passage of time. it is true also that since arbitration is essentially a one-off process, which once encountered the user never hopes to meet again, it is peculiarly difficult to find out what the user really wants. This means that assertions on what is the best legal and institutional framework for the practical conduct of arbitrations tends to be based on anecdote and personal conviction, rather than hard and quantitative evidence. This is a pity. We should try harder than we do to draw the user into our discussions, and it is a pleasure to see that some of them are represented here today.

My two remaining comments relate to attitudes rather than principles. The first is to emphasise the crucial importance of the Arbitration Bill, which I most earnestly hope will soon be brought into, and taken through, the legislative process. It involves no revolutionary principles, for indeed there is very little new law in it at least in its present form. But it is likely in my opinion to inspire a wholly new attitude. For too long has English arbitration law been the preserve of the text-writers and the experts impenetrable to the users for whom it is designed, and forbidding to those who want to assess its merits and possibilities before they choose to apply it to their future disputes, and who need to know what they are up against when a dispute draws them into its orbit. In is present shape the draft Bill, which now lives up to the standards prescribed by the first report of the Departmental Committee, brings a new and overdue transparency to the law. I think that we shall see the process opened up and made effectively available in a wholly new way.

Finally, I want to make a contribution to the English language. There are plenty of ugly words, so here is another: "Demachoisation", which I have patched together from some most interesting papers offered here today. Intransigence and cynicism are the curses of modern arbitration. Perhaps they can to some extent be designed out of the system by careful drafting of rules and contracts, to provide a less confrontational framework for dispute resolution, but I doubt whether Sir Michael Latham himself would suggest that this is a complete answer. Just as much an I believe be achieved by the simple creation, or more accurately re-creation, under the leadership of the lawyers of a culture of courtesy and moderation, neither of them of course the same as weakness or lack of zeal for the interests of their clients; and by arbitrators demonstrating the confidence, personality and skill to impose on those concerned the atmosphere of order and respect without which the resolution of disputes is so much more consuming of effort and skill than it has need to be.

I mentioned a short while ago the presence of users. I noticed the name of Sir Alastair Morton as the immediately following speaker with the same stimulation as the holiday swimmer who looks up to see the surface of the sea broken a few metres away by a triangular fin. Whatever he has to say is sure to be original, topical, unequivocal and forceful. Looking forward to this I will detain the audience no longer, and will simply light the blue touch paper and stand well back.

Part I

Adversarialism in Construction

1. The Channel Tunnel Contract: Conflicts and Interests

Sir Alastair Morton

Synopsis

This paper presents a personal view of the nature and extent of the inherent problems with the structure, objectives and outcome of the Channel Tunnel project.

Introduction

From the outset the significant difference with the Channel Tunnel project was that its construction was to be funded entirely by private capital. One could say, or might not wish to say, that was the fundamental problem, in that it confounded both British and French custom and practice in public works. However, the most important lesson the exercise teaches is the importance of original sin—the way in which the project was set up before the client even existed. On this point I am claiming absolution in advance for some of us on the client side.

The Nature of the Project

The client was not present at the start of the Channel Tunnel, it was promoted by a grouping of two parties—contractors and banks. Indeed, Margaret Thatcher, as she then was, said it would be done by private enterprise or not at all. This governed the process of promotion. The competitive process for the award of the concession agreement and the granting of the concession for an initial 55 years revolved around a bidding contest. The lowest price tender did not win. The winner submitted the most comprehensive and satisfactory bid on a number of counts. However, before a concession could be granted the two governments wanted to know that heads of terms with the railways had been signed, heads of terms with bankers were in place, and that heads of terms for a construction contract existed, and all of which appeared to fit together as a whole. Everything rushed forward to the front end, still with no client.

During the selection process, as it unfolded, the parties found themselves in a large room with two ante-chambers, or side rooms. The contractors left first, saying 'We've promoted our project, we specified its outline, the government has accepted it, we are now retiring into the room next door, and we are going to make money from building and transferring the project—"build, claim and deliver".' The own and operate, the 'O's in B.O.O.T., fell by the wayside. Build and transfer was the contractor's ambition, and they were quite clear about it. The bankers retired into the other side room, and said: 'We're going to make money out of arranging the financing and providing a part of it over the coming years'.[1] When the two promoters left the room, this left an empty room with a table in it and a sheet of paper upon it. On this piece of paper was written one word—'Eurotunnel'—the name given to the future client. Everything had to go on from there. The history is available to interested parties.

Basic Problems for the Project

Two types of original sin have surfaced so far; the failure to recognise the nature of the interaction between conventional public works procurement in two countries with the notion that it is executed exclusively by private enterprise, and secondly the promoters not forming a part of the client; in fact forming the opposition to the client. Then between us all we managed to stir into the pot a number of other things.

Procurement

In Britain, the public sector client traditionally appoints a consulting engineer to produce documents on his behalf which are then put out to tender. The result is often a less than satisfactory contract. This

---

[1] And make money they have, until yesterday. Something over £700,000,000 in margins and waiver and other fees have been paid to the bankers from that moment until this—that is £700,000,000 over and above the cost of money.

invariably results in a plethora of claims, and a good living is invariably made by many external parties in the course of the negotiation and settlement.

In France, there is less involvement of outside consulting engineers. The Engineering Services are not a strong element of the French construction industry, because much more is done in house by *les entreprises*. French construction firms are used to dealing with governments on a basis peculiarly their own—a lot of negotiated settlements are effected by the senior members of the project team retiring to a back room on a Friday evening or weekend; a great deal of furniture gets smashed, but when everybody comes out only one person speaks and then the cheque is put in the bank. That is a great over-simplification of the process but it is the tradition in France of public works contracting, and it depends on the expectation of a lot of repeat business. There is, however, only one Channel Tunnel!

Legal Environment

There are many people who could recite the governing law provisions perfectly,[2] so I won't even try. Put very simply, the governing law of the construction contract was "the common principles of English and French law"—these have not been found yet. I will, however, make the point that, culturally speaking, in French law there is a very important body of principle which considers the intention of the parties at the time of contract to be fundamental to the interpretation and enforcement of the contract. There are other markedly different principles, so one has some sympathy with all of the parties. For example, I have seen a memorandum written in the British Treasury on the subject of the railway contract, which happens to be governed by French law. One dating back to 1986 contains one of those famous marginal notes from a senior civil servant who concludes, with great insight, that 'there will be trouble over this clause sooner or later'.

Arbitration on the railway usage contract is now in progress. The duties of the parties—particularly the public sector parties to it—are at issue. We are seeking to rely on some pretty arcane and refined

---

[2] The paragraph alluded to is clause 66 of the contract.

principles of French administrative law, principles which have led to what any Anglo-Saxon lawyer would define as trouble—for those who think of it in English terms. It is hoped to settle this arbitration quite soon, so there's no case for commenting on it, other than to underline that cultural problems and legal drafting problems loom in the background.

The financing was arranged under English law. We have from time to time had occasion to grapple with vagaries of insolvency law in the two countries in which the assets of Eurotunnel are located—it would appear that these systems are totally incompatible, although French insolvency law has been updated. Under the present system at a certain point in the proceedings an action can be commenced by a much wider range of parties than is possible or even conceivable in England—any one individual shareholder can commence proceedings in France. From that moment on, once the court decides to involve itself of its own free will and without even sitting, the ability of the parties to continue with the enterprise is severely affected. Even so, continuity of the project is deemed the paramount concern, the secondary duty being the continuation of employment in the enterprise, and thirdly the interests of the creditors. This is rather different from the somewhat brutal practice more familiar in England, and in fact very difficult to administer in sympathy with other systems. There were many other cultural differences in the origin of Eurotunnel, each of which had discrete consequences, and some (not all) of which led to legal differences.

Environment on Site

It is common in France for the engineering profession to draft a plan, and secure investment for that plan before it goes ahead. Thus, the amount of capital invested into the ground by the contractors before any tunnelling began was much greater on the French side than on the British side, even allowing for differences in working or ground conditions. A lot more sophisticated control equipment, service equipment, logistical support equipment and so on was put into the ground by the French, and the benefit showed. A further practical cultural difference was the attitude towards the client and claims in site management on the two sides. On the French side, good records were kept, good information was exchanged from contractor to client on a monthly basis on the evolution of contentious matters, and every claim was resolved with the minimum of dispute, either during the period or towards the end. The result was that the final cost of the terminal on the French side came out above the original price, but by no means so far above it and with very little dispute and difference as to the outcome in the end between the parties.

On the British side there was a paranoid unwillingness to present claims. This was partly caused by the chaotic nature of the site records and the reality of five firms working together in explicit unwillingness to agree. This factor was underlined by the site-cost-control computer package—no-one could agree which was best, therefore the five built a new one. This computer system crashed twice in the first year, thus making it rather difficult to keep good records even if they were trying. They were, however, consistent in their unwillingness to present claims on a regular and measured basis, rolling them up and presenting a great big bang-crash-wallop of claims at the back-end of the project. Tremendous argy-bargy, minimal evidence, maximum noise—that's the British style.

This peculiarly British approach to disputes and claims created particular problems. The problems were perpetuated by two breeds of professionals, the more significant of which in my opinion was the quantity surveyor, followed by the lawyer. I will never forget a presentation early in the project by a TML engineer to our largely non-executive board. At the end of an extremely good presentation, one of the French directors enquired of the engineer what his role in the project was. He replied that he was a 'claims engineer'. The director, well-educated and logical of mind, said 'You engineer claims?'; 'You design and build claims?' The engineer replied in the affirmative on both counts. Everyone in the room collapsed with laughter; it was a perfect summary of exactly what was happening.

In his paper, Edward Lightburn deals with machismo amongst British contractors.[3] I think he may have included me in that category. I would not wish to argue lest I perpetuate the stereotype, but, in my

---

[3]   See Lightburn, E., *Machismo in Construction Industry Disputes*, Paper 2, *infra* p. 17.

defence, I would like to put machismo in context. Eurotunnel was always on the defensive—it was created after the agreement had been made and had no position of strength at all. For a variety of contractual and financial reasons examined above, Eurotunnel scarcely existed as a party—it could not control its purse, this was the bank's; and the banks would not permit amendment of contracts without their consent and agreement. In addition, the contractors had the right to stop work if they were not paid on time and, in the event of stoppage, compensation would be paid by the banks, therefore, every effort was made by the banks not to have work stop—and the contractors knew that.

There is an obvious need to contend with the machismo of contractors, and with the 'dynamic inertia'—as the newspapers call it—of 225 banks who never agree about much with each other, let alone with their borrowers. As a result it has been necessary for the client to be forceful, always recognising that we had little or no bargaining power. The art to the trick was similar to ju-jitsu; using one's opponent's strength to bring about the opponent's discomfiture, shall we say, rather than downfall. At the end of all that I was awarded the Institution of Civil Engineers' Gold Medal for my contribution to the construction industry.

Commercial environment

The construction works contract included elements of a target price contract, a lump sum contract and a procurement management contract—in effect it was a three part contract. This contract was held together—and at the back-end by bank insistence—by warranties and performance guarantees that put the fear of God into the contractors. This very quickly to led to confusion between the client and the contractor. The commercial reality of construction is that as things begin to go wrong the parties need to be able to get together and work things out. But there was soon fear on the part of the contractor as they began to design the project on the basis of their lump sum tender. The contractors soon realised they had not thought it through fully, desperation set in and they engaged a contract manager whose brief seemed to be, more or less, to blow the contract wide open. This strategy very nearly succeeded. We had to go all the way through the

disputes resolution process—which went in the contractors' favour—
and then the arbitration process—which went in our favour very
strongly—to halt the effort to break the contract open. The disputes
panel was favoured by TML—about which they have spoken
separately and regularly. Our view is that it did not work very well,
for a variety of cultural background, foreground and methodological
reasons. But the disputes panel was there, and one of the big problems
it caused was that its findings had to be paid for before you went to
arbitration.

The first though about "dispute resolution" that comes to mind is that
the English Court of Appeal had said that if a foreign arbitration
clause exists there can be no parallel *locus* for the English judiciary.
Since almost every contract known to me has a ICC arbitration clause,
and usually sited outside London, I thought we might not see the City
of London and most of the law firms in it much longer with us. Maybe
I misunderstood. The House of Lords sorted it out later.[4]

The incidence of disputes also increased when civil engineering
consortia became involved in mechanical and electrical works, and
then into the 'clever end' of it, signalling and the like. The original sin
there was the nature, the relationship and the structure of the parties,
and what criteria were introduced into those contracts. One wonders
whether it was an example of the contractors' Machiavellian skill of
the drafting of their lawyers at the outset coupled with there being no
client, or pure Sod's Law, that led to a situation that meant that the
cost of ensuring the interaction between the 'clever end' and basic
equipment, such as a plain ordinary tunnel and terminal, was under a
lump sum. Was it also Sod's Law, that this interface was being
designed as part of the lump sum, and that the client could not
intervene in the process at all, except by paying for variations. TML
was to design the solution but the design, before it could be built, had
to be approved by the Intergovernmental Organisation. Eurotunnel as
the client had the responsibility to get the scheme approved. One can
easily imagine the problem: if TML was to design a less-than-
adequate solution—shall we say, a design that was not good enough
even though they tried hard—and submitted it to Eurotunnel who, in

---

[4] *Channel Tunnel Group and Another v. Balfour Beatty Construction Ltd and Others* [1993] AC 334.

turn, submit it to the international body of expertise and consultancies for approvals. When comments and changes are suggested, the contractor interprets the changes as representing variations and waits for the instruction; the client refused to issue an instruction and a dispute arises. This is essentially what happened when the tunnel's equipment and transport system went into place. All in all, I think it's an absolute miracle and a tribute to a great many people that we've come through, and we've got a working and very safe system is in place at the end.

In spite of the difficulties and somewhat amazingly the Channel Tunnel got built; it got built because people had pride in what they were doing, because gradually the weaker parties from the original lead partition of work were weeded out, and gradually people who really knew what they were doing, who really cared about what they were doing, got a grip on it and finished it. Disputes, however, had by the end of the contract reached a deafening crescendo. The price for the tunnelling works came out well in the end, only 50% over original estimate. For a construction project as massive as the Channel Tunnel, the out-turn cost was not out of line when read together with on average a 45% cost overrun for every trunk road built in Britain in the past decade.

Conclusion

It goes without saying that a great deal of the foregoing is to be taken in the context of the current Private Finance Initiative. I have been until now the chairman of the Private Finance Panel and I fear this is where the blockage is. We are beginning to see a way through for the PFI, including just how much less the accepted bids on these projects are than the true public service comparators from the past; i.e. not what the budget price was when the public service sector project was launched, but what the out-turn cost was.

Under the PFI, Civil servants are now required to negotiate specifications, contractual terms and deals, and to transfer risk to people who are much more practised at it than they are—contractors, bankers, the operators and such like. It is, therefore, proving very difficult to achieve progress on PFI projects at the necessary pace—of the many projects under consideration, even with the approximate knowledge of what can be achieved by way of savings, achieving a signed contract is proving difficult, and no doubt, after the contract has been signed, the project will be tested for a period of time before it is allowed to proceed.

It is in this context alone that I wish to comment on Eurotunnel's current situation as announced yesterday—I mention this because it is philosophically relevant, not because I have a ready-made PR opportunity. Eurotunnel is currently engaged in discussions with its bankers, whether it wanted to or not, or whether it likes it or not, to re-consider the financial engineering carried out at the front end of the project. As an aside, this exercise has reopened the debate as to whether the Channel Tunnel project would ever have got off the ground with a more appropriate financing structure, or even with more parties, such as state-entities, included in the financing package—the answer is that it probably would have, but it would have looked very different. Reconsideration is now necessary because the facts dictate that we have to, and it is the facts that are driving us. We—Eurotunnel and the financiers—are reconstructing the financial superstructure to fit the operating infrastructure, and this is being undertaken mindful of the timing of the flows of money, as much as the directions or the quantities, although quantity does come into it. With hindsight, it is a great pity that Eurotunnel neither had endowed to it a truly long-term finance strategy, nor someone to shoulder the initial interest costs at the outset of the project.

2. Machismo in Construction Industry Disputes

Edward Lightburn

Synopsis

This paper presents the writer's observations of attitude and culture prevalent in the construction industry, and examines briefly specific problems and how they can be rectified.

Introduction

I have practised law as a solicitor for 35 years both in the City and with public and private sector conglomerates. For the past 12 years or so I have had my own consultancy practice advising construction sector clients and contractors in the UK and abroad. I am also Commercial Director of the Centre for Dispute Resolution—CEDR. Although I am a lawyer, in this paper I will touch on legal matters only indirectly when examining the wider issues, and then only to give an overview of the principles involved. Machismo is my underlying concern.

Construction Practice

They say first impressions are important. What immediately struck me when I came to construction law was that it was very different from other commercial worlds, even those which are closely related such as electrical and plant engineering and of which I had some experience. In the construction industry, people have been a part of it all of their working lives, often there were (and still are) families who have been involved in the construction industry for generations; people seem to work immensely hard within a hierarchical structure, and, somewhat refreshingly, without much 'side'. A tremendous amount of shouting goes on in all directions—without seeming to matter whether this is at one's own or the other side. The ability to listen or communicate is not commonplace, whereas interference in everyone else's business is.

The most striking analogy to a newcomer was that of the self-absorbed and tetchy white rabbit in "Alice"—quite why one was late, or where the important date was often remained a mystery.

Of course the above thumb-nail sketch presents a somewhat exaggerated—some would say wildly exaggerated—picture, but there has to be a degree of exaggeration to tease out what I believe to be the underlying problem in settling disputes in the construction industry. The root-cause of the trouble is, simply, the way people work together. This does not relate to the words of the contract, important though they are. At best words are only indirectly able to manage the way in which people work—attitudes do not change over night.

In the example I give below, let me just say the project is big. What of course is meant by big nowadays is absolutely huge, perhaps the entire annual budget of a small country; often the project will be international and involve a variety of disciplines; engineers, bankers, governments, planners, environmentalists, economists, lawyers, accountants, and so forth. My example indicates what typically takes place with this type of project.

Procurement

A short list of tenderers is chosen and intense lobbying begins; politics, with a large 'P' and small 'p' enters the fray. Prior to the contract being let the project will be under continuous review and change will be rife—this project is already streets apart from the sort of precision lawyers, and money men, like. In particular, design criteria will be in flux in a response to the conflicting aims of 'getting it right' and 'getting it cheap'. The prospective tenderers are invariably expected to take responsibility for these proposals. As a backdrop to the hard work, struggle, tears, misunderstandings, false deadlines and cut corners, the contract wording is being cobbled together from standard forms, frequently not in consort with the more subtle engineering picture emerging. As the roller coaster cannot go on for ever, the contract is placed with the engineering design criteria still under development.

Claims

Not very long after work starts the contractors make their first claims for more time and money, sometimes quoting contract conditions, sometimes not. At this stage nothing much is done about the claims, except that the client may make some deductions from certificates for reasons of its own. The pace gradually hots up; the claims and counter claims get bigger, cloaked with and backed by contractual argument. In the old days, this would go on for ever with hysteria mounting, global claims escalating and senior reputations at stake with the 'Emperor's new clothes' syndrome to the fore. The claims were destined all to be settled say, some years later if lucky and at great expense, in terms of both time and money, by playing a game akin to russian roulette in either the courts or in arbitration. Nowadays there is the growing use of adjudication or mediation at early stages in the process of dispute resolution, but this is by no means common practice. This aside, the real problem—whether or not modern methods are used to settle these disputes and claims—is the confrontational approach which is historical and endemic in the Construction Industry.

... and so to battle

The problem is therefore the automatic drawing up of battle plans based on the premise of attempted precision, which just is not there. Of course what this is all about is money. Simply put, A has told B that he is going to get the job done for £x, yet wants to be paid £y for it. Naturally, both are completely different figures, and, short of a miracle, there is only a slight chance of attaining the higher figure, or anything remotely near to it. A further absurdity is that the end figure can go way out of kilter when lawyers' and experts' charges are added in. It is virtually impossible for a judge properly to understand the fundaments of a complicated construction case when they are buried under myriad disputes concerning past events— actually, as time passes, neither side really understands the position itself in the mounting general confusion of contractual postulation, technical claim and counterclaim. The only certainty is that nobody can predict the result with any degree of accuracy—least of all the lawyers, because disputes of fact and differing expert opinions as to engineering matters rule, not matters of law.

Specific Solutions to Specific Problems

Culture

Schemes should be put into place where sufficient numbers of professionals, drawn from all levels of management are seconded to, for example, banks, potential clients including government departments or contractors to see how the other side lives. The object of this exercise would be that when they came back to roost they have a better understanding of *how* others get to where they want to get to, as opposed to understanding *what* they want which is usually fairly obvious anyway. Secondment initiatives are already in place, but not, I believe, Industry-wide. They are usually done on an ad hoc basis. Secondment is generally opposed as being "a waste of time", or on the basis of not being able to "spare him or her", or "I don't want them messing around here" (contractor about a potential sub-contractor exchange).

Prevailing in the construction industry is the fear of trying something new, something which may be outside the familiar pattern of work, or which might lead to the boss losing control. Mediation is a case in point. Most construction firms when asked to mediate, if a mediation clause is not in the contract, tend to refuse, but those few who do mediate almost always settle. The reasons given for not mediating are invariably:

- loss of control through the intermediary; or
- mediation is a sign of weakness..

On the first count, it is the parties who decide how to achieve settlement, not a third party mediator; on the second count, the 'real men don't mediate' attitude, this is machismo and plain nonsense. Based on my experience, I submit that the real reasons are more likely to revolve around:

- the parties' desire not to pay anything yet; and
- on the contractor's side, the fear of being bullied into settlement; or
- on both sides, the fear of admitting that the size of the claims and counterclaims are unsustainable.

This reasoning is terribly out of date and should be discarded.

"Neutralising" the cause of argument

A striking aspect of the dispute process on big construction projects is that as they escalate so does the acrimony they generate. The acrimony increases by each party believing that it is absolutely right and that the other side is at best incompetent or, at worst, a crook— again, fear is often the motivating factor. This attitude completely fails to recognise that the inevitable interplay between client, contractor and other advisors must mean that each will be less than perfect from time to time.

Responsibility for design is a particular case in point. It is often the case that the contractor is in theory made responsible for carrying out the design, when the client or his advisors have considered it necessary to intervene. Whether these interventions are made rightly or not, this practice inevitably erodes exact contractual responsibilities. In any large project, major lacunae in the design may occur and it is stupid to try to attribute precise blame when the project is in a necessary continuous state of change and development. In the neutralisation of disputes, it would seem sensible to have substantial sums of money set aside pre-contract, outwith contractual responsibility, to cover development contingencies under the direction of joint management teams and without necessarily attributing blame.

I quite realise that in putting this idea forward, I will raise the hackles of some in the industry; they will claim that this scheme is impracticable and anyway has been tried before. However, I well remember one Chief Executive saying to me that he could take anything but surprises when the finger just had to be pointed at someone. In other words, why not cater for a degree of uncertainty, which is inevitable anyway, in advance, as opposed to striving for absolute precision—*i.e.* what is the point in telling shareholders, financiers and others that something is going to cost £x when it is going to cost at least £y.

Contractual procedures

At the heart of a contract is the insistence that as far as possible problems are catered for and can be sorted out as, when, or if they occur. It has always seemed strange that where something technical goes wrong it is dealt with immediately, but disputes are left festering for months and even years, then handed over to the lawyers to deal with at arms-length. After all, the management and settlement of disputes is really only part and parcel of effective quality control—why hand over control to outsiders, unless one absolutely must, to play the game and only watch from the sidelines.

Apart from the Latham report,[1] whose practical importance is open to debate, I refer particularly to the experience gained on the new Dartford River Crossing and the Hong Kong Airport Project.[2]

An example of this in operation is the dispute resolution procedure on the Hong Kong Airport Project. On the ascent of that particular dispute resolution staircase, one can negotiate, mediate with an informal, confidential and "without prejudice" opinion if requested, adjudicate, arbitrate and finally, if not too exhausted, litigate. The general idea is that a dispute resolution obstacle course is created. In theory a disputant will have settled well before the final stair. Litigation will only take place in truly disastrous circumstances, most issues having been dealt with at stages 2 or 3 by trained mediators or adjudicators. These independent and trained professionals will have been on standby well before the contract was signed and before any dispute has actually risen. This approach is in its infancy and there will inevitably be teething problems, but it is, I believe, an important step forward in the management of disputes.

---

[1]   Latham, Sir Michael, *Constructing the Team*, HMSO, London, 1994.
[2]   Uff, J. & Higgins, J., *Structured Avoidance of Disputes* (1995) 4 ADRLJ 179.

The essence of mediation is that neither side 'wins', but interests are addressed, settled and paid off—this takes care of the machismo factor. Lawyers will have to relearn their roles as men and women of business, as opposed to mere technicians of litigation—this includes the ability to draft concise intelligible settlements. On the basis of this experience, mediation clauses should soon start appearing in numbers of commercial contracts.

Statutory procedures for settlement

There are very welcome signs that Arbitration in the UK is really getting to grips with reform of its procedure, in particular through the proposed New Arbitration Act. If arbitration returns to being a relatively quick and inexpensive process, lawyers may then again start putting arbitration clauses back into contracts. We also have the Commercial and High Court Practice Directions.[3] Hopefully these will impel the parties to settle early in the proceedings and without recourse to arbitration or litigation. If the judiciary really means business there will also perhaps be penalties for default.

In my experience, quite often the parties do not wish to settle because they want to keep their high claim and counterclaim figures on their books for some years—'virtual reality' in the construction industry accounts if you like. With any luck in the meantime other better contracts will come along to enable these claims and counterclaims to be settled at lower acceptable figures. This is commercial life and I do not condemn it. However, the judiciary has become a party to the game and ludicrous, lengthy and complex cases jam the courts—this makes a mockery of the legal process. The remedy is for the courts to instruct litigants to settle earlier, perhaps through the medium of non-binding mediation prior to the litigation continuing. Access to justice through the court surely means access for those who really need to get to court quickly, in particular the small and medium sized businesses, whether in construction or industry at large.

---

[3]   [1995] 1 WLR 262

Conclusion

I believe that the Construction Industry has to show a real will to alter its confrontational and somewhat devious attitudes. If we remain as medieval knights with our retinues clanking around in full armour but often with no wish to enter into combat, the construction industry will sink under its own weight. Lawyers and legal contract procedures in tandem with mediation and/or streamlined arbitration can help to corral disputes, but the real challenge to construction is to change its culture, a change which can be helped by the courts themselves being stricter with litigants. The signs are hopeful because the necessity for speed of action and rapid results will of necessity dictate good and timely commercial and judicial practice.

3. Adversarialism, Pro-active Management and the NEC

Andrew Baird

Synopsis

This paper draws on the author's extensive practical experience gained by introducing and using the NEC to control an annual capital expenditure programme of over £1bn. The effect of the NEC in reducing the severity of disputes is examined in this context. An action list for the various participants in the construction process is given in conclusion.

Introduction

The Latham Report [1] states that, "Endlessly refining existing conditions of contract will not solve adversarial problems. A set of basic principles is required on which modern contracts can be based. A complete family of interlocking documents is also required. The New Engineering Contract (NEC)[2] fulfils many of these principles..."

However, neither the Latham Report nor the words in the NEC family of documents will in themselves bring about the change the industry needs. Changes in behaviour come from the heart and have never come about overnight. Change has a better chance of success if it is motivated and supported by decisions and leadership at the highest level in the industry, and followed through with total commitment until the acceptable behaviour becomes a way of life. The various implementation committees arising from the Latham Report are now

---

[1]   Latham, Sir Michael *Constructing the Team , Joint Review of Procurement and Contractual Arrangements in the United Kingdom Construction Industry. Final Report, July 1994*, HMSO.

[2]   The Institution of Civil Engineers London. The NEC System is published as a series of documents of which the *Engineering and Construction Contract Second Edition 1995* is one. The NEC is published by Thomas Telford Services Ltd, London.

in place, these seek to facilitate the 'top down' change process. A question remains as to whether the same attention is being given to the basics of organisational strategy, and actions within the project team itself.

In South Africa ESKOM has committed itself to the NEC philosophy and are treating it as a Management Board project. To date ESKOM has let over 50 contracts using the NEC and has pioneered the use of a Minor Works version of the NEC on over 1500 contracts in its £100mn per annum electrification programme. Product Design & Supply, and Maintenance versions of the NEC are also under trial, ahead of the ICE's publication of these documents for general consultation. Many of the changes to the First Edition NEC, now available in Second Edition form as the Engineering & Construction Contract, are the result of the ESKOM experience to date.

Understanding construction industry behaviour

The best way to reduce the number of disputes is to avoid getting into them in the first place. However, disputes are only the visible part of the low productivity iceberg. It is time for a complete reorientation by comprehensive training from board room to college and across the service providers from draughtsman and consulting engineer to solicitor and construction judge. The NEC can be used as the basis of that reorientation.

Before a change of attitude and culture can be brought about, it is necessary to understand what makes people do the things they do. Human nature is pretty consistent. People are not usually born with an attitude problem; they simply respond to the environment around them. People develop a culture from the company they keep, again responding to the environment around them. A pschycologist will point out that in all areas of human activity, an *event* is usually the response to a *pattern of behaviour* which in turn is the reflection of a *system*. This simple analogy holds good in religion, parenting and politics and must surely apply to the construction industry.

Focusing on disputes within the construction industry, the legal profession must shoulder some of the blame for the high level of adversarialism in the industry. However, lawyers and even corporate legal advisors are only undertaking the duties asked of them by those who instruct them. Sadly these managers are often senior engineers within the controlling boards of clients and contractors' organisations who, cocooned in their Ivory Towers and remote from the judgmental realities of the construction site, believe they know best usually with the benefit of hindsight. Clients have responsibilities too and as the Latham Report states "implementation begins with clients".[3] It can be seen that *events* will only change if there is a fundamental overhaul of the *system*.

The main causes of disputes

A comprehensive research report conducted in Australia,[4] and in consultation with over 90 construction related organisations in 16 countries, concluded that:

> *"The comment was made repeatedly around the world, including Asia, that the greatest cause of claims and disputes in the construction industry is related to problems in contract documentation, including errors, contradiction, ambiguity and the late supply of documents, which gives rise to delays and inefficiencies and hence claims."*[5]

This echoes the author's experience, if anything the situation is now worse than in 1988 when those observations were made. This is not surprising. Even ignoring a possible decline in drafting skills, clients faced with the high cost of finance and increased competition within their sphere of operations take longer to sanction the go-ahead for their projects in order to be more sure of success. However, once the

---

[3]   *Op cit*, page vii.
[4]   Australian Construction Services, Department of Administrative Services and several other participants . *Strategies for the Reduction of Claims and Disputes in the Construction Industry A Research Report*. Queensland, November 1988
[5]   *Ibid*, Summary p. 2.

decision to invest has been taken, clients naturally expect construction to start almost immediately. Inevitably documentation is rushed or, if standardised specifications are used, every standard document which may be considered to have some relevance is included in the contract with little thought as to how it may relate to other documents.

How the NEC can address each of the main causes

Ambiguity and contradiction

Most contract documents are developed by a team of people. Organisational structures (the *system*) have a substantial influence on the *behaviour* of that team. In many project teams, particularly of the matrix type commonly used in multi-discipline projects, the Project Manager is often seen as the 'gatherer of consensus', or the person who looks after time and cost. Technical disciplines or the lead discipline dominate the structure and quite naturally each discipline wishes to use the standard form of contract prescribed by its professional institution or the in-house version of it. Head office design teams are often structured on the basis of discipline yet site execution is on a regional or system basis.

With each discipline endeavouring to do its professional best the 'gatherer' can only attempt to placate the various technical interests. Little account is taken of the relevance of different pricing or design-procure-construct strategies and forms of contract are 'adjusted' to accommodate sub-contract work of a different discipline. To make matters worse, when free issue materials are the order of the day, the corporate materials manager with an inflated centralised buying ego *tells* the project manager when he can expect his materials and often responds only to the project manager who shouts the loudest. Corporate commercial then require their 'corporate directives' to be included in each contract document 'by decree' again irrespective of how these may relate to all the other specifications or to the conditions of contract. The project manager armed with his sophisticated critical path planning software is then expected to use his communication skills so as to complete the project on time and within budget.

Such an arrangement is hardly likely to minimise ambiguity or contradiction and simply means that the project team will be fighting fires from day one of the contract. Furthermore, the natural work breakdown of a project is usually into a series of multi-discipline operating systems which inter-relate with each other to work as an operating whole. Functional discipline is irrelevant to the end user[6].

A strategic policy to use the NEC (the System) as the only form of contract for the whole project team corrects the above mis-alignments overnight. Being multi-discipline it allows project teams to be structured and develop contracts on a system *or* lead discipline basis. All members of the project team are working to the same commercial terms. Discipline flexibility is enhanced because there are no discipline related terms in the contract and hence fewer special conditions are required. A back-to-back form of subcontract is available for use by contractors with their subcontractors. Even use of the term *Project Manager* in the NEC helps to redirect authority for project performance, and the actions of the *Project Manager* in the contract back this up.

For his part, the Project Manager must now (with the correct system in place) change his behaviour and take ownership of all the contract documents before they are issued for tenders and check, check, and check again for ambiguities and contradictions. The Project Manager's actions under NEC are clear and he can be held accountable for them. Part of his skill as a Project Manager is to then ensure that he passes components of that accountability to the relevant contributing member of the project team. He must of course be ruthless in his rejection of any requirements which deviate from the NEC terms, conditions and procedures. He is no longer the gatherer of consensus.

Clients must change (or check) their behaviour by ensuring that they have given the Project Manager the authority, training and support he needs to exercise his role correctly and of course have appointed the appropriate person in the first place.

---

[6] Baird, P.A., *System Orientation for the Project Team— the key to greater customer satisfaction.* INTERNET 90 Paper and International Journal of Project Management, Vol. 9 No. 2 May 1991 Butterworth-Heinemann.

Errors

It goes without saying that a single point of responsibility for the preparation of contract documentation as described above, as well as for subsequent change control and contract administration—which the NEC requires—must promote a reduction of errors. The key to such benefits being available to the Employer is that, unless there is a problem of performance, the Employer must exercise his responsibility by ensuring that the same Project Manager, as far as it is practicable, sees the project through from conception to close out.

The rush to 'start construction tomorrow' with all the errors of both fact and judgment that such action brings about can also be tempered by adoption of the NEC. The Project Manger simply needs to take one document (the System) to the meeting with his client and explain that his client has a choice of strategies. Starting tomorrow could mean using Options E or F, which are cost reimbursable forms of contract, but if the client requires more definitive budgets the Project Manager has Options A and B in his tool kit and can explain that in order to use these tools properly he needs the time to prepare complete scopes of work. With design by either Party included in the NEC, the time to construction start can be reduced if the client is prepared to let his project manager develop performance specifications for contractors to offer their services on a design and construct basis rather than the longer design - procure - construct method.

An *error* control aspect of the NEC often not readily appreciated is that the Project Manager and his designers can concentrate on complete scopes of work but not necessarily correct scopes of work— if Options A B, C or D apply. Some project data are inevitably provided later than other data. However a practice which so often causes major errors and delays is one in which scopes or designs are prepared on an interrupted basis by several people and held back until the missing data are made available. When the missing, but correct, data arrives they are either too late or hurriedly inserted without due care of the inter-relationships with other existing data. The inevitable errors and delays lead to disputes.

With changes being measured in the NEC on the basis of Actual Cost plus Fee—which the effect of the change causes—the Employer is not so exposed to opportunistic pricing of changes which traditional bill rates or lump sum contracts often lead to. The project team can therefore concentrate at one sitting to prepare a fully integrated design using assumed 'best estimate' data where the correct data is missing and then when the correct data does arrive, deal with the effect of the change, if any, on the Actual Cost plus Fee basis—this is also fairer to both parties. The overall project is not delayed by late supply of the total scope package, only by the effect of the change, and continuity of design effort reduces errors.

Errors of understanding and commercial judgment by both Parties due to the prolix language of traditional forms of contract are legion. Some users may not like the way NEC allocates risk in its Core Clauses, but at least there is clarity which a tenderer can allow for and the Employer knows and is prepared to pay for. The correction of Defects and the list of compensation events are examples of this point.

Late supply of information

The NEC's early warning system,[7] Accepted Programme[8] and compensation events[9] deal specifically with delay to information, they are a powerful combination and provide a stimulus for good project management. Because of the possible uncertainty as to how Project Managers will use Clause 61.5, Contractors are already making good use of the early warning procedure—and it works. Other changes to behaviour as discussed above are having a similar effect. Because of the comprehensive compensation event procedure, Project Managers will only fall behind on information delivery once. Many a hot fax machine and the tight time periods in the compensation event procedure have motivated Project Managers to stand firm on their commitments and the commitments of others to them.

---

[7] Clause 16
[8] Clause 31
[9] Clause 60

Other features of NEC which can reduce adversity

The previous section highlighted some suggestions for restructuring of the project team and how the NEC (the System) can be used as a catalyst to change *behaviour* and reduce the number of 'built-in disputes waiting to happen' (the Events). Equally important is the NEC's role in changing the nature of adversity that will occur by reducing the impact and cost of it to the Parties as well as preventing it developing into a recognised dispute with a life of its own to the ultimate cost of clients. This section provides some examples.

Procedural precision : The 'is-it' or 'is-it-not' test

On one early ESKOM NEC contract some 34 unresolved compensation events had been in debate for over four months and relationships were deteriorating. The Contractor exercised his right to refer to the Adjudicator and the daunting task of dealing with 34 claims commenced. The Adjudicator, having studied the details, convened a meeting with both the Project Manager and Contractor present. All 34 issues were resolved on merit in a single meeting leaving only the extent of cost to be finalised. The compensation event procedure is so precise that a very simple test could be applied to each issue. Namely, was it a compensation event or not, and if so which one. Changes to the Works Information were the main culprit and not difficult to determine.

The requirement for method statements in the Accepted Programme will obviously further reduce adversity that may still exist relating to quantum. Again the 'is-it' or 'is-it-not' test can be applied to the Contractor's resources. Further debate then relates only to admissible cost as defined by the Schedule of Cost Components. The point being made is that the *nature* of adversity has changed from being judgmental sessions between people determined not to lose face over rigidly held opinions of merit and contract interpretation, to issues of fact relating to application of resources and their Actual Cost as defined in the contract. This is far less damaging to relationships and does not require expensive man-hours or legal advice for its resolution.

Allocation of risk

The clarity of risk allocation and liability can lead to heated debate during the tender phase, particularly in the process plant sector of the industry, with NEC's silence on the matters of direct and indirect losses and force majeure being the main stumbling blocks. This is now being attended to as described later in this paper.

The process of selecting *conditions of contract* in the Contract Data and completing the task itself is another area where NEC contributes to the avoidance of formal disputes. The user can no longer habitually quote the standard form he feels comfortable with and complete a few details relating to dates. He has to think about how risk it to be allocated. A steep learning curve for some. On early use of NEC the Project Manager had a tendency to allocate all the risk to the contractor and for good measure impose monstrous monetary constraints in the Secondary Options. Many clients and their project managers think that such punitive action will at last get the job done on time. Until they realise who is paying for their actions and at what cost. Realism eventually prevails and client and project manager armed with a better understanding of the procedures in the NEC, which already have the effect of improving contract control, arrive at Win-Win data rather than Win-Lose data. Open debate in the NEC Users Group assists greatly in this regard, and for the good of the industry.

The project manager and his client have now learnt that passing all risk to the contractor and imposing excessive damages for poor or late performance is probably not in his best interests. The contractor realises too from the list of compensation events that his days of being able to pass the implications of anything outside his control onto the client (as per the FIDIC Yellow Book Clause 26.1(h)) are also over. He now has to plan for float in his programme to cater for strikes and supplier delays and ensure that critical node points in his network are given maximum management attention with alternative plans in place in case problems arise. This is the level of performance clients require and, in return, the float in the programme under the NEC is the contractor's and remains so.

Although the debate at tender stage can become a little heated and prolonged as each side haggles about the Contract Data, once agreed at least both Parties know where they are going and which are the critical issues they have to manage.

Flow Charts and Guidance Notes

The provision of comprehensive Flow Charts and Guidance Notes is unique to the NEC system of documents and should assist greatly in enhancing the commercial role of the NEC system. Although not to be relied upon for interpretation of the contract terms, it is common sense that they will be extremely persuasive for contract practitioners in both Parties. This in itself should prevent many potential disputes from going any further than the coffee bar.

The role of the Adjudicator

Clients generally employ at least one if not a team of legal advisors. It is a fact of corporate life that these advisors are usually higher up the corporate ladder than the average in house project manager, often reporting directly to the Chief Executive. If they are costed as a corporate overhead, their services are "free" to the project budget and the total cost of procurement is distorted. It is also usual for these lawyers to operate across the full spectrum of the clients' operations. Hence that all important in-depth experience of the nature of construction disputes is not always present, consistent or appreciated. Construction contracts are regarded as just another "agreement". The idea that an Engineer or Architect, particularly one that is not in the client's direct employment, should have the contractual role of solving disputes on the client's behalf, and what's more as judge and jury of his own performance, is quite unpalatable to the corporate lawyer. The Chief Executive, having hired his legal advisor to protect his interests in the first place would readily agree. Arbitration using yet another engineer or architect as the arbitrator is just as unpalatable even if he has all the necessary legal qualifications. So it is off to court we go, or to an arbitrator. The use of formal legal process becomes the behaviour of the day.

The author is continually amazed that contractors and professionals in private practice are so surprised by this behaviour. It is the inevitable result of the corporate system. This is why many clients, including ESKOM, took instant dislike to the dispute resolution clauses in the First Edition of the NEC with its default of using only arbitration. The Second Edition overcomes this.

The role of the *Adjudicator* as intended to be used in the Second Edition of NEC (now the Engineering & Construction Contract) has many advantages. Some are listed here :

- For the corporate lawyer, apart from its novelty value, at least some form of independence is assured, the incumbent is known before a dispute arises and the lawyer may feel he could influence or advise on the selection. The option to litigate (although under very limited circumstances) after the adjudicator's decision is still there.

- Contractors, although at first objecting to sharing costs equally for resolution of disputes which inevitably they are likely to raise, realise it is a much quicker route to a definite outcome (whether favourable or not) as distinct from a global recommendation so often the outcome of the Engineer's quasi-judicial role or that of a mediator often used as the first line of dispute settlement.

- An ironic feature of human behaviour pertinent to the role of the Adjudicator is that the Project Manager is not likely to allow much for his services or indeed budget for them at all. If in private practice, the Project Manger would have to highlight this potential cost to his client, and the in-house Project Manager's superiors would also need some convincing to allow for such costs. In both cases, it could be seen as an indication of poor performance. The outcome is that the Project Manager is likely to be motivated to foster satisfactory relations with his Contractor in order that they resolve problems between them or before they arise, thus avoiding the use of the Adjudicator at all. This is certainly the ESKOM experience.

- Although not required by the contract, the Parties could agree at the outset to use the Adjudicator pro-actively by requiring him to perform a periodic review at agreed intervals of the health of the project and in particular the relationships on site. The apparent additional cost to the Parties could even become a saving as potential disputes are nipped in the bud and the Adjudicator's cost of familiarisation is not incurred if and when a dispute does arise. The client could be more easily convinced to budget for such cost as it could be proposed as an insurance in his interests and not the cost of poor performance.

The improved procedure for the use of an Adjudicator now included in the Second Edition of the NEC is one of the main reasons for ESKOM abandoning its 'licensed version' of NEC and in future using the "Black Book" unamended.

The tribunal

In the Second Edition of the Engineering and Construction Contract provision is now made for the formal dispute resolution process to be selected in the Contract Data. The obvious choice is arbitration or litigation.

The author has designed for ESKOM a two stage process within the *tribunal*. A Senior Executive Tribunal may be followed by litigation in the Supreme Court. This ensures that the benefits of ADR are included in the dispute resolution process before rushing to formal legal process. The Adjudicator clearly can only act for the Parties in accordance with the contract. He cannot allow commercial relationships or other external influences to cloud his judgment and the Parties would not wish that he did. However the stark reality of arbitration or litigation being the next step is something most clients would like to avoid. The ESKOM Executive Tribunal is designed as an informal process to apply experts to the matters in dispute with the default that should the process not produce a settlement or should the time periods within the process be violated, then either Party can withdraw and revert to litigation.[10] The process provides for the Parties, by agreement, to use arbitration to settle the dispute if it is felt that given the nature of the dispute this would be the more objective path to follow.

The Executive Tribunal is attached as an appendix to this paper and comment from readers would be welcome. The outcome of the ESKOM approach will be of interest. However, as the *Adjudicator* has only been called twice in around 1500 NEC contracts let by ESKOM—with speedy resolution being possible on both occasions— the Executive Tribunal is likely to remain untested for some time to come. With the unknown—'not tested in the courts'—aspect of the NEC, the Executive Tribunal approach is comforting to both contractors and ESKOM senior management.

The opportunity to retrain *all* contract practitioners

With the NEC being so radically different to other forms of contract used in the industry, and certainly to ESKOM's previous in-house forms, training in the use of NEC before applying it is considered essential. This in itself can make a substantial contribution to an increase in productivity and the reduction in disputes; not just because of the introduction of the NEC and the benefits this might bring with it, but in the realisation as soon as training commences that the level of expertise in contract development and contract administration is appallingly low. The lack of understanding at all levels within the organisation of the simple inter-relationship of time, cost and quality much less the basics of good project management is frightening. What is more frightening is that ESKOM is not alone in this respect.

Initially training was provided for by ESKOM Commercial Resource Management to staff in all operating Business Units. This training was charged for on a cost recovery basis, but did not attract those who thought they did not need training. More recently in-house training

---

[10] See also Uff, J. & Higgins, J., *The Structured Avoidance of Disputes.* (1995) 4 ADRLJ 179, the similarity between the ESKOM tribunal and the recommendations included in this paper are significant and merit further appraisal.

has been charged as a corporate overhead and augmented by a hypertext software package developed for ESKOM by educational experts from Pretoria University. This has attracted more trainees, but there is still a long way to go. It is not a one-off exercise either. Staff turnover and problems with continuity of application require training to be on a continuous basis. With some 25 Business Units letting contracts this is a daunting task. Accreditation principles are now being negotiated with the Staff Unions as practitioners will eventually be examined on their knowledge and 'licensed' to operate NEC documents.

Such training can of course be arranged for any form of contract, but the benefit to ESKOM of having only one system to prepare for and teach with all disciplines mixed in the one session speaks for itself. In fact it is doubtful if training on all the Mechanical & Electrical, Civils and Building discipline-based documents published by the various joint industry committees and FIDIC would be practicable and at best would be generic in nature. There are plenty of courses on contract law but these do not teach administrators how to operate a contract. The introduction of the Product and Maintenance Contracts is of course made much easier by the similarity they have to the Engineering and Construction Contract. The benefit to ESKOM of the Minor Works version for inexperienced staff to cut their teeth on has been substantial. It is also quite gratifying to receive similar feedback from the Consultants and Contractors working for ESKOM who regularly demand places on the ESKOM courses.

The role which NEC is playing in the awareness of and increase in contract administration skills deserves the highest recognition. It *must* change attitudes and reduce adversity as the level of understanding spreads.

Does the commercial role of the NEC really work ?

There are three categories of problem areas which are worth mentioning. Problems with the NEC itself, problems associated with its introduction and problems associated with its role as the agent of change (the catalyst) described above.

The contract document

The NEC Engineering and Construction Contract is claimed to be a contract suitable for international use in all sectors of the construction industry. However its critics claim it falls short of this and is biased towards works of Civil Engineering. The critics are often reluctant—or unwilling—to be specific about the shortfalls. But from tenders received in the Process Plant sector (usually for M & E works), it is obvious that these relate partly to the absence of references to "technical" matters such as procedures for testing and commissioning, import permits, provision of operating manuals and 'as-built' drawings. The answer to this criticism is the obvious one that such matters do not belong in Conditions of Contract and can better be dealt with in specifications, *i.e.* as part of the Works Information. Indeed, NEC is designed to act this way including in its relevance to 'Civil and Building' works. This drafting principle not only broadens the application of the NEC but also provides its users with greater flexibility to define such needs as each client requires them to be handled without the need for special conditions of contract. Its seems, however, that as long as there are references to adverse weather and physical conditions within the site, the document is considered a 'Civil' document. This is unfortunate, both matters relate to risk allocation, but clearly have a less significant—but never non-applicable—impact on scopes of work which have a predominant M & E component.

The far more serious criticism is that clauses dealing with limitation of liability and force majeure are absent, thus rendering the Contractor's risks unlimited. This may not have such a serious—again, never non-applicable—impact on Civil and Building works, but clearly it does for Mechanical and Electrical works and for all works in a process plant environment. The NEC Panel has convened a task team of experts to deal with these issues and the resulting changes will be included in a future third edition. It can be expected that the NEC approach to these matters will be a refreshing improvement on the prolix and vague language so often found in traditional plant related contracts or as drafted by contractors' lawyers in qualifications to their tenders.

Implementation of the NEC contracts

Forms of Agreement, Performance Bond, Guarantees and other standard documents often included in traditional construction contracts are not provided in the NEC documents themselves, although some assistance is now provided in the Second Edition Guidance Notes with examples of the drafting which may be used. Traditional Conditions of Tendering may need to be revised if only to have matching terminology and to delete the prolix language now out of keeping when matched to the NEC style of drafting. Other in-house documentation and procedures will need review and revision, but this will result in a welcome rationalisation and alignment of a number of similar procedures previously required for the several different documents. It is then a case of education, education and education. The overall cost of implementing the NEC documents should not be underestimated. For some organisations this will be regarded as just that—a cost. For others it will be regarded as an investment.

The NEC's role as the agent of change: a health warning

As with the introduction of any other new management system, especially one which highlights inefficiencies, there is bound to be a tendency to blame the system for all the organisations' new ills, and for some parts of the organisation to resist the change on the grounds of cost, and comfort with the existing status quo. The ESKOM implementation programme has highlighted an almost complete ignorance of the presence and function of conditions of contract, (particularly in the technical disciplines) and knowledge of the benefits and techniques of Project Management even in well established project management teams.

There is no doubt that the clarity of the NEC documents will demonstrate to many project managers—particularly in client organisations—that they are grossly under resourced, both in manpower numbers and skills. There are no "extra" procedures in the management of an NEC based contract over the management of a contract based on the traditional forms. Traditional contracts often state a right or an obligation of a Party. As the early sections of this paper illustrated, however, many of those obligations are not recognised or practiced. The NEC drafts those same obligations in the form of time limited actions. People must be available to act within the stated time limits, suitably empowered and capable of carrying out the actions of them or the Party they represent will be in breach of contract. It is that simple.

With the current trends of down-sizing and out-sourcing by many large capital works clients, there will be a grave danger that, upon realisation of their lack of manpower resources and skills, they will out-source the total capital works development programme, and thereby 'throw the baby out with the bathwater'. Hence, the opportunity for real change through industry wide synergy—that which Latham considers to "start with clients"—will be lost. It is dangerous to assume that the manpower and skill base in the independent project management companies and consultancies is any better than the client may perceive his is. It might only be a matter of degree and one for which it is not worth selling the family silver and losing overall control.

The benefits are beginning to show

It is still early days yet, but the objectives set for NEC are already being recognised. ESKOM's Majuba Power Station Project Manager has described NEC as a breath of fresh air. The main comment from the Majuba Project team—£2.5 Billion and over 700 contracts involving every discipline—are that they wish all their other contracts were based on NEC. The more tangible observations so far can be listed briefly as follows:

The need to exercise contract options and complete extensive contract data has forced users to gain a much greater awareness of what the (general conditions of) contract actually means and requires of them. Younger engineers and technicians have appreciated this enormously. Day-to-day discussion is now about risk allocation and responsibility, neither of which were uppermost when using the previous conditions of contract.

The accountability placed on the Project Manager causes him to act more professionally and diligently. The powers given to the Project

Manager still cause some anxiety to contractors and to more senior in-house staff who feel they have lost a degree of control. A "Project Managers Manual" outlining all his actions and responsibilities would assist. An awareness of contract strategy has developed overnight for all engineering disciplines who were hitherto locked into the common practices of their respective professions.

The interest being shown in the NEC by many clients, professionals and contractors in South Africa can be ascribed to many things. The mood of the 'rainbow nation' to do things differently to the way it did things in the past is undoubtedly a contributing factor. The will to want to work together in a spirit of mutual trust and co-operation is another. This is demonstrated vividly in the SA NEC Users Group Association meetings. Issues of the day are dealt with head on and not pushed under the carpet. However the major factor has to be the need for an increase in productivity, skills and the drive for standardisation. The South African Government intends to standardise forms of contract and considers this to be the only way to break down vested interests in the industry and operate as the means to accelerating its huge Reconstruction and Development Programme. Many people in the Republic feel that the NEC with its more complete lateral and vertical coverage of the procurement and skill spectrum has a good chance of becoming that standard.

ESKOM had no choice but to do something about its previous forms of contract, both from a legal and management point of view. Emerging from the days of plenty into of an era of tight money, improved management behaviour and an incredible emphasis on the control of cost reinforced this non-option. Making the choice in 1988 was not easy but looking again at the selection of documents ESKOM could have adopted shows that, even today, there are no others which better fit its requirements. The choice today would be the same. The NEC is here to stay. It will not be without its trials and tribulations. Any system used to regulate two parties with diametrically opposite objectives is bound to have its critics and cynics, and produce a certain amount of strife.

Conclusion

The needs of a major user of commercial contracts have been illustrated. If meaningful change is to take place there must be a change in the (management) systems used in the industry, in order to cultivate a better working environment of mutual trust and co-operation.

Clients, at all levels in the chain, need to educate themselves about the industry with particular emphasis on the influence which organisational structures have on the main causes of disputes through the reduction in ambiguity, errors and late supply of information, and how best to balance the allocation of risk in the interests of their project and future business relationships, whilst maintaining an adequate and skilled project control team to ensure that their needs are met and that they can maintain sufficient influence within the industry to protect their future investment potential.

Construction Professionals must divest themselves of their protectionist practices and claims of discipline exclusivity and replace such behaviour with improved recognition of the commercial requirements of their clients. If they do not do this, their "status" will continue to decline. The NEC is the unification catalyst they can use to demonstrate their commitment.

Contractors and specialist subcontractors must recognise that the days of passing risks associated with their performance and activities common to the construction industry on to their client are gone. Hopefully their support for using the NEC will enable them to negotiate a reasonable balance of risk before the contract starts.

The supporting legal and commercial professions need to recognise that it is in their long term interests to promote a pro-active educational role in the interests of risk awareness, rather than risk avoidance and profit by their clients misfortune after the facts are known. Constructive support for the NEC both as it is and in the improvements which they could bring to it, rather than sniping in the wings, would be a good place to start.

4. Major Infrastructure Projects: Contracts, Risks and Disputes

Joanna Higgins

Synopsis

This paper deals with the needs of major infrastructure projects with reference to risk allocation, dispute avoidance and dispute 'channelling', specifically how identification of the relevant risks inherent in the project, and their proper allocation is fundamental to avoiding disputes. Finally, the importance of appropriate mechanisms for channelling disputes is discussed and consideration given to factors relevant to the methods by which infrastructure projects are procured.

Introduction

One fundamental principle underlying this paper is that advance consideration of the risks of the project is essential in the avoidance of uncontrolled disputes. For the purpose of this paper, the expression "uncontrolled disputes" is intended to connote those disputes which do not fall within part of the dispute channelling process provided for.

In order to consider the requirements of infrastructure projects it is necessary first of all to assess the factors which characterise such projects and to distinguish major infrastructure projects from traditional construction projects. It is assumed in this paper that the method of infrastructure procurement will include an element of private finance rather than the project being entirely in the public sector. There has been a growing tendency worldwide for governments or their agencies to place major projects into the private sector, frequently through the mechanism of BOOT contracts (Build, Own, Operate, Transfer).

The procurement of an infrastructure project is likely to involve several or all of the following factors:
- the existence of an external funder who has an active role in determining the structure of the project.

- the presence of a State or State owned entity as client.
- probable foreign element, either in terms of venue for the works or foreign investment.
- possible participation by the contractor in the role of client through the use of concession agreements or otherwise.
- significant risk assumed by the contractor.

These factors taken together tend to distinguish infrastructure projects from traditional construction projects although any one or more of these factors may also be present in traditional construction projects. The most significant aspect of infrastructure procurement when compared with traditional forms of contract is the greater risk assumed by the contractor.

Identification of risk

Risk and uncertainty (ie. the probability of certain outcomes being unknown) are inherent in all construction projects. In major infrastructure projects, the length of concession, the type of facility and the location, the number of organisations involved and the uncertainty of meeting the required revenues greatly increase the risks over those expected in a traditional contract.

The web of contracts giving rise to the relationship between the parties will be determined by the individual characteristics of the project. Whatever the form of the project, however, it is vital that early consideration is given to appropriate risk allocation. In order to allocate risk, one must first analyse the project risks.[1] As with all negotiations relating to future contractual relations between the parties, the tendency at the outset of the project is for each party to focus on its own needs and desires, to the potential detriment of the project. This will particularly be the case where there is an imbalance of bargaining power between the parties. This difficulty is exacerbated by the number of inter-related contracts which make up an infrastructure project. It is

---

[1] For a discussion on the nature and scope of the risks see Payne, H., '*Major Infrastructure Projects and Their Environmental Impact*' in Uff, J. & Odams, A.M., *Risk, Management and Procurement in Construction* Centre of Construction Law & Management, King's College London, 1995.

also relevant to bear in mind the financial risks which each party runs by its involvement in the project may be considerably larger than would normally arise in the course of their business. This has implications therefore not only for the contracting parties but also their shareholders, insurers and so forth.

In analysing risk at the outset of an infrastructure project, it is not just a matter of each party identifying and valuing the risks which he is to bear. Each party needs also to have satisfied itself that other parties have appropriately identified risk and have the capacity to bear those risks. If this is not the case then the ultimate success of the project may be threatened. It may also threaten the economic viability of the participants themselves. At the very least it means that disputes during the course of the project become more likely.

It is vital that risks are analysed in order to determine which of them cannot be "priced" and how project-threatening risks are to be managed. It may be the case that risks, once identified, are so onerous that the project structure originally envisaged may need to be altered in order to accommodate those risks. It will be the case that the project funders, normally risk-averse in respect of their own participation, will ensure that as far as possible risks are both identified and allocated to parties best able to bear them.

Accurate risk identification should be coupled with transparent risk allocation in order to avoid "unnecessary" disputes. It is important also to anticipate the impact of outside forces on a project. This is particularly important in relation to many infrastructure projects which traditionally take place in the less developed parts of the world. There may therefore be significant risks relating to political changes, civil unrest or currency fluctuations. Although certain of these risks can be laid off, it may be very difficult or impossible to cater for political or social change. An unexpected change of government may lead to a fundamentally different approach by the host country to the project in question.

The role of the financiers

Project promoters must be satisfied that the uncontrollable risks generated by the role of parties outside the project are within realistic parameters before they will be prepared to take on the project. Privately financed infrastructure projects are also characterised by the significant role which the providers of that finance take. The project funders' perception of the risks of the project will be fundamental to the participation of the promoter in the project and the legal structure for the project.[2] It is therefore vital that the project promoter identifies and allocates risk in a fashion which will enable him to obtain appropriate funding for the project. This will frequently involve much of the project risk being passed on to the contractor.

The bankers' perspective on the allocation of risk is frequently connected with the theory of financial pain. This particularly characterises their relations with project sponsors and project contractors even where the project is limited recourse or no recourse at all. Funders will undertake risk sensitivity analysis in order to determine the significance of the risks to the project. It is important that risks are not over-estimated or under-estimated, since this would affect the profitability or viability assessment of the project.

Risk sensitivity analysis is in theory capable of scientific evaluation and analysis. In practice however funders' appraisal of risk sensitivity will be affected by subjective factors such as the track record of the promoter company. They will also seek to ensure through their legal team that the project documentation deals with the more sensitive risks by for example providing for protection against inflation risk by price escalation clauses in power supply contracts or the provision for increase in tolls in the case of a road or bridge toll project.

It may be appreciated by the host government that the risks which the project promoter would otherwise run are such that it will be difficult and/or uneconomic for project promoters to take on those risks or to

---

[2]   See Scriven, J. '*A Funder's View of Risk in Construction*' in Uff, J. & Odams, A.M., *Risk, Management and Procurement in Construction* Centre of Construction Law & Management, King's College London, 1995 for a detailed analysis of how funders perceive risk in infrastructure procurement.

obtain the private sector finance to do so. The principal may therefore be prepared to reduce the risk to the private sector. This acceptance of the need to find an appropriate means of dealing with risk is in the author's view a fundamental part of the dispute avoidance process. It is axiomatic that parties should carry the risks and price for them only where it is appropriate for them to do so. It is more likely that disputes will arise if this is not the case and such disputes will tend to be intractable.

Contractors' risk

The traditional structure of a construction contract means that the contractor frequently takes limited responsibility or financial risk in relation to the successful outcome of the project. Infrastructure project procurement tends to take the form of either design and build/turnkey contracts or BOOT projects. Both of these methods of procurement significantly shift risk and reward to the contractor. This high level of responsibility will therefore cause the contractor to approach the project differently to his approach to the traditional construction contract. From the point of view of the procurer of the project, this increased responsibility of the contractor is perceived to have certain advantages:

- There is a single point of responsibility for production of the works. This potentially reduces the management load on the employer and makes seeking redress for default easier in that it is not possible for the contractor to blame the designer and vice versa.
- Savings and cost due to improved "buildability". The contractor will have responsibility for co-ordinating his design to ensure that it is buildable. This is a more difficult process to manage where the design is carried out by a third party.
- The greater risk taken by the contractor reduces the potential for cost increase once work is commenced.
- Potential time-savings can be made as work can theoretically commence before design details for the whole process are complete.

From the perspective of the contractor on the project, the risks which he undertakes relate primarily to the size of the project and the degree of engineering innovation required. The projects considered for private finance are usually large and complex, involving a multitude of inter-related design and engineering problems. The level of engineering innovation necessary may also be considerable. Current technology may be advanced, as in the case of the Channel Fixed Link project.

The construction related risk is a major contribution to the overall risk for a privately financed project. The input of construction organisations is therefore important and they are often better able to assess the financeability of the project than the project promoter. In order to avoid financing difficulties it is frequently the case that constructors are part of the main promoter organisation thereby reducing the potential for conflict between the interests of the constructor and those of the promoter. The use of an appropriate form of contract may of itself act in minimising the prospects of disputes and in creating significant savings in the overall project costs. The construction contract will frequently take the form of a turnkey contract but in certain projects other contract strategies will be more appropriate. In the case of the Channel Fixed Link, the three types of construction contract used were lump sum contracts for the terminals and fixed equipment in the tunnels, a target contract for the tunnelling works and a provisional sum in respect of locomotives and rolling stock. The transportation system and mechanical and electrical equipment was however based only on performance specification.

Contract strategies suitable for construction contracts for major infrastructure projects may include:

- **Lump Sum** This form of contract fixes the amount payable by the promoter to the contractor leaving the contractor to profit from cost savings or take the risk of cost overruns.
- **Guaranteed Maximum Price** This form of contract is on a reimbursable cost basis giving the benefit of cost savings to the promoter and the cost over the guaranteed maximum to be paid to the contractor.
- **Target Cost** This form of contract is executed on a reimbursable basis with cost overruns or savings shared by the promoter and the contractor.
- **Reimbursable Cost** This form of contract is where all costs are reimbursed by the promoter to the contractor.

A fixed price turnkey contract is often the preferred procurement contract in major infrastructure projects since promoters and lenders need to obtain maximum certainty of the final construction price. Since the contractor is committing himself to a fixed price this inevitably means that the price which he bids will be higher in order to give him protection against those increased risks. Often contractors are required to provide completion guarantees and assume responsibility for delays arising within their control and should provide performance bonds, advance payment guarantees/bonds, advance payment guarantees/bonds and retention money guarantee/bonds.

Completion of the construction work on time is frequently paramount in these projects since the construction phase will frequently be carried out as part of the concession period. This means that construction overruns cut short the length of the operating period with adverse effects on income stream. This may leave the promoter to wish to adopt a fast track method of construction to order to maximise the revenue phase. The contractor may therefore be facing a project which has design evolving as the construction proceeds, engineering innovation and pressure to complete the project on time and at cost where the number of parties involved in the construction process may be large and may include local labour as a project requirement.

Unavoidable disputes

The appropriate allocation of risk is unlikely to eradicate disputes but will minimise the frequency of their occurrence and should affect the severity of their impact. Some disputes may however be both unforeseeable and unforeseen at the time of preparation of the project documentation. Alternatively, the potential for conflict may have been predictable but was nonetheless something which could not be catered for at the outset. The relationship between the parties will usually endure for a considerable number of years and the basis of agreement between the parties may no longer be seen as appropriate by one or more of the parties. It is important therefore that the parties and their lawyers determine in advance how such disputes are to be dealt with. As with any group of contracts affecting numbers of parties, it is fundamental that as far as is possible the dispute resolution mechanisms are compatible between interconnected contracts.

With infrastructure projects it is particularly significant that disputes should be defused during the course of the works rather than being allowed to escalate into a dispute at the end of the contract. During the construction period there will always be a powerful incentive for the parties, or at least one of them, to resolve any disputes rapidly. Disputes that have not been capable of resolution during the project will probably become difficult to resolve quickly and economically subsequently, partly because the parties' positions may have become entrenched but also because of the need to prove after the event what the relevant facts were. This problem will be exacerbated in infrastructure projects which tend to be on larger scale and of longer duration than other construction works. This means that resolution of disputes after the event may have to be based on documentary records since the works themselves will have been completed, potentially removing relevant evidence by the nature of the process. Finding the relevant witnesses may also become a difficult process as they may well be scattered all over the world to other construction projects.

Given that infrastructure projects are frequently set in an international context, the difficulties may be increased by the possible relevance of foreign laws or regulations which one or more of the parties may not be familiar with ; cultural differences between the parties and "political" difficulties associated with the public knowledge that a project has not gone entirely to plan if a dispute is in the public domain. Given these difficulties, it is vital that all the parties at the outset of the project consider how disputes are to be dealt with. This means that equal care must be given to the disputes clauses as is given to the commercial and financial aspects of the contract. It is necessary first to acknowledge the different factors which are relevant to the concession agreement. These are unlikely to be the same as those affecting the construction contract. It is important to note however how the terms of the concession agreement dispute resolution clause will affect the equivalent provision in the construction contract.

It may be that the dispute channelling or resolving mechanisms between the State and the concession company will be subject to little or no flexibility. It is frequently the case that only the national courts of the sponsoring government will be acceptable to the principal. If this is the case, a concession company must determine how significant a risk this method of dispute resolution represents. This stance is particularly probable in countries in the Far East such as China. An alternative may be sought but if this is a non-negotiable issue, the question of the impact on the project of potential disputes may be perceived by both the contractor and funders as fundamentally different from a project whose disputes could be dealt with by a recognised international arbitration body. A compromise solution may be to provide for arbitration in a neutral country and this is frequently acceptable to for example South American state entities. It will however be necessary for the contractor and funders to analyse carefully the potential consequences of providing for arbitration in a neutral country, whose procedural rules may affect the outcome of proceedings.

It may be that this will become a significant factor in whether the company bids for the concession or is able to obtain financing for the project. The dispute resolution mechanism with the host country is likely also to affect the way in which the concession company deals with his relationship with the contractor. One important example is the question of compliance with specification by the contractor where the dispute resolution clause in the concession agreement is draconian. Such a default could offer to the government an opportunity to refuse to pay without there being effective remedies for the concession company against the government. The concession company will therefore be particularly anxious to ensure that the contractor must comply with specification and can only raise issues such as additional payment for overcoming unforeseen conditions in a way which will not affect progress.

If however the dispute resolution clause in the concession agreement is subject to discussion then the concession company needs to take into account a number of issues.

Finality and Enforceability

The host government or state agency may wish any disputes to avoid coming to public attention in view of potential political embarrassment. This may lead a desire to have some form of alternative dispute resolution as a first stage in the dispute resolution process. In certain countries such as Japan this is regarded as the most appropriate method of resolving disputes. If such an approach is unsuccessful, the contract should provide for some form of enforceable decision so that deadlock does not take place. The degree of enforceability and finality of judicial or arbitral decisions will depend upon applicable national legislation and treaty obligations. In selecting between arbitration or litigation a relevant factor will be the right of appeal from unacceptable decisions. It may be regarded as desirable to have finality but with an attendant risk of being adversely affected by an erroneous decision rather than having rights to appeal which might delay the project.

Neutrality

A party, particularly a state entity or government, may feel uncomfortable agreeing to resolution of disputes in the court of another party's country. This therefore may lead to arbitration as a part of the dispute resolution mechanism given that a tribunal may sit in any country of the world, outside the jurisdiction of the courts of either party.

Nature of the Disputes Likely to Arise

One method of dealing with the risks associated with disputes is to consider the nature of the relief that may be required and the party who is most likely to be a claimant. For the party who considers itself most likely to be a claimant, its desire will be for a dispute resolution process which is rapid and efficient. On the other hand, the party that considers it more likely that it will be the defendant may be more concerned to ensure that the forum selected will be one in which it will have a full and proper chance to defend itself with the greatest possible review or appellate proceedings available.

At this international level therefore different issues arise from those which are relevant to the relationship between the concession company and the contractor. In its contract with the contractor, the concession company is concerned with how best to protect its position vis a vis the purchaser of the project. The contractor on the other hand is obviously interested in ensuring that any grievances he has can be properly aired and that he is not disadvantaged by the process. The extent of the incompatibility of these interests will be affected by whether or not the contractor itself participates in the concession company. The contractor will however be expected to take on much of the risk of the project construction. His rights of recourse will be limited by the contract and his obligation to deliver the project on time and budget will be paramount. Without such a requirement, and limited rights of the contractor, the funders would be unwilling to agree to participate.

One of the fundamental considerations for this dispute resolution mechanism is the extent to which each party is entitled to pursue disputes at all. The contract may be so drafted that only certain forms of grievance may be pursued. Claims for work done by way of variation could be limited by requiring such work to be done only on the basis of an agreed all inclusive price with an express provision that this agreed compensation is to be taken as the full measure of the contractors loss or right to compensation. Alternatively, a third party may be imposed between the parties to try to resolve disputes. One current favoured mechanism is adjudication. It is vital that disputes are channelled so that they do not escalate into issues which would affect the progress or financial viability of the project. It is particularly crucial therefore that issues are resolved as soon as they arise. It is also possible to provide for arbitration during the course of the works rather than as is currently the norm leaving it to the end of the contract. In major infrastructure projects it is undesirable from both parties' perspective to leave disputes to fester.

Infrastructure projects have tended to use relatively sophisticated dispute resolution processes in order to avoid projects becoming delayed or relationships soured. International projects such as the Channel Fixed Link have used a variety of mechanisms and governing laws in an attempt to provide processes which are both effective and politically acceptable. Such dispute resolution clauses frequently include layers of dispute channelling before the traditional dispute determination by court or arbitrator takes place. Two examples are set out below of how projects have dealt with potential disputes.

Examples :

Third Dartford River Crossing

The Dartford Bridge was a BOOT project. A concession was granted by the Department of Transport to a company known as Dartford River Crossing Limited. They were to design, build and operate the new bridge as well as take over the operation of the two existing tunnels for a period thereafter. The project was funded by the company raising the finance which they would then recoup from the tolls charged for both the bridge and the tunnels. There were complicated mechanisms for the handing back of the bridge to the Department of Transport, dependent upon the speed at which the original debt was recovered. Conflicts could potentially arise between any of the company, the Department of Transport, the company's design and build contractor and the Department of Transport's appointed professional advisers. In order to avoid entrenched disputes, the Parliamentary Bill, the Concession Agreement and the Construction Contract all contained elements of adjudication provisions.

The decision as to who should be the adjudicator is likely to be fundamental to the success or failure of the mechanism in question. The choice will depend upon the nature of the disputes which it is envisaged may arise. In the case of the Dartford River Crossing it was necessary to find someone capable of dealing with the engineering and legal issues together with issues concerning the operation and maintenance of cable stay bridge design In order to obtain the appropriate level of expertise and given the potentially serious financial consequences of the decisions in question, it was originally intended to appoint a company to fulfil the role rather than an individual. But after consideration of the issues in more detail, it was decided to appoint a single adjudicator, experienced in major projects and contractual disputes, supported by a panel of technical assessors whose expertise would be drawn on if the adjudicator considered the areas of dispute to be outside his own expertise. The panel was approved by all the concerned parties. There was also provision for the appointment of an assessor who was not on the panel if the parties agreed it was appropriate.

A crucial aspect of this procedure was the appointment of the adjudicator in advance of any disputes arising. This involved payment of a retainer to enable the chosen adjudicator to keep himself up-to-date on the progress and problems with the work on site, so that he would have a background knowledge of the contract which would save the parties time and money if any disputes were referred to him. A material consideration for the adjudicator was his own personal potential liability. In order to deal with this, the parties agreed that the adjudicator would be immune from actions for negligence. The parties also undertook that in the event of any action being brought against them by a third party, they would not plead negligence of the adjudicator as a defence. The adjudication procedure was based loosely on the Short Procedure of the ICE Arbitration Procedure, except that the exchange of "pleadings" was consecutive rather than simultaneous.

No legal representation was permitted and the parties bore their own costs as well as sharing the costs of the adjudicator and the assessors. The adjudicator was not to give a reasoned decision unless he believed that the giving of reasons might assist the parties in the resolution of any disputes in the future.

Two references were made to the adjudicator, both related to design issues. For the first reference, the parties agreed that the technical assessor should be a specialist whose name had *not* been included in the list of assessors. In the second reference the assessor was drawn from the original panel. Outside these formal references it was found that the periodic site visits of the adjudicator were themselves of benefit. During these visits the parties raised matters which could potentially have led to disputes, and the adjudicator gave informal indications of his views on the relevant questions. It was considered that these informal indications were helpful in avoiding future disputes. Another advantage which the process gave the parties, and which had been the original rationale for adopting the process, was the speed at which decisions could be obtained albeit that these were not binding after the completion of the works. This appears to have had the effect of limiting the diversion of resources from construction into disputation.

Hong Kong Airport Core Programme

The construction of Hong Kong's new airport is in two parts: the airport itself, which is the responsibility of the Provisional Airport Authority; and the approaches to the airport, which are the responsibility of the Hong Kong Government Works Branch. The airport and the approaches are effectively known as the Airport Core Programme. The Government ACP contracts contain dispute resolution procedures which are in four tiers:

1. Submission of a dispute for a decision by the Engineer;
2. Mediation;
3. Adjudication;
4. Arbitration.

The contracts contain, in schedules, rules for mediation, adjudication and arbitration. There is provision that no action in law in relation to any dispute can be commenced unless and until all the applicable dispute resolution procedures in the contract have been exhausted. It is also expressly provided that the contractor is to continue with the works during the dispute process unless the contract is terminated.

The mediation rules provide for the mediator to inform himself of the nature and facts of the dispute in any way he sees fit and to conduct the mediation in such manner as will permit the parties to present their views to him. He may see the parties together or separately and if he considers appropriate, or if the parties so request, he may express preliminary views as to the matters in dispute. During the course of the mediation, the mediator may attempt various compromise solutions with the parties. If it becomes clear to him that a settlement is unlikely then the mediator is to submit to the parties a report setting out the facts as he sees them, his opinion on the matters in dispute and his proposal for terms of settlement.

The adjudication rules provide for a more formal procedure. Provision is made for a Request for Adjudication which is to contain details of the issues and a statement of the relief claimed, together with copies of relevant documents. The adjudicator has a wide discretion as to the procedure to be followed. Witnesses may be called and the adjudicator may commission expert evidence. The adjudicator is to give his decision within forty two days. That decision is to be in writing, must give reasons and be signed and dated by the adjudicator. In the event of an arbitration, the submissions of the parties, the documents and the decision of the adjudicator *are* to be admissible in the arbitration.

The final recourse of the parties is to arbitration. The Arbitrator is given a wide discretion in relation to the conduct of the proceedings, unless the parties agree otherwise. Provision is made for the submission of written statements and documents. The parties may be represented by lawyers. The arbitrator is given power to rule on the existence and validity of the contract and on his own jurisdiction. The evident purpose of this structure is to ensure that disputes, which inevitably arise on any construction project are resolved in appropriate ways before the project itself is affected.

Conclusions

Certain features have been identified as fundamental to the procurement of infrastructure projects where private finance is utilised. Each of these features will impact upon the way in which it is appropriate to deal with disputes. Because of the potentially huge risks undertaken in the sector, risk allocation is undertaken in as transparent a means as possible. The active participation of the funders means that projects with unduly onerous risks will be unlikely to obtain funding, acting as a safety mechanism. The funders' role means also that there will be two sets of advisers analysing risk, thereby increasing the prospect that relevant risks will be identified.

The vital importance of delivery of the project on time by the contractor will lead to mechanisms in the contract to defuse disputes before they become "uncontrolled". The parties are in theory at least able to choose between a whole range of dispute channelling mechanisms, from ADR through various forms of expert determination to litigation or arbitration. Each dispute channelling process needs to be that which is designed to meet the needs of the particular project.

The construction industry has much to learn from this relatively sophisticated sector. It is apparent that many of the larger UK contractors are becoming increasingly involved in infrastructure procurement and in this way some beneficial effect on traditional construction procurement may be expected. It is important to recognise that disputes may arise on any project but by a careful analysis and allocation of risk, together with dispute channelling mechanisms, that projects should be completed without a fundamental breakdown in the relationships between the parties.

Part II

Comparative Arbitration Issues

Part II.

Comparative Adjudication Process

5. The Policy in Favour of Arbitration in England and in the United States

Andrew Berkeley

Synopsis

This paper seeks to compare the law relating to separability of the arbitration agreement and multiparty arbitration in England and in the United States, and examine how the law is affected by, and relates to, policy considerations in both jurisdictions.

Introduction

The first of the following quotations is from an opinion of Mr. Justice Brennan delivered in the Supreme Court of the United States in 1983, the second is from a speech in the House of Lords in England made by Lord Diplock in 1991.

> *"The Arbitration Act establishes that, as a matter of federal law, any doubts concerning the scope of arbitrable issues should be resolved in favour of arbitration, whether the problem at hand is the construction of the contract language itself or an allegation of waiver, delay, or a like defence to arbitrability"*[1]

> *"I agree with the passage I have cited from the arbitrators' award and I take this opportunity of re-stating that if detailed semantic and syntactical analysis of the words in a commercial contract is going to lead to a conclusion that flouts business common sense, it must be made to yield to business common sense"*[2]

Both seem to express some favour for arbitration as a means of resolution of disputes.

---

1 *Moses H. Cone Memorial Hospital v. Mercury Construction Corporation* 460 US 1; 74 L Ed 2d 765; 103 S Ct 927 (1983), at p 941.
2 *Maritime Transport Overseas GmbH v. Unitramp Salem Rederierna AB (The Antaios)* [1981] 2 Lloyd's Rep 284.

That the question deserves attention first became evident to the writer when sitting as an arbitrator in the United States. The following are extracts from a brief to a Federal Court by counsel seeking a stay of litigation in favour of arbitration:

" ... *The Federal Arbitration Act manifests a 'liberal federal policy favouring arbitration agreements'.* [3]
... [The FAA] *is applied in the light of the strong federal policy favouring arbitration.* [4]
.. *This policy favouring arbitration dictates that 'any doubts concerning the scope of arbitrable issues should be resolved in favour of arbitration ...'* " [5]

The reiteration of the theme of policy and the freedom with which the United States courts felt able to call upon it as a ground for their decisions was noticed by the writer, coming, as he did, from a background of English law. There has been a reluctance amongst the English Judiciary to rely on policy considerations (at least explicitly).

On further consideration it became evident that there were several areas of the law of arbitration where, although the legal systems of both countries had, broadly, moved in the same direction with respect to arbitration, there were important differences in methods and perhaps even in ultimate goals.

In dealing with the topic it has been quoted as a guide that:

"In England a cooperation has developed - according to some harmonious, according to others discordant - between arbitration and the courts. The English courts have a wide discretionary

---

3   *Gilmer v. Interstate/Johnson Lane Corp*, 111 s. Ct. 41, 112 L. Ed. 2d 18 (1990); *Moses H Cone Memorial Hosp. v. Mercury Constr. Corp.* 460 US 1, 24 (1983).

4   *Shearson/American Express Inc v. McMahon*, 482 US 220, 226 (1987) ("The Arbitration Act thus established a federal policy favouring arbitration ... requiring that 'we rigorously enforce agreements to arbitrate' "); *Dean Witter Reynolds Inc v. Byrd*, 470 US 213, 221 (1985) ("must rigorously enforce agreements to arbitrate").

5   *Moses H. Cone Memorial Hospital v. Mercury Construction Corporation* 460 US 1; 74 L Ed 2d 765; 103 S Ct 927 (1983); see also *United Steel Workers of America v Warrior & Gulf Navigation Company* 363 US 574, 582 (1960) (arbitration should be compelled "unless it may be said with positive assurance that the arbitration clause is not susceptible of an interpretation that covers the asserted dispute".

power in the matter of arbitration. In effect, arbitration is integrated into the English judicial system. In the United States, on the contrary, arbitration is considered as a private procedure which is ruled solely by the will of the parties. The intervention of the courts is confined to verifying formal regularity and the fact that the equality of the parties has been observed. It is in this that the fundamental difference with English law lies."[6]

Policy or Principle?

It has been noted that judgments in the United States authorities continually refer to the "policy" of the law regarding arbitration—to a much greater extent than appears in English judgements. In England a classic statement of the judicial attitude to policy was made by Lord Scarman in *McLoughlin v. O'Brian*[7]

"The distinguishing feature of common law is this judicial development and formulation of principle. Policy considerations will have to be weighed but the objective of the judges is the formulation of principle. And if principle inexorably requires a decision which entails a degree of policy risk, the court's function is to adjudicate according to principle, leaving policy curtailment to the judgement of Parliament. Here lies the true role of the two law making institutions in our constitution. By concentrating on principle the judges can keep the common law alive, flexible and consistent and can keep the legal system clear of policy problems which neither they nor the forensic process which it is their duty to operate are equipped to resolve. If principle leads to results which are thought to be socially unacceptable, Parliament can legislate to draw a line or map out a true path."[8]

---

6 René David, *L'Arbitrage dans le Commerce International*, Paris 1982. Page 166. (Writer's translation).
7 [1983] 1 AC 410
8 *Ibid* at 430.

This eloquent passage shows clearly that policy is something which, in England, the courts would aspire to avoid. However, some authors are sceptical about the clear distinctions which are there made.[9]

By contrast, in the United States, the judges are not by any means so reluctant to admit policy as an element leading to their decisions. Indeed, as will be amplified later, the existence of a judicially identified policy in the United States can sometimes appear to be an important part of the *ratio* of a judgement. Thus, in the important cases which brought anti-trust, Securities Exchange Act, and the Racketeer Influenced & Corrupt Organizations Act (RICO) disputes within the field of arbitrability, the Supreme Court explicitly made reference to policy as determinative of its decision.[10] It is submitted that this direct use of "policy" is not merely a difference between the United States and England in judicial use of language in relation to statutory interpretation, but that it is indicative of a much more profound difference in the way that courts in the two countries recognize the authority of law.[11]

In England the courts do sometimes become involved in policy and, even in the creation thereof but there is rarely a direct appeal to it as a ground of decision. It is, for instance, instructive, in this context to cite the decisions in *The Nema*[12] and *The Antaios*[13] where the House of Lords undoubtedly laid down policy for the interpretation of the 1979 Act. In his speech in *The Nema* Lord Roskill said when criticising Robert Goff J's, as he then was, approach in *The Wenjiang:*[14]

---

9   See, for instance, Bell, *Policy Arguments in Judicial Decisions* Oxford 1983, especially at page 35, where the author points out that where judges feel that there is a broad consensus on the substantive reasons, they may not articulate them, or they may call them "common sense". *"Policy need not be invoked where reason and common sense will at once point the way"* Lord Morris in *Dorset Yacht v Home Office* [1970] AC 1004, 10 .

10 *Mitsubishi Motors v Soler Chrysler Plymouth* 87 L Ed 2d 444, 454; *Shearson/American Express v McMahon* 96 L Ed 2d 185, 193; *Rodriguez de Quijas v Shearson/American Express* 104 L Ed 2d 529, 534.

11 Atiyah, P.S. & Summers, R.S., *Form and Substance in Anglo-American Law*, Oxford 1987 reprinted 1991

12 *Pioneer Shipping v. B.T.P. Tioxide Ltd. (The Nema)* [1982] AC 724

13 *Antaios Compania Naviera v. Salen Radierna A.B. (The Antaios)* [1985] AC 191

14 *International Sea Tankers Inc v. Hemisphere Shipping company Ltd. (The Wenjiang)* [1982] 1 Lloyd's Rep 128

" [I]*f the learned judge's view were allowed to prevail, I find it difficult to see what useful purpose had been served by the passing of the 1979 Act which had as one of its primary targets the abolition of the special case, since it seems to me that, if leave to appeal from an arbitral tribunal to the High Court is to be given in accordance with the principles which the learned Judge there enumerated, the notoriously unsatisfactory results to which special cases have given rise in recent years will be perpetuated, albeit in different form.*"[15]

The passage is phrased in terms of remedy of past defects; there is there no direct appeal to policy, still less a reliance on a policy in favour of the (final) resolution of disputes by arbitration, but it is a statement of policy nevertheless. On this issue, Professor Duncan Wallace states that the revolution in the law of arbitration brought about by *The Nema* and *The Antaios*, "possibly the greatest for more than a century, was virtually invisible in the wording of the 1979 Act itself".[16]

The Agreement to Arbitrate

The Statutory Background

The law in England, American Federal Law and the laws of the great majority of the States afford the mechanism to make simple executory agreements to arbitrate disputes irrevocable and enforceable.[17] The law in all such cases is now statute law. It can thus be said that arbitration in all the jurisdictions under consideration is a creation of statute.

---

15 *Pioneer Shipping v. B.T.P. Tioxide Ltd. (The Nema)* [1982] AC 724, *per* Lord Roskill at 745-746.
16 Uff, J. & Jones, E. (Eds) *International and ICC Arbitration*, Centre of Construction Law and Management, King's College, London, 1990, p. 242.
17 Arbitration Act 1950, s. 1; The United States Arbitration Act 1925 (as codified in 1947, 9 USC 1-14), 9 USC 2; 'Modern' State Arbitration Statutes as cited in 'Commercial Arbitration for the 1990's, Section of Litigation, American Bar Association, Chicago, 1991 at Appendix 1. ('Modern' Statutes are those enforcing agreements to arbitrate existing controversies and any arising in the future. Forty eight States, the District of Columbia and Puerto Rico have modern statutes. Alabama and West Virginia have statutes which enforce the arbitration of existing disputes only, App. 1 *ibid.*)

It is not the purpose of this paper to deal with the history of arbitration. However it is worth observing that arbitration agreements as they originally developed under the common law, including various early enactments such as that of 1698 in England did not possess, or possess fully, the attributes of irrevocability and enforceability. Indeed these attributes are taken as criteria of modernity and as essential to the process of arbitration as it exists today.[18] It would still be possible today to have a "common law" (as opposed to modern) arbitration because all of the statutes require, in order that they be applicable,[19] that the agreements be in writing. Oral agreements to arbitrate would still fall under common law jurisdiction and, perhaps, be revocable unilaterally by a party.

This progress leading to arbitration governed by modern statutes making written agreements to arbitrate irrevocable and enforceable is the most fundamental support for the freedom of arbitration, as that term has been defined here, which has been laid down by the law. With the exception of two States in America, it applies in all the jurisdictions under investigation and so, in that basic context, the policy in favour of arbitration can be said to have attained a uniform development.

The Status of the Agreement

When attention is turned towards an analysis of the agreement itself, differences between the United States and England begin to become evident and it is useful to begin by citing the words of the Federal Arbitration Act:

> "*A written provision in any maritime transaction or a contract evidencing a transaction thereafter arising out of such contract or transaction, or the refusal to perform the whole or any part thereof, or an agreement in writing to submit to arbitration an existing controversy arising out of such a contract, transaction or refusal, shall be valid, irrevocable, and enforceable, save upon*

---

18 Macneil, I. R., *American Arbitration Law*, Oxford, 1992 at page 15.
19 Arbitration Act 1950, s. 32; Federal Arbitration Act s. 2; Uniform Arbitration Act s.1 (the modern State codes are based on this model which was adopted by the National Conference of Commissioners on Uniform State Laws and approved by the American Bar Association in 1955).

such grounds as exist at law or in equity for the revocation of any contract."[20]

Two Federal cases dealing with this section show the judicial application of a policy in favour of arbitration with great clarity. The first is *Robert Lawrence*[21] decided by the Second Circuit (Federal Appeal Court) in 1959 and the second, *Prima Paint*,[22] a Supreme Court case of 1967.

In *Robert Lawrence* the plaintiff sought damages for allegedly fraudulent misrepresentations made by the defendant inducing it to purchase a quantity of woollen fabric. The purchase contract contained a broad arbitration clause. At first instance the court denied a stay of proceedings pending arbitration holding that "... The question whether or not there is a valid agreement to arbitrate must be decided by the court prior to the issue of a stay and cannot be submitted to arbitration as 'a controversy arising out of such contract' within s.2." Judge Medina in the Federal Court of Appeal however held that Congress intended by the Arbitration Act to create a new body of federal substantive law affecting the validity and interpretation of arbitration agreements:

"It is also clear that the Congress intended to exercise as much of its constitutional power as it could in order to make the new Arbitration Act as widely effective as possible. One of the dark chapters in legal history concerns the validity, interpretation and enforceability of arbitration agreements. From the stand point of businessmen generally and of those immediately affected by such agreements they were beneficial and salutary in every way. But to the courts and to the judges they were anathema. In England and in America the Courts resorted to a great variety of devices and formulas to destroy this encroachment on their monopoly of the administration of justice, protecting what they called their "jurisdiction". Suffice it to say that for a considerable time prior to the passage of the Arbitration Act in 1925 the Congress had come to the conclusion that an effort should be made to legislate on the subject of arbitration in such fashion as to remove the

---

20 9 USC 2
21 *Robert Lawrence Company v. Devonshire Fabrics Inc.* 271 F 2d 402 (1959).
22 *Prima Paint Corp. v. Flood & Conklin 388 US 395*, 18 L Ed 2d 1270 (1967).

hostility of the judiciary and make the benefits of arbitration generally available to the business world."[23]

The dictum of Judge Medina has a degree of frankness which does not appear to have an equivalent in the English cases. Finally, the court also frankly stated that the policy of the Act also existed "to help ease the current congestion of court calendars".

In *Prima Paint* the Supreme Court approved the decision in *Robert Lawrence*. Flowing from these two decisions, Federal law establishes that the arbitration clause is severable from the substantive (or "principal" contract, to use the expression of the court in *Robert Lawrence*), that the invalidity of such contract need not affect the arbitration clause and, further, that if the arbitration clause is broad enough, the arbitrator can try questions of fraud relating to it.

Macneil makes a further relevant observation. He points out[24] that for the thirty five years or more between the passing of the Federal Arbitration Act in 1925 and the early Sixties, the Act was merely a procedural statute applicable only in the federal courts. This was the "narrow" interpretation that it had been enacted under the power to regulate procedure in the federal courts "It was, at most, policy neutral respecting the desirability of arbitration relative to other contracts". The results of the 1960s revolution, two of which have been described above, flow from "a shift of the Constitutional underpinnings of the Federal Arbitration Act from power to control federal courts to congressional power to regulate commerce".

It is important to note, when comparing the American system with the English, that this degree of freedom of the courts in the United States (and not just the Supreme Court) to interpret legislation by "choosing" the Constitutional power with reference to which Congress intended to legislate, is not available in England. To that extent, therefore, the English courts are less free to initiate policy and the conventional view is that the courts must wait until Parliament chooses to move by passing fresh legislation as declared by Lord Scarman.[25]

---

23 *Robert Lawrence Company v. Devonshire Fabrics Inc.* 271 F 2d 402, 406 (1967)
24 MacNeil, *op. cit.* p 148,149
25 See also, for example the words of Lord Simonds in *Magor and St Mellons Rural District Council v. Newport Corporation* [1951] 2 All ER 839 when striking down Lord Denning's judgement in the English Court of Appeal that the courts should try

However, in *Heyman v. Darwins*[26] the House of Lords had already anticipated one of the results of *Prima Paint*. They decided that the arbitration clause had an existence independent of the "substantive" contract:

> "... [A]n arbitration clause in a contract....is quite distinct from the other clauses. The other clauses set out the obligations which the parties undertake towards each other...but the arbitration clause does not impose on one of the parties an obligation in favour of the other. It embodies the agreement of both parties that, if any dispute arises with regard to the obligations which the one party has undertaken to the other, such dispute shall be settled by a tribunal of their own constitution... "[27]

This case deals with a situation where the contract, having existed, had come to an end, or rather the mutual obligations of performance had come to an end—the finding was that the arbitration clause was capable of surviving that eventuality. The proposition is thus placed on an analytical basis without any mention of the external influence of policy; the results of the analysis flowed from the facts of the situation themselves.

In 1993, the members of the Court of Appeal found themselves able to refer to policy. In *Harbour Assurance*[28] the question was not, as in *Heyman*, whether the arbitration clause could survive the end of the performance obligations of the contract, but rather whether it was still valid where there was the possibility of illegality affecting the whole contract.

---

to find out the intention of Parliament—and of ministers too. Lord Simonds said: "It appears to me to be a naked usurpation of the legislative function under the thin disguise of interpretation. And it is the less justifiable when it is guesswork with what material the legislature would, if it had discovered the gap, have filled it in." This echoes Justice Black in *Prima Paint* except that the Supreme Court could, and did refer to the congressional record.

26 [1942] AC 356
27 *Ibid per* Lord MacMillan at 373-374, 375, 377. Cited by Mustill and Boyd as "the true *ratio decidendi*" of the case, *Commercial Arbitration, 2nd Edition*, Sweet & Maxwell, London, 1991, p.110, n.14.
28 *Harbour Assurance Co (UK) Ltd v. Kansa General international Insurance Co Ltd.* [1993] QB 701.

The plaintiffs in a reinsurance claim alleged that the defendants were not registered under the Insurance Acts to carry on the business necessarily involved in performing the contract, which included an arbitration clause, and that therefore the agreement was void for illegality. At first instance Steyn J (as he then was) reluctantly held that the issue of illegality was not within the jurisdiction of an arbitrator and therefore dismissed an application for stay. In the Court of Appeal, Hoffman LJ said:

> "*In every case it seems to me that the logical question is not whether the issue goes to the validity of the contract but whether it goes to the validity of the arbitration clause. The one may entail the other but ... it may not. When one comes to voidness for illegality, it is particularly necessary to have regard to* **the purpose and policy** *of the rule which invalidates the contract and to ask, as the House of Lords did in* Heymans *whether the rule strikes down the arbitration clause as well ... In deciding whether or not the rule of illegality also strikes down the arbitration clause,* **it is necessary to bear in mind the powerful commercial reasons for upholding the arbitration clause** *unless it is clear that this would offend the policy of the illegality rule.*"[29] (emphasis supplied)

After finding that there was nothing in the judgments in *Heymans* which would prevent the separability of the arbitration clause, which was established in that case, from extending to some cases where illegality of the contract was alleged the Lord Justice concluded:

> "*In construing the contract one is assisted by the presumption in favour of one-stop adjudication. As Lord Bingham said in* Ashville Investments v. Elmer Contractors Ltd.[30]: '*I would be slow to attribute to reasonable parties an intention that there should in any foreseeable eventuality be two sets of proceedings*' "

---

29 *Ibid* at 724.
30 [1989] QB 488, 517

It can thus be concluded that the two jurisdictions (English and Federal) have arrived at similar conclusions with respect to the independence of the arbitration clause[31].

Multiple parties and consolidation of actions

The position where there are multiple potential defendants, only some of which have an arbitration agreement with the plaintiff, is one which exhibits clear differences in treatment between England and the United States. This was considered by the Court of Appeal in England in *Taunton Collins* v. *Cromie*.[32] The plaintiff employed an architect and contractors to build a house. The building contract was in the RIBA form which contained an arbitration clause. The house was alleged by the Plaintiff to be unsatisfactory; he sued the architect who in his defence partly blamed the contractors. The Plaintiff joined the contractors as co-defendants. The contractors applied for a stay under s.4. of the 1950 Act and the refusal at first instance to grant the stay was appealed. The matter was, of course, 'domestic'.

In the judgment the point as it was perceived was dealt with directly:

> *"The matter is of considerable importance. There is a great number of contracts in the RIBA form, but there is very little authority on this point. It seems to me most undesirable that there should be two proceedings in two separate tribunals ... to decide the same questions of fact ... The decision of the official referee might conflict with the decision of the arbitrator. There would be much extra cost .... there would be delay. There would be procedural difficulties.....as to who should call the contractors and so forth ... Everything should be dealt with in one proceeding before the Official Referee."*[33]

Lord Denning cited with approval the words of McNair J in *The Pine Hill:*[34]

---

31 *Prima Paint* has been followed in New York, *Schachter v. Lester Witte & Co.* 41 NY2d 1067 (1977) and it is thought that most State jurisdictions would do likewise.

32 [1964] 1 WLR 633

33 *Ibid*

34 [1958] 2 Lloyd's Rep. 146

"I think that a serious risk would be run that our whole judicial procedure, at any rate in relation to this claim, would be brought into disrepute if ... there was a serious possibility of getting conflicting questions of fact decided by different tribunals ..."[35]

It is submitted that, at least in the speech of Lord Denning, this case shows clearly the working of a policy. The court had a discretion and it decided that the possibility of multiple proceedings, with consequent procedural difficulties, was so unwelcome that arbitration should give way to litigation.

Taunton Collins and *The Pine Hill* were distinguished in 1973 in the *Bulk Oil* case.[36] In his judgment, Kerr J (as he then was) referred to the conflict of the two "well established and important principles". One was that the parties should normally be held to their contractual arrangements, the other the multiplicity of proceedings was very undesirable. There were two important features which distinguished the instant case from *Taunton Collins* and *The Pine Hill*. In the first place the possibility of the multiplicity of proceedings did not arise solely from the choice of the party wanting the whole dispute to be dealt with by way of litigation and, in the second, multiplicity in each of those two cases could have resulted in substantial injustice to the plaintiff because their alternative claims might both be defeated if different conclusions were reached by the two tribunals. The judge continued:

"Taking these two distinguishing features together, it seems to me that the principle underlying these cases is really as follows. Where there are disputes under two related agreements only one of which contains an arbitration clause, the court will exercise its discretion to allow both disputes to proceed to litigation together if ... a stay of the litigation relating to one of these disputes would be liable to cause substantial injustice to the party which wants them to be litigated together. In this connection the court will take into consideration whether or not the party seeking to litigate both disputes together is in some way to be held responsible for the dilemma in which he finds himself."[37]

---

35 *Ibid* at 152.
36 *Bulk Oil (Zug) AG v. Trans-Asiatic Oil Ltd. SA* [1973] 1 Lloyd's Rep 129
37 *Ibid* at 137.

There is there a reference to principle as a decisive factor and the judges usage of that concept accords with that of Lord Scarman. In describing the conflict of principle with which he was confronted, the judge did not refer to policy in favour of arbitration but rather simply to the desirability that parties should be held to their bargains—in this case the bargain to arbitrate.

The position in the United States stands in sharp contrast. There policy is appealed to openly. And, of course, the statutory context is different because the Federal Arbitration Act and state statutes do not give the courts a discretion of the type which the Bulk Oil court had under s. 4(1).

In the *Moses Cone* case[38] the hospital had entered into a contract with Mercury, the contractors, for the construction of additions to the hospital building. The contract contained an arbitration clause. Disputes arose and there were consequent actions by the hospital against Mercury and the Architect in state and federal courts. Mercury sought to have the action against it stayed in favour of arbitration and the consequent appeals and cross appeals reached the Supreme Court. At IV A of Justice Brennan's judgement it is stated:

> *"The hospital points out that it has two substantive disputes here — one with Mercury concerning Mercury's claim for delay, and the other with the architect, concerning the hospital's claim for indemnity for any liability it may have to Mercury. The latter dispute cannot be sent to arbitration without the architect's consent since there is no arbitration agreement between the hospital and the architect. It is true therefore that, if Mercury obtains an arbitration order for its dispute, the hospital will be forced to resolve these related disputes in different forums. That misfortune ... occurs because the relevant federal law requires piecemeal resolution when necessary to give effect to an arbitration agreement. Under the Arbitration Act, an arbitration agreement must be enforced notwithstanding the presence of other persons who are parties to the underlying dispute but not to the arbitration agreement. If the dispute between Mercury and the hospital is arbitrable under the Act them the hospital's two*

---

38 *Moses H. Cone Memorial Hospital v. Mercury Construction Corporation* 460 US 1; 74 L Ed 2d 765; 103 S Ct 927 (1983).

disputes will be resolved separately, one in arbitration and the other (if at all) in state-court litigation."

The court then went on to hold that the dispute between Mercury and the corporation was arbitrable because "the Arbitration Act establishes, as a matter of federal law, that any doubts concerning the scope of arbitrable issues should be resolved in favour of arbitration". The court was influenced in its decision "by the clear intent of Congress, in the Arbitration Act, to move the parties to an arbitrable dispute out of court and into arbitration as quickly and as easily as possible". Reference was made by the court to s. 3 of the Act which states that if a suit is brought on the merits of a dispute covered by an arbitration agreement: "the court in which such suit is pending, upon being satisfied that the issue involved in such suit or proceeding is referrable to arbitration under such agreement, **shall** on the application of one of the parties stay the trial of the action...." (emphasis supplied)

There is thus a two step process under Federal law; first the court is to satisfy itself that the issue is referrable to arbitration (and under *Moses Cone* the Supreme Court has laid down that any doubts are to be decided in favour of arbitration); second, the court must mandatorily stay—it has no discretion. The position under s. 4 of the 1950 Act in England is, where, in a domestic arbitration, the court has a discretion to stay, it is not bound by any authority specifically to favour arbitration—although the burden of proof is on the party opposing the stay of the litigation[39]—and may take factors, such as convenience[40] and the undesirability of bifurcated proceedings into account.

In *Dean Witter Reynolds Inc. v. Byrd*,[41] decided shortly after *Moses Cone*, the Supreme Court confirmed that, on issues with respect to which an arbitration agreement has been signed, a district court has no discretion, but is mandated to direct immediate arbitration. "The principal purpose of the Arbitration Act is to ensure judicial enforcement of private arbitration agreements and **not** to promote the expeditious resolution of claims" (emphasis supplied).

---

39 *Bulk Oil (Zug) AG v. Trans-Asiatic Oil Ltd. SA* [1973] 1 Lloyd's Rep. 129
40 *Tritonia Shipping Inc v. South Nelson Forest Products Corp. (The Tritonia)* [1966] 1 Lloyd's Rep. 114
41 470 US 213; 105 S Ct. 1238; 1985 US Lexis 57; 84 L Ed. 2d 158.

In *Volt*[42] the Supreme Court considered *Moses Cone*. A standard form construction contract which was used for Volt's for work in the State of California for Stanford contained a choice of law clause stating that: "the contract shall be governed by the law of the place where the Project is located." Unlike its federal counterpart, the law of California permits a court to stay arbitration pending resolution of related litigation. Stanford sued Volt and Volt moved for a stay—the motion was denied at first instance and on appeal to the California Court of Appeals. The Supreme Court had jurisdiction (the case involved commerce and *Volt* was not a California company) and it affirmed the rejection of the motion for a stay. In argument *Volt* had relied on *Moses Cone*. The Court said:

> "... [W]e *do not think the Court of Appeals offended the* Moses Cone *principle by interpreting the choice-of-law provision to mean that the parties intended the California rules to apply to their agreement. There is no federal policy favouring arbitration under a certain set of rules: **the federal policy is simply to ensure the enforceability, according to their terms, of private agreements to arbitrate.**"*[43] (emphasis supplied).

The court went on, however to affirm the cases showing the policy (including *Moses Cone*) which have been cited.

Conclusion

The decision in *Volt* has caused some consternation in the American arbitration community.[44] Matters have been clarified by two subsequent cases in the Supreme Court—*Mastrobuono* v. *Shearson*[45] and *First Options* v. *Kaplan*.[46] These two cases restate the primary policy, that agreements to arbitrate shall be enforced in accordance with their

---

42 *Volt Information Sciences Inc. v. Leland Stanford Junior University* 109 SC 1248 (1989); YB Comm Arb XV 131 (1990)
43 *Ibid* at 135.
44 Coulson,. R., *High Court Jolts Arbitration* The Arbitration Journal, June 1989. A the time of writing, Mr Coulson was President of AAA.
45 1995 US Lexis 1820.
46 115 S Ct 1920; 131 L Ed 2d 985 (1995).

terms. *Kaplan* however draws a distinction which may be important in the continuing development of the policy:

> *"Just as the arbitrability of the merits of a dispute depends upon whether the parties agreed to arbitrate that dispute ... so the question 'who has the primary power to decide arbitrability?' turns upon whether the parties agreed to submit that question to arbitration. If so the court should defer to the arbitrator's decision. If not, the court should decide the question independently.* **These two answers flow inexorably from the fact that arbitration is simply a matter of contract between the parties.**"[47] (emphasis supplied)

In England, the traditional means of development of policy by legislation is, we hope, shortly to be invoked. Under the proposals for a new Arbitration Act in England[48] the law as to the separability of arbitration agreements is codified.[49] This provision corresponds closely to Article 16(1) of the UNCITRAL Model Law[50], although in the Draft the provision is not mandatory. In the explanatory note[51] the Department of Trade and Industry (the sponsoring department for the legislation) ("DTI") states that the Draft "aims to restate the major aspects of the current law on arbitration in a clear and accessible way so that it is readily understandable to all ... [and] ... to introduce changes which will help to facilitate speedy and cost effective dispute resolution."

Although the Model Law is not considered appropriate for incorporation onto England's legislative landscape, its structure, language and spirit has been carried through wherever possible into the Draft. It is clear that the desire to facilitate international arbitration, to attract international arbitration to England, and to safeguard England as a forum has been a leading policy motive in the drive towards modernisation.

---

47 *Ibid*
48 *Consultative Paper on an Arbitration Bill*; *Draft Clauses of an Arbitration Bill*, Department of Trade and Industry, July 1995.
49 Section 7(1).
50 United Nations Commission on Uniform Trade Law, Model Law on Arbitration, 1985.
51 *Consultative Paper*, Section I p.1 *et seq.*

6. Sanctity Revisited: The Efficacy of Commercial Arbitration in Australia

Peter Towson

Synopsis

This paper analyses the law in Australia pertaining to autonomy of the arbitral process.

Introduction

Arbitration is an attractive alternative to litigation in that the parties are more in control of the process. Three facets are cited in support of this contention; the proceedings are private and the documents confidential, the proceedings are unlikely to suffer judicial interference, and the award is not subject to wide-ranging judicial review. However, these mainstays of are currently under judicial fire in Australia. The judiciary has recently examined the proposition that confidentiality is not an essential element in arbitration and, in the absence of an express term in the arbitration agreement has said it need not be implied. There has also been great judicial interest in the residual powers of the Court to intervene in interlocutory matters and the procedure and rules under which arbitration awards may be reviewed has been considered and expanded. This paper examines the present state of the law on these aspects of the law governing arbitration.

Confidentiality

A recent decision of the High Court of Australia dealt with the issue of confidentiality in private arbitration. In *Esso Australia Resources Limited & Others v Plowman (Minister for Energy and Minerals) & Others* [1] the High Court held that confidentiality was not an essential attribute of a private arbitration imposing an obligation on each party

---

1   (1995) 128 ALR 391.

not to disclose the proceedings or documents and information provided in and for the purposes of the arbitration. This decision did not entirely accord with the English authorities *Dolling-Baker v Merrett* [2] and *Hassneh Insurance v Mew*.[3]

The proceedings arose from arbitrations between State Government instrumentalities in Victoria and Esso/BHP under contracts for the supply of natural gas. The disputes concerned a claim for an increase in the cost of gas supplied as a result of certain fiscal amendments. The disputes had been referred to arbitration and preliminary steps had been taken. The Minister for Energy and Minerals commenced proceedings in the Supreme Court of Victoria seeking declarations that information disclosed to the instrumentalities in the course of the arbitrations was not the subject of any obligation of confidentiality. Esso/BHP sought to prevent disclosure of certain commercial aspects of the cost of supply of natural gas.

At first instance[4] Esso submitted that the requirement of confidentiality was based on an implied term in the arbitration agreement. The judge in rejecting this submission concluded that the mere fact that parties to a dispute arbitrate in private does not import any legal or equitable obligation not to disclose to third parties any information obtained during the course of the arbitration.

The Appeal Division of the Victorian Supreme Court[5] allowed the appeal by Esso against the declarations made but left two declarations in the following terms:

> "6C GFC *(Gas Corp.) is not restricted from disclosing information to the minister and third persons by reason only that:*
> (a) *the information was obtained by it from Esso/BHP in the course of or by reason of arbitration pursuant to the 1975 sales agreement; and*
> (b) *the information has not otherwise been published.*

---

2   [1990] 1 WLR 1205.
3   [1993] 2 Lloyd's Rep. 243.
4   Unreported, Supreme Court of Victoria, Marks J.
5   [1994] 1 VR 1.

6F SEC (Elec Corp.) is not restricted from disclosing information to the minister and third persons by reason only that:

(a) the information was obtained by it from Esso/BHP in the course of or by reason of arbitration pursuant to the 1981 sales agreement; and

(b) the information has not otherwise been published. "

Esso appealed to the High Court of Australia on the question of confidentiality. Mason CJ noted that one of the reasons why arbitrations are commercially attractive is their privacy. His Honour referred to *Dolling-Baker v Merrett* [6] and said that the fact that a document is used in an arbitration does not confer on it any confidentiality or privilege which can be availed of in subsequent proceedings. However in questions of production of documents by subpoena or discovery the Court should have regard to the normal rules of confidentiality.

Mason CJ identified several reasons why complete confidentiality of arbitration proceedings can never be achieved:

- No obligation attaches to witnesses
- The award can be enforced in the same manner as a judgment and be subject to judicial review
- An arbitrating party may be bound to disclose under an insurance policy the existence and nature of arbitration proceedings and any award made

His Honour stated that if the parties wished to secure the confidentiality of materials used in the arbitration, they could insert provisions to that effect in their arbitration agreement, but he also noted that the contractual obligations would not bind the witnesses to confidentiality.

Mason CJ stated that the Courts have consistently viewed government secrets differently from personal and commercial secrets; the government must show that the public interest demands non-disclosure.[7] He used the present case as an example of "compelled

---

6   [1990] 1 WLR 1205.

7   See *Commonwealth of Australia v John Fairfax & Sons Ltd* (1980) 147 CLR 39 at 51.

openness", stating that the public in Victoria has the right to know because the price increases will be chargeable to the consumers by the public utilities. After noting that documents produced by one party to another in the course of discovery should be subject to the same undertaking of confidentiality as in a court, i.e. not to use the documents disclosed for any purpose other than in relation to the litigation in which it was disclosed, his Honour held that there was no implied contractual term of confidentiality in an arbitration.

In agreeing with the Chief Justice, Brennan J stated that if a party to an arbitration is under any obligation of confidentiality, then the obligation must be contractual save for confidentiality in respect of discovered documents. Toohey J dissented and the majority remitted the declarations to the judge at first instance for reformulation in accordance with the reasons of the majority.

Intervention in Arbitral Procedure

The extent of a Court's power to intervene in relation to interlocutory or procedural orders made by arbitrators has been considered by different State Supreme Courts.

In *South Australian Superannuation Fund Investment Trust v Leighton Contractors Pty Limited* [8] the Full Court of the South Australian Supreme Court allowed an appeal from a Master who refused to intervene in an arbitration. The Arbitrator had held that the particulars of a global claim comprising six volumes of material was sufficiently precise for the respondent to provide a defence. The Full Court held that it had a supervisory role over arbitrators in relation to pre-hearing and procedural matters. The basis of this supervisory role was said to be found in *Commercial Arbitration Act 1984 (NSW)* s.44 (dealing with misconduct), the structure of the Act and, particularly ss. 47 [9] and 43. [10]

---

8 (1990) 55 SASR 327.
9 **47. General power of the Court to make interlocutory orders**
   The Court shall have the same power of making interlocutory orders for the purposes of and in relation to arbitration proceedings as it has for the purposes of and in relation to proceedings in the court.

It was considered that s. 47 was superfluous, unless it expressed the supervisory powers and s.43 must necessarily be dealing with interlocutory matters since s. 38 deals with the position after an award has been made. [11]

The South Australian decision was rejected in strident terms by the New South Wales Supreme Court in *Imperial Leather Company Pty Limited v Macri & Marcellino Pty Limited* [12] where Rogers J considered all reasons advanced by the South Australian Court in the light of the House of Lords decision in *Bremer-Vulkan*.[13] He held that the legislative purpose and intent of the Act was such that the Court does not have power under s. 43 to review the conduct of or procedural orders in the course of arbitration proceedings unless they are inconsistent with the requirements of natural justice.

In a recent decision of the Victorian Supreme Court, *Nauru Phosphate Royalties Trust v Matthew Hall Mechanical and Electrical Engineers Pty Limited*,[14] Smith J expressly agreed with Rogers J. Dissatisfied with the particulars of nexus between delay and damages in a global claim, the proprietor sought an order for further particulars which was refused by the arbitrator. In Court the proprietor made alternative claims for either striking out the global claim, or for an order for further particulars, and sought an order for the removal of the arbitrator for misconduct. The applications were dismissed, primarily on the basis that s.47 of the 1984 Act did not confer a special supervisory jurisdiction on the Court for dealing with procedural error by arbitrators. However the Court held it had a discretion to intervene in appropriate cases of infringement of natural justice.

---

10 **43. Court may remit for reconsideration**
Subject to section 38(1), the court may remit any matter referred to arbitration by an arbitration agreement together with any directions it thinks proper to the arbitrator or umpire for reconsideration.

11 Section 38 **Judicial Review of Awards**, reproduced below, echoes the provisions of the section 1 of the English Arbitration Act 1979.

12 (1991) 22 NSWLR 653 at 666-7.

13 *Bremer-Vulkan Schiffbau und Maschinenfabrik v South India Shipping Corporation Ltd* [1981] AC 909.

14 [1994] 2 VR 386.

In *Commonwealth of Australia v Cockatoo Dockyards Pty Ltd* [15] Rolfe J dealt with an application to set aside orders by an arbitrator permitting amendment to the Points of Claim during the course of the proceedings and the introduction of further evidence which put the claim on a different basis. The proceedings were brought in reliance upon ss. 43 and 47 of the Act.

Rolfe J held that s. 47 does not give the Court power to make orders the effect of which is to overrule decisions of the arbitrator, but gives the Court "an ancillary or concurrent power to make orders touching on the conduct of the arbitration".

> *"In my opinion s.47 does not provide any jurisdiction to allow this Court to review an arbitrator's decision or to hear an appeal against it. In my opinion it is intended to grant, although in more general terms, power to make the type of orders provided for in s.12(6) of the Arbitration Act 1950 (UK), to the extent those matters are not dealt with specifically in other sections."* [16]

He further held that s. 43 did not grant jurisdiction to the Court unless there has been a successful challenge to an award under s. 38, and that the remission of "any matter referred to arbitration" might include a decision on practice and procedure.

The power of the Court under s. 47 has been held to include orders for security for costs,[17] to grant a Mareva injunction,[18] and the power to direct the hearing of an arbitration along with a Court reference pursuant to Pt 72 of the Supreme Court Rules.[19] In New South Wales there are rules of Court made pursuant to the Commercial Arbitration Act (Pt 72A r. 4)[20] which provide that the Court may refuse to make an order under s. 47 where the Court considers that the arbitrator has power to make the order.

---

15 Unreported, Supreme Court of New South Wales, 3 November 1994, Rolfe J.
16 *Ibid.* at 13.
17 *Johnson v Macri & Marcellino Pty Ltd* (unreported, Supreme Court of NSW, 8 June 1990, Cole J).
18 *Imperial Leather op cit.* at 666.
19 *Aerospatiale Holdings Australia Pty Ltd v Elspan International Ltd* (1992) 28 NSWLR 321.
20 See also Supreme Court Rules (ACT) O.83 r 8.01

The Cockatoo Dockyard arbitration proceedings involved a claim, inter alia, by the Commonwealth for breaches of covenants of a lease of the dockyard and an assertion that the defendant was obliged to hand up the dockyard in good repair and condition. The site is an island in Sydney Harbour which has been used as a naval dockyard since 1857. The Commonwealth claimed damages based on the cost of "remediating" the island to a standard suitable for residential sub-division. The issues arising in this aspect of the claim and many of the reports concerning alleged contamination and pollution were obviously of considerable public interest, and certainly of interest to the State Government of New South Wales.

At the request of the respondent, the arbitrator gave directions restricting disclosure of documents "prepared for the purposes, or to be in any way used in" the arbitration. The arbitrator made various directions in March, June and September 1994. The Directions made in June 1994 which were in issue were to the following effect:

> "1. *Direct that neither party to the proceedings disclose or grant access to:-*
>
> (a) *any documents or other material prepared for the purposes of this arbitration;*
>
> (b) *any documents or other material, whether prepared for the purposes of this arbitration or not, which reveal the contents of any document or other material which was prepared for the purposes of this arbitration;*
>
> (c) *any documents or material produced for inspection or discovery by the other party for the purposes of these proceedings;*
>
> (d) *any documents or material filed in evidence in these proceedings.*"

The directions included a proviso permitting disclosure to legal advisers etc. and a direction that, on twenty-four hours' notice, either party "having formed the view that its interests so require" advise of any proposal to disclose documents, and apply to set aside the earlier directions. The arbitrator wished to maintain confidentiality of information on the environmental issues during the currency of the arbitration. He was concerned about the potential impact on witnesses and their evidence if those issues were sensationalised in the media. In October 1994 the Commonwealth requested the arbitrator, inter alia, to set aside his earlier directions. The arbitrator dismissed this application.

In proceedings separate from those referred to earlier, the Commonwealth sought the intervention of the Court and a declaration that the arbitrator did not have power to make the directions. It relied upon ss. 43 and 47 of the Act, and upon the inherent jurisdiction of the Supreme Court supported by s. 23 of the Supreme Court Act 1970 (NSW). Rolfe J[21] refused the application, citing the reasons set out in his earlier opinion.[22] He further rejected the submissions that the Court had inherent jurisdiction to intervene and that s. 23 of the Supreme Court Act 1970 (NSW) advanced that jurisdiction. He held that there was no power to intervene under the Commercial Arbitration Act outside the power reserved for removal of an arbitrator for misconduct under s. 44. The Court of Appeal granted leave to appeal from the decision and on 27 June 1995, by majority, allowed the appeal.[23]

The President of the Court of Appeal, Kirby P, gave the leading judgment of the Court. He agreed with Rolfe J that it would be extraordinary if the Commercial Arbitration Act limited appeals against final awards yet provided a mechanism to review interlocutory orders made during an arbitration. The Court also agreed with Rolfe J that it had no power under ss. 43 or 47 of the Act to intervene, and held that the interlocutory direction was not an award to which s. 38 applied. The Court considered the question of misconduct under s. 44 which might have entitled an application for removal of the arbitrator; this however was a course the Commonwealth chose not to pursue.

Kirby P then considered the inherent power of the Supreme Court supported by s. 23 of the Supreme Court Act 1970 which provides:

---

21 Unreported, Supreme Court of New South Wales, 15 November 1994.

22 *Commonwealth of Australia v. Cockatoo Dockyards Pty Ltd*, unreported, Supreme Court of New South Wales, 3 November 1994.

23 *Commonwealth of Australia v Cockatoo Dockyard Pty Ltd*, unreported, Court of Appeal New South Wales, 27 June 1995.

"23. The Court shall have all jurisdiction which may be necessary for the administration of justice in New South Wales."

Reference was made to the jurisdiction derived from the Court's establishment to receive the royal prerogative to do justice, which provides an extremely large inherent jurisdiction. This inherent jurisdiction or the jurisdiction provided by s. 23 was able to be ousted by specific legislation. The respondent to the appeal relied upon the specificity of the Commercial Arbitration Act 1984 and the Court's decisions in *Promenade Investments Pty Limited v New South Wales* [24] and *Natoli v Walker*[25] as establishing a general policy against intervention.

Counsel for the respondent agreed that if the interlocutory directions were beyond the arbitrator's competence, then the Act allowed for his removal for technical misconduct. Counsel also argued that the decisions were not final in that the Commonwealth had leave to request the lifting of the order against specific documents but had chosen not to adopt that course.

The President referred to the finding of Steyn J, as he then was, in *Biakh and Biali v Hyundai Corporation Limited* [26] that there was no inherent jurisdiction left to intervene at an interlocutory stage which did not otherwise fall to be dealt with as misconduct by the arbitrator. Kirby P admitted that he would have agreed with Counsel's reasoning if the matter was within the scope of the arbitration. In the present arbitration he held that there was a public interest to be observed and therefore the Court should use its inherent powers to administer justice to overcome the statutory requirement of non-intervention. He said that it was the scope of the arbitration itself and the ambit of the orders that may properly be made by an arbitrator within that scope which should be of concern to the Court. In effect, the President held that the Court had the power to define the boundaries of an arbitration beyond which

---

24 (1991) 26 NSWLR 203 at 225-227.
25 Unreported, Court of Appeal of NSW, 26 May 1994.
26 [1988] 1 Lloyds Reports 187.

the powers to issue interlocutory orders would intrude into the domain of legitimate public interest.

While he realised that the concept of a boundary around the legitimate activities of an arbitrator may be inconsistent with the majority decision of the House of Lords in *Bremer-Vulkan*, [27] the President still upheld the primacy of applications for interlocutory orders to the arbitrator. But he did question the general proposition that, by the act of submission to arbitration by private contract, parties can be deprived of relief by a Court if the orders of the arbitrator go beyond the legitimate boundaries of the arbitration.

> *"Where such an excess of jurisdiction exists, it is both proper and necessary that the jurisdiction of this Court should remain to uphold the rule of law and to safeguard other competing lawful rights and duties. Whether this Court's residual jurisdiction arises from its large inherent powers derived ultimately from the sovereign ... I do not have to decide. The powers survive because the Commercial Arbitration Act will support only such directions as are lawfully made within the large ambit of the operation of that Act. Stray outside that ambit, and the supervisory power of this Court remains to provide relief at the behest of a party showing a requisite interest to invoke that relief."*

The Court of Appeal made reference to the public's legitimate interest in obtaining information concerning Government dealings and the inclination of the judiciary of Australia to view the disclosure of Government information "through different spectacles". The Court considered that the same approach should apply to arbitrators and said:

> *"Where an arbitrator, in the course of giving a procedural direction, goes beyond the establishment of procedures necessary for the commercial arbitration between the parties and makes orders which impinge upon the public's legitimate interest, the arbitrator goes outside the arbitration. Certainly, the arbitrator cannot then point to s.14* [28] *of the* [Commercial

---

27 [1981] AC 909
28 14. **Procedure of arbitrator or umpire**

Arbitration Act 1984 (NSW)], *unelaborated, as a basis to sustain directions made. There will be a fine line between procedural directions which are **within** the large ambit that s.14 permits and those which go **beyond**. To the former, the Court will show restraint, reserving any complaint to be made to the end of the arbitration in any challenge that may lawfully be brought from a final (or interim) award or for the removal of the arbitrator for misconduct. But where the Court concludes that the direction made has gone beyond the purposes of the arbitration proceedings, and is thus extra-jurisdictional and unlawful, it will, in a proper case, provide relief. In my view, this is such a case.*"

In the light of earlier and repeated statements as to the necessity for arbitrators to observe the principles of natural justice in interlocutory orders, this decision may offer a remedy where otherwise the only apparent course for an aggrieved party is to seek the removal of the arbitrator for technical misconduct. This might occur, for example, if an arbitrator, clearly without power, nevertheless ordered a stay of a cross claim in the proceedings pending provision of security for costs.

The more probable result of the decision of the Court of Appeal will be that it is confined to rare cases involving government bodies where an issue of significant public interest is involved.

Judicial Review of Arbitration Awards

Following the introduction of the Uniform Commercial Arbitration Acts, some courts in Australia took a liberal view of the approach to be taken by the court on an application for leave to appeal from an arbitrator's Award under s.38. The approach taken was not consistent in all courts. In *Qantas Airways Limited v Joseland and Gilling*,[29] the Court of Appeal in New South Wales considered the scope of the

---

Subject to this Act and to the arbitration agreement, the arbitrator or umpire may conduct proceedings under that agreement in such manner as the arbitrator or umpire thinks fit.

29 (1986) 6 NSWLR 327.

discretion to grant leave to appeal and referred to in *The Nema*,[30] but held:

> *"We are not convinced that the statements of Lord Diplock, based as they are on a different background, are applicable to s 38 of our Act. The matters to which Lord Diplock refers are important factors in determining whether leave should be given. But the exercise of the discretion conferred by s 38 does not depend on whether the claimant has made out a strong prima facie case or fulfilled the other requirements to which his Lordship refers. It is a discretion to be exercised after considering all the circumstances of the case. We will postpone the question of granting leave until we have discussed the substantial issues in the case."* [31]

and later

> *"The form of agreement is in general use in New South Wales. The arbitrator's decision affects the construction of a number of important clauses in that agreement. Leave to appeal should be granted and the appeal should be allowed."* [32]

The Nema guidelines were rejected in some New South Wales decisions[33] and yet were accepted in others.[34] In Victoria, the Nema guidelines were applied in *Karenlee Nominees Pty Limited v Robert Salzer Constructions Pty Limited*,[35] but in other decisions the approach taken in Qantas Airways has been followed.[36]

---

30 [1982] AC 724, 742-43.
31 *Qantas v Joseland & Gilling* (1986) 6 NSWLR 327, 333.
32 *Ibid.* at 337.
33 *Jennings Construction Limited v Q H & M Birt Pty Limited* (1987) 8 NSWLR 18.
34 *Donvito v Diekman* (1989) 6 BCL 30.
35 [1988] VR 614.
36 *Leighton Contractors Pty Limited v Kilpatrick Green Pty Limited* [1992] 2 VR 505.

Section 38 in the *Commercial Arbitration Act 1984 (NSW)* was amended in 1990.[37] The amendments nevertheless do not, as was intended, specify the circumstances in which the Court may exercise its discretion or the matters which should be taken into account.

The leading case on the interpretation of s. 38 dealing with applications for leave to appeal from awards is *Promenade Investments Pty Limited v New South Wales*.[38] The Court of Appeal noted that the terms "error of law on the face of the award" and "manifest error" were well known

---

37 **38. Judicial Review of Awards**
  (1) Without prejudice to the right of appeal conferred by subsection (2), the court shall not have jurisdiction to set aside or remit an award on the ground of error of fact or law on the face of the award.
  (2) Subject to subsection (4), an appeal shall lie to the Supreme Court on any question of law arising out of an award.
  (3) On the determination of an appeal under subsection (2) the Supreme Court may by order -
    (a) confirm, vary or set aside the award; or
    (b) remit the award, together with the Supreme Court's opinion on the question of law which was the subject of the appeal, to the arbitrator or umpire for reconsideration or, where a new arbitrator or umpire has been appointed, to that arbitrator or umpire for consideration,
    and where the award is remitted under paragraph (b) the arbitrator or umpire shall, unless the order otherwise directs, make the award within 3 months after the date of the order.
  (4) An appeal under subsection (2) may be brought by any of the parties to an arbitration agreement -
    (a) with the consent of all the other parties to the arbitration agreement; or
    (b) subject to section 40, with the leave of the Supreme Court.
  (5) The Supreme Court shall not grant leave under subsection (4)(b) unless it considers that:
    (a) having regard to all the circumstances, the determination of the question of law concerned could substantially affect the rights of one or more parties to the arbitration agreement; and
    (b) there is:
      (i) a manifest error of law on the face of the award; or
      (ii) strong evidence that the arbitrator or umpire made an error of law and that the determination of the question may add, or may be likely to add, substantially to the certainty of commercial law.
  (6) The Supreme Court may make any leave which it grants under subsection (4)(b) subject to the applicant complying with any conditions it considers appropriate.
  (7) Where the award of an arbitrator or umpire is varied on an appeal under subsection (2), the award as varied shall have effect (except for the purposes of this section) as if it were the award of the arbitrator or umpire.
38 (1991) 26 NSWLR 203 at 225-227.

to the Courts and held that the construction promoting the purpose or object underlying the Act must be preferred to other constructions, so that it was permissible to obtain assistance from material not forming part of the Act if the meaning was obscure. The final question of whether to grant leave must take account of matters referred to by Lord Diplock in the *Nema*.[39]

If a judge was required to determine "manifest error" it would be preferable for the judge to hear adversarial argument. The Court referred to the decision of Brownie J in *Graham Evans & Co. Pty Ltd v SPF Formwork Pty Ltd*.[40] where his Honour said that if an appellant asserted an error of law because the award omitted reference to some essential ingredient in the chain of reasoning, it would be wrong to exclude evidence showing that the matter not mentioned in the arbitrator's reasons was conceded during the hearing.

The Court of Appeal also considered the comments of McHugh JA in *Larkin v Parole Board* [41] where he said "manifest" connotes an error of law that is more than arguable.

It may be necessary and permissible to consider extrinsic material on a leave application if the error of law is not manifest, however the requirement that the question must add substantially to the certainty of commercial law reflected the limitation which Lord Diplock[42] had in mind, and should not be construed narrowly. An appeal in any event will only lie on a question of law arising out of the award.

A recent case illustrating the approach to be taken by the Court on an application for leave under s. 38 is *Natoli*,[43] where the judge at first instance granted leave from an award under a residential building contract which rejected three cross claims. On the appeal, the judge reversed his grant of leave in respect of one matter but allowed an appeal in respect of two items which were a claim that payments to nominated subcontractors were within the contract and not extras, and a claim that painting of the residence was included by reference in a

---

39 [1982] AC 724, 742-743.
40 (1992) 8 BCL 147.
41 (1987) 10 NSWLR 57.
42 *The Nema* [1982] AC 724 at 742-3.
43 *Natoli v Walker* (unreported, Court of Appeal of NSW, 26 May 1994).

tender letter. By a majority, the Court of Appeal allowed the appeal and the arbitrator's award was reinstated.

Having referred to the modest amounts involved and to the objects of the amended s.38 "to promote the finality of arbitral awards even at the price of denying a party its usual entitlement to the determination of the dispute by a Court of law", and considering at length the questions raised in the appeal, the Court was satisfied leave should not have been granted.

The President of the Court of Appeal granted leave primarily to emphasise the concern that the Courts should have to ensure finality of the award made by the arbitrator and to reflect the intention of Parliament reflected in debate on the Commercial Arbitration (Amendment) Bill 1990 that "all too often arbitration had become simply a 'dry run' for the litigation which followed".[44]

Kirby P said that the Courts were "too tender to the achievement of justice and insufficiently attentive to the needs of finality". He said that it was evident that the intention of the Parliaments throughout Australia was to have a much narrower focus on appeals; the approach now favoured is to follow the House of Lords.[45]

The decision in *Promenade* [46] has been followed by courts[47] in other States indicating a preparedness to adopt a consistent approach. Since *Promenade* there has been one case only where the Court of Appeal has provided leave where it was refused by a judge at first instance. In *Friend and Broker Pty Ltd v Council of the Shire of Eurobodalla* [48] it appeared to the Court that there had been a clear and simple oversight by the arbitrator of the principle of law that if a breach of contract has two causes, both co-operating and of equal efficacy in causing the loss, a party responsible for the breach is liable to the plaintiff.

---

44 New South Wales Parliamentary Debates (Legislative Assembly) 29 November 1990 11569.

45 *The Nema* [1982] AC 724

46 *Promenade Investments Pty Limited v New South Wales* (1991) 26 NSWLR 203.

47 For example *Commonwealth v Rian Financial Services and Developments Pty Ltd* (1992) 36 FCR 101; and *Re Tiki Village International Ltd* [1994] 2 Qd R 674.

48 Unreported, Court of Appeal, 24 November 1993.

Conclusion

Following an initial liberal approach, in some cases, to the review of arbitration awards under the Uniform Commercial Arbitration Acts, and consequent upon amendments to the provisions dealing with judicial review of awards, the Court of Appeal in New South Wales has now prescribed an approach more consistent with the stringent "Nema" guidelines. It is therefore evident that the restrictive rights of appeal from an arbitrator's award that apply in England now apply similarly in Australia; the emphasis on finality has been beneficial to litigants, at least from the point of view of the costs of dispute resolution. However, English cases on the subject of confidentiality exemplify the impossibility of establishing a general rule because of the unlimited and undefinable exceptions to any statement of a rule. The High Court rule in *Esso* [49] holds that confidentiality is not an essential element in arbitration and, in the absence of an express term in the arbitration agreement, will not be implied. Such judicial consistency has unfortunately not been applied to the issue of the residual or inherent power in a Court to intervene in interlocutory arbitral matters—two down, one to go.

---

49 (1995) 128 ALR 391.

7. Commercial Arbitration in Canada: A "Model" Law for Others?

Richard Potter

Synopsis

This paper examines how arbitration law in Canada has developed and adapted to incorporate the UNCITRAL Model Law.

Introduction

Canada has become a proving ground for many of the key issues of commercial arbitration in the 1990s, from the desirability of adopting the UNCITRAL Model Law, to the relationship between common law courts and arbitrators, to the use of court-annexed ADR. As a result, legislators and commentators alike will want to observe the Canadian experience, a jurisdiction which largely inherited 19th Century English law (yet has within it a Civil law jurisdiciton with markedly different origins and traditions), a federal jurisdiction, a multilateral trading economy with strong bilateral trade and investment ties to the United States, and a country which has embraced the UNCITRAL Model Law with considerable enthusiasm. In addition, those same legislators and commentators will want to observe the relationship between these developments and other aspects of court reform such as the creation of a commercial court in Ontario.

The discussion below is not intended to be exhaustive or completely comprehesive but, rather, is a general introduction to the way in which Canada has rather quickly adapted to changing circumstances in the commercial world.

The pre-Model-Law law

There may be only mild exaggeration in the assertion of Professor Paterson[1] that "the almost unqualified enthusiasm with which Canada adopted the Model Law was largely explicable by the primitive state of its arbitration law". Professor Graham, with only slightly more restraint, has described this state of Canada's pre-Model Law arbitration law as "static"[2].

However described, the status of arbitration law in Canada prior to the adoption of the Model Law was not such as to give confidence to a commercial lawyer. He or she could not safely predict whether the courts would uphold the parties' choice and permit them to forsake the courts for the resolution of their disputes. This stemmed not only from the undeveloped form of the various provincial arbitration statutes, but also from the prevailing judicial attitude towards commercial arbitration and lesser tribuals.

Although the typical arbitration statute in common law Canada[3] might refer to the possibility of staying parallel legal proceedings in favour of arbitration, there was a heavy onus on an applicant in that regard which was seldom met. Exclusion of appeals to the courts were drafted, but there was no legislative assurance that an intention to exclude appeals would be respected, and there was no mention of any power to grant interim relief, whether by the arbitrator or by the courts. Legislative intentions regarding judicial review were barely hinted at. Generally speaking, however, the courts kept a watchful eye on what were seen as markedly inferior tribunals.

To the extent that parties attempted to grant autonomy to arbitral tribunals, the courts were seldom willing to support this without reservation. This was particularly the case if the position could be stated so as to frame the question as one of law on which the arbitral tribunal had erred or as one putting into question the tribunal's jurisdiction. No distinction was made in the pre-Model Law legislation between domestic and international disputes; rather, the legislation appeared to apply to

---

[1]   Paterson, "Implementing the UNCITRAL Model Law: The Canadian Experience", (1993), 10 *Journal of International Arbitration* 29

[2]   Graham, "The Internationalization of Commercial Arbitration in Canada: A Preliminary Reaction" (1987-88), 13 *Canadian Business Law Journal* 2

[3]   For example, the *Arbitrations Act* (Ontario), RSO 1980, c 25

virtually all arbitration, domestic and international, commercial and otherwise.

With such an archaic legislative underpinning, it is not surprising that commercial arbitration, as an institution, was relatively undeveloped. This could be contrasted with a more modern infrastructure that supported grievance and collective bargaining arbitration, an institution that had pervaded industrial relations throughout Canada for several decades. In this legal sector, which was the subject of its own *sui generis* legislation in each jurisdiction[4], an extensive network of private, professional arbitrators, mediators and facilitators had grown up to service the need for the rapid settlement of labour disputes.

It was a continuing curiosity, therefore, until the 1980s that in Canada the relative sophistication of dispute resolution in the field of labour relations could coexist beside the relative primitiveness of the same process in the world of commerce.

The New Legal Landscape

By 1987, the Canadian arbitration landscape had a dramatic new look. By then, each of the ten Canadian provinces and the two Territories had adopted a form of the Model Law for all arbitration that within their respective terms fell within the relevant definitions as being "international" and "commercial"[5]. In addition, because the division of powers under the Canadian Constitution allocates several industry sectors, such as telecommunications, atomic energy, and interprovincial transportation, exclusively to the federal jurisdiction, the federal government also adopted the Model Law,[6] for application to all arbitration within federal jurisdiction, whether domestic or international.

There are variations amongst the several versions of these 13 Model Law enactments, but, for purposes of a general discussion, they can be considered to be virtually a single body of law. In itself, this has been a

---

[4] In each jurisidiction, the final and binding settlement of labour disputes by arbitration was and is required by law, and this process is specifically exempted from the general arbitration law. For example, see the *Labour Relations Act* (Ontario), RSO 1990, c L.2, sections 45 (1) and (12)

[5] See Graham, *op. cit.* 2, for the respective statute citations

[6] *Commercial Arbitration Act* (Canada), RSC 1985, c 17 (2nd Supplement)

considerable advance. So far as international commercial arbitration is concerned, the benefit of a relatively uniform law across the 13 jurisdictions is obvious. A concomitant benefit, however, was the re-thinking of the way in which domestic, or non-international arbitration, should be treated. Since the old statutes, albeit inadequately, covered both domestic and international arbitration, the carving out from them of international commercial arbitration for special treatment via adoption of the Model Law forced the legislatures to reconsider their treatment of domestic arbitration. As a result, each Canadian jurisdiction now has modernised its statute governing those arbitrations which fall outside the purview of the international statutes[7].

The relationship between courts and arbitrators

There is no doubt that one of the motives in the adoption of the Model Law in Canada was simply to provide a more coherent "internal" code for the governance of the arbitral process in international commercial arbitration proceedings. However, the more controversial motive which was never far from the surface in the discussion and debates leading up to the adoption of the Model Law was the goal of better regulating the relationship between the courts and the arbitral process. In fact, this discussion and debate was so central to the reform process that evidence of it (in effect, a strong criticism of the prevailing legislative and judicial attitudes of the day towards arbitration) was enshrined, uniquely, in the preamble of the adopting legislation in British Columbia:

Whereas British Columbia, and in particular the City of Vancouver, is becoming an international financial and commercial centre;

And *Whereas disputes in international commercial agreements are often resolved by means of arbitration;*

And Whereas Bristish Columbia has not previously enjoyed a hospitable legal environment for international commercial arbitration;

---

[7]   For example, see the *Arbitration Act* (Ontario), SO 1991, c 17. This statute specifically addresses in a comprehensive way the staying of parallel legal proceedings (section 7), appeals to the courts (section 45) and applications for judicial review (section 46), although it should be noted that the threshold over which a court must leap before setting side a domestic arbitration award is somewhat lower than that provided for under the Model Law legislation

And *Whereas there are divergent views in the international commercial and legal communities respecting the conduct of, and* ***the degree and nature of judicial intervention in, international commercial arbitration***;

And *Whereas the United Nations Commision on International Trade Law has adopted the UNCITRAL Model Arbitration Law which reflects a consensus of views on the conduct of, and **degree and nature of judicial intervention in, international commercial arbitration;***

Therefore Her Majesty by and with advice and consent of the Province of British Columbia ... [emphasis added][8]

The manner in which this surprisingly blunt legislative language has been received by the courts is examined below.

Judicial attitudes in the field of labour arbitration

Although not a prerequisite to an exposition of the reception of the Model Law in Canada, it is instructive to observe the parallel question of the relationship between Canadian courts and labour arbitral tribunals. In part this is because English case law (decided in a commercial and non-collective bargaining context) is still occasionally, although decreasingly, cited by Canadian courts. In part this is because it fills in the backdrop against which judicial attitudes about curial deference are formed.

The leading authority is a 1993 case in the Supreme Court of Canada[9] which held that curial deference will be extended to labour arbitrators interpreting a collective agreement (even in the absence of a clause in the governing labour relations statute governing privity), although the extent of that deference may not extend to errors in the interpretation of statutes or the common law.

The *Bradco Construction* case has brought into focus a lingering anomaly which is the result of arbitration developing divergently in

---

8   *International Commercial Arbitration Act*, SBC 1986, c 14

9   *United Brotherhood of Carpenters and Joiners of America, Local 579 v. Bradco Construction Limited*, [1993] 2 SCR 316

commerical and labour fields in Canada. We now apply one standard of curial deference in international commercial arbitration, another standard for domestic commercial arbitration, a further standard for labour arbitrations involving interpretations of collective agreements and yet another standard for labour arbitrations involving interpretations of statutes and common law. Since the seemingly watertight compartments between labour arbitration and commercial arbitration are seldom breached, perhaps this is "merely" a socalled "academic" question.

A new role for the judiciary: motions to stay

The acid test for the Model Law was how it would be accepted by the judiciary. Not surprisingly, the first few cases displayed a variety of judicial attitudes. In a pair of cases decided in 1988, *Boart Sweden AB* in Ontario[10] and *ODC Exhibit Systems*[11] in British Columbia, and on surprisingly similar facts, courts showed quite different approaches to applications to stay parallel legal proceedings .

Both cases involved a Canadian company and a Swedish party in a distributorship arrangement in which the Canadian company received or claimed to receive the exclusive rights to sell a product in a territory which included Canada. The Swedish grantor of the rights purported to terminate the distributorship agreement. The relevant agreements provided for arbitration of disputes. In each case, the Canadian party launched legal proceedings in Canada and the foreign party moved to stay the legal proceedings relying on, among other grounds, article 8(1) of the Model Law which provides that the court should refer the matter to arbitration "unless it finds that the agreement [to arbitrate] is null and void". In both cases, the respondent plaintiff alleged that the defendant was guilty of tortious conduct in the carrying out of the contract and that this was sufficient justification for the respective plaintiffs to proceed in court.

In the *ODC Exhibit Systems* case, the stay application was denied without any reference to the underlying policy considerations which the British Columbia legislature set out in the preamble to the statute. Rather, the court used conventional contract analysis to conclude that by the time the matter came before the court the distribution agreement had been

---

[10] *Boart Sweden AB et al. v. NYA Stromnes AB et al.* (1988), 41 BLR 295 (Ont HCJ)
[11] *ODC Exhibit Systems Ltd v. Lee et al.* (1988), 41 BLR 286 (BCSC)

discharged. In addition, a secondary agreement in which the agreement to arbitrate was ignored on the basis that an allegation that the agreement had been, or might have been, entered into fraudulently could not be a dispute "arising out of [the] Agreement".

By contrast, in the *Boart Sweden AB* case, the Ontario court could hardly have been more supportive of what it conceived to be the underlying legislative policy in adopting the Model Law:

> *"Public policy carries me to the consideration which I conclude is paramount having regard to the facts of this case, and that is the very strong public policy of this jurisdiciton that where parties have agreed by contract that they will have the arbitrators decide their claims, instead of resorting to the Courts, the parties should be held to their contract."*[12]

In 1993 in the *Automatic Systems* cases[13], the Ontario Court of Appeal specifically endorsed the findings in the *Boart Sweden AB* case and strongly articulated its support for a limited judicial role in the supervision of commercial arbitrators operating in the setting of the Model Law. As this author has commented elsewhere,[14] these cases involved Ontario's construction lien statute, a legislative scheme which is peculiarly rooted in the locality. In these circumstances, therefore, a court might have felt that it had ample justification not to enforce the parties' expressed wish for foreign arbitration to settle disputes arising out of a construction project in Ontario. Instead, the Ontario Court of Appeal deferred to an arbitration process to take place in the State of Missouri. Most significantly, it did so with little hesitation.

At this juncture it is especially appropriate to review the facts and circumstances of the *Automatic Systems* cases.

A dispute arose from a construction project to be carried out in the Canadian province of Ontario. Automatic Systems Inc. (ASI) was a company located in the American State of Missouri that agreed to

---

[12] *Op. cit.*, 302

[13] *Automatic Systems Inc v. Bracknell Corp.* (1993), 12 BLR (2d) 132 (Ont CA) and *Automatic Systems Inc. v. ES Fox L*td (1993), 12 BLR (2d) 148 (Ont CA)

[14] Potter, R.B., "The Coming of Age of the UNCITRAL Model Law in Canada", (1994-95), 24 *Canadian Business Law Journal* 429

supply a conveyor system for inclusion in an assembly line being constructed at a Chrysler Canada plant in Ontario. The prime supply contract contained no arbitration provisions. The electrical portion of the job was subcontracted by ASI to Bracknell Corp., an Ontario firm. The subcontract was on ASI's standard form, and contained an arbitration clause that, in effect, provided for arbitration of disputes in Kansas City under Missouri law and the rules of the American Arbitration Association.

After disputes arose between ASI and Bracknell under the subcontract, Bracknell commenced an action in Ontario against ASI and Chrysler Canada under the *Construction Lien Act* (CLA), an Ontario statute.[15] ASI responded with a demand for arbitration in Missouri of both parties' claims. A bond for the full amount of Bracknell's claim was paid into court by ASI. This discharge the lien on the real property which had been created under the CLA. ASI then moved in the Ontario court to have the action under the CLA stayed in favour of arbitration in Missouri, invoking the provisions of section 8 of Ontario's *International Commercial Arbitration Act*[16] (ICCA) and Article 8 of the Model Law.

Bracknell urged the court to dismiss the motion to stay the Ontario action primarily on the grounds that the CLA does not permit parties to contract out of its application to them that the choice of Missouri law in the subcontract was therefore void and that an arbitrator in Missouri would not be bound to apply Ontario law; and, that, accordingly, the court ought not to refer the parties to arbitration. ASI, on the other hand, submitted that referral to arbitration under the ICAA was mandatory once all the conditions for application of the statute were met. In ASI's submission, the thrust of the CLA was to provide lien rights on the real property comprising a construction site, while the common law of contract governed the proof of the amounts that were owing between the parties. An arbitrator's award, wherever made, would merely quantify the amount of Bracknell's lien claim to be asserted against the bond, in accordance with the procedure set out in the CLA. There was room, therefore, within the scheme created by the CLA, for a foreign arbitration to determine the liability for and amount of such a claim.

---

[15] RSO 1990, c.30
[16] RSO 1990, c I.9

In the court of first instance, the motion to stay was dismissed on two bases. The first basis was that because the CLA expressly recognises arbitration of a domestic claim, but does not mention international claims, the Legislature must have intended to exclude the latter from the ambit of this recognition. The second basis was that sound policy reasons favoured applying Ontario law to construction lien claims because the application of a foreign law could be unfair if it skewed the result by either augmenting or diminishing a particular claim or type of claim.

On appeal, the applicants ASI, was successful in reversing the decision of the court below and the CLA action in Ontario was stayed in favour of Missouri-based arbitration. In the view of the Ontario Court of Appeals the readily available recourse to the security which had been posted (a bond or letter of credit) reduced questions of claims against trust funds and lien rights in real property to purely a question of contract between ASI and Bracknell. The parties had chosen to arbitrate their contractual differences by arbitration in Missouri and, faced with the mandatory provisions of the ICAA, the Court of Appeal found no reason not to respect the parties' choice. As a matter of interpretation of the CLA, there was no basis for any distinction between an arbitration that is purely domestic or one that is interprovincial or international.[17]

The Ontario Court of Appeal's views at a policy level are found in this strong endorsement of the Model Law:

> *Having regard to international comity, and to the strong commitments made by the Legislature of* [Ontario] *to the policy of international commercial arbitration through the adoption of the* [ICAA] *and the Model Law, it should, in my respectful view, require clear language indeed to preclude it.*[18]

---

[17] This paraphrase of the Court of Appeal judgment could be misinterpreted. To say that the CLA should be interpreted equally as regards domestic and international arbitrations does not in any way impinge on the separateness of the two schemes for administering arbitration in Ontario—the ICAA for international arbitrations, and the Arbitration Act for domestic arbitrations—of which more below

[18] *Automatic Systems Inc. v. Bracknell Corp.*(1993) 12 BLR (2d) 132 (Ont CA) at 144

Despite this strong support from Ontario for the ICAA and the Model Law in favour of party autonomy, a cloud on the horizon has emerged in the form of a more recent judgment of the British Columbia Court of Appeal, *Burlington Northern Railroad Company v. Canadian National Railway.*[19]

A dispute arose under an 80-year old track-sharing agreement. One party, Burlington Northern Railroad Company (BNR), wrote to the other, Canada National Railway (CNR), stating that it wished to use the arbitration provisions in the agreement to settle the dispute. BNR enclosed a draft of arbitral questions for determination, recommended a venue for arbitration and enclosed a draft agreement regarding arbitration procedures. Although CNR undertook to search for qualified arbitrators, it did not respond to BNR's letter and did not make a nomination. BNR brought an action to enforce its claim. On a chambers motion, CNR successfully moved for an order staying the legal proceedings. On the appeal, however, a 2-1 majority of the British Columbia Court of Appeal reversed the court below.

In the view of the majority, given in perfunctory reasons, because CNR did not make a nomination, the agreement to arbitrate was 'inoperative' or 'not in operation' within the meaning of Article 8 of the Model Law. As a result, the mandatory stay provisions regarding concurrent legal proceedings were not binding on the court. The minority judgment was also grounded on a reading of Article 8, but with opposite result and supported by much more fully articulated reasons. In the view of the minority, Article 8 does not require that an arbitration clause be invoked in a certain procedural manner, but merely requires that the dispute be one which the parties have agreed to resolve by arbitration, as opposed to recourse to the courts.

The *Burlington case* leaves a number of unanswered questions;

- If there is doubt whether an arbitration agreement is "inoperative", why should not this be left, in the first instance, for the arbitrator to make this decision? The writer of the majority reasons, Madame Justice Southin, had this to say on the point in an earlier case "When it is not plain that the matters in dispute fall outside the arbitration agreement,

---

[19]   (1995) 20 BLR (2d) 145 (BCCA)

the question whether they fall within it is not, in the first instance, for the court, but for the arbitrator."[20]

- Why should the party that intended to start the arbitral process be rewarded for later changing its position and starting legal proceedings?

- Does the *Burlington* case represent a change in direction of judicial attitude towards growing arbitral autonomy or is it merely an aberration from the generally more hospitable approach represented by *the Bracknell* case?

At the very least, as a result of this case, solicitors will be giving more careful scrutiny to their clients' strict adherence to procedural matters in arbitration proceedings. Although a definitive assessment is hampered by the limited scope of the majority reasons, the result seems to have been arrived at in a somewhat circular and mechanistic manner. As such, it does not seem to be representative of the general trend of the case law. On balance, Canadian courts have become increasingly accustomed to giving greater deference to arbitral tribunals when parallel proceedings arise. For international arbitrations under the Model Law, this trend will continue.

A new role for the judiciary: post-arbitration judicial review

Following the adoption of the Model Law, most of the early reported case law in Canada involving the interaction of courts and arbitrators has arisen from motions under section 8 of the Model Law. That is, as in the *Automatic Systems* cases discussed above, the disputants have come to the courts before the arbitration proceedings were completed and at a time when they were disputing which arbiter should take precedence, judge or arbitrator. The other key juncture in the parallel systems that can produce conflict is after the issue of the arbitration award. At that point, one party may consider whether there exists grounds on which to found an application for judicial review of the award.

---

[20] *Gulf Canada Resources Ltd. v. Arochem International Inc.* (1992), 43 CPR (3d) 390 at 401

For international disputes, the barrier over which an applicant for judicial review must leap is set at a high level. The Model Law starts from a strong presumption of party autonomy. On a plain reading of Article 34 of the Model Law, only in the most egregious circumstances should a court be able to set aside an award.[21] However, given the long history of close supervision of inferior tribunals by Anglo-Canadian courts, until the advent of the *Quintette Coal Ltd.* case[22] in 1990, it could mot be presumed that activist judges would not attempt to emasculate Article 34.

Quintette Ltd. (Q) was a British Columbia coal supplier which had entered into a long-term supply contract with a Japanese steel consortium, Nippon Steel Corp. (N). The price of the coal was to be adjusted in accordance with a complex series of formulae and could take into account unforeseen circumstances. Disputes arose over the price to be charged over a particular four-year period, 1987 to 1991. The disputes were referred to arbitration, as contemplated by the contract. Expensive hearings were held over a two-year period. The award did not represent acceptance of either party's position, but was a melding of the two theories contended for by the parties.

Q applied for judicial review of the award, arguing that the arbitration board's jurisdiction was confined to fixing a price as at a fixed date, and that it was not open to the board to set a series of prices over the four-year period. The Chief Justice of British Columbia dismissed the application for judicial review, noting that the Model Law gives no power to the court to set aside an award on the ground of errors of law. Instead, an arbitration award can be set aside only if it deals with a dispute not falling within the terms of the arbitration.

The court observed that the relationship between the older law of arbitration, developed in a wholly domestic context, and that applicable to international arbitration was considered in the leading *CBINZ Ltd.* case in New Zealand[23] which cited the *Mitsubishi* v. *Chrysler* case in

---

21 The grounds listed are party incapacity, improper notice, the award dealing with a dispute not falling within the submission, improper composition of the tribunal, improper subject matter and a conflict with public policy.

22 *Quintette Coal Ltd v. Nippon Steel Corp.* (1990), 48 BLR 32 (BCSC) and see the writer's Case Comment at 74.

23 *CBINZ Ltd. v. Badfrer Chiyoda*, [1989] 2 NZR 669 (CA)

the United States Supreme Court.[24] These cases, according to the British Columbia court, illustrate a world-wide trend toward restricting judicial control over international commercial arbitration awards.

International vs. domestic arbitration

All of the above discussion, as to both principles and case law, has dealt with international commercial arbitration, the arbitration that is defined as both 'international' and 'commercial' by the relevant provincial, federal or territorial legislation. In addition, each provincial and territorial jurisdiction has legislation designed to apply to arbitration that does not fall within the international commercial field. Here, there is much less uniformity amongst the various pieces of legislation, both because the unifying effect of the Model Law is missing, and because the historical antecedents of the older, general arbitration codes still have life.

This paper is not an appropriate forum to outline in detail the differences between the various Canadian international and domestic arbitration statutes in respect of, (i) motions to stay, and (ii) post-award appeals and judicial review. The reader is however referred to a comprehensive study by John Chapman which can be found in the Canadian Bar Review.[25]

As noted by Chapman, in the late 1980s when all the provinces adopted the Model Law for international commercial arbitrations, several provinces took the opportunity to overhaul their domestic arbitration statutes. In general, the result was a more modern approach to court supervision. For example, the new Ontario domestic statute, the *Arbitration Act*,[26] permits court intervention only in accordance with listed criteria. While this codification is an improvement, there has not yet been sufficient case law under the new legislation to conclude what level of deference Ontarion courts are likely to accord to domestic commercial arbitrators. For example, the courts in Ontario could follow the House of Lords decision in *The Nema*,[27] later applied and

---

24 *Misubishi Motors Corp. v. Soler Chrysler Plymouth Inc.*, 473 US 614 (1985)
25 Chapman, J.J., *Judicial Scrutiny of Domestic Commercial Arbitral Awards* (1995) 74 CBR 403
26 SO 1991, c. 17
27 *Pioneer Shipping Ltd. et al. v. B.T.P. Dioxide Ltd.*, [1982] AC 724

followed by British Columbia courts in the *Belkin* case[28] under a statute not identical to the Ontario one, and further limit judicial review beyond what might be taken from a literal reading of the statute.

In principle, it is possible that Ontario and other Canadian courts will take an interventionist position on this question. That is, any common law court free from binding authority on the question could take the view that non-specialist private tribunals need close supervision to maintain the purity of commercial law. However, in the writer's opinion this day has passed. It is highly unlikely, given the growing acceptance that ADR is an issue of public interest (and not a question only for obscure debate by professors of commercial law) that such a view would prevail. On the one hand, domestic arbitration statutes in Canada may never be interpreted to give arbitrators quite the same high degree of autonomy as they will receive in the international sphere; on the other hand it is unlikely that this difference in treatment will have a significantly dampening effect on the flowering of ADR in Canada.

Conclusion

The question of the degree of party autonomy sanctioned by the courts will be one of the most important factors in the success of the new legislative scheme in Canadian commercial arbitration law. In this writer's experience, when the parties to a commercial negotiation are given the opportunity to negotiate fully for a comprehensive ADR provision that reflects the parties' interests and the particular fact situation at hand, the result of this process is that the parties come to believe that the responsiblity for the enforcement of the agreement lies, in large measure, in their own hands. This increases immeasurably the likelihood that the culminating steps of the dispute resolution procedure will never be used at all, because the parties will settle their dispute within the system they have tailored to meet their needs. As a result, the parties should be given the maximum freedom to contract out of conventional legal proceedings.

The Canadian experience may be relevant to other jurisdictions, such as England and Wales, as they consider the implications of the adoption of the Model Law. Whether other countries wish to emulate Canada in its

---

[28] *Domtar Inc. v. Belkin Inc.*, [1990] 2 WWR 242 (BCCA)

wholesale embrace of the Model Law is, of course, for them to decide, but to date the Canadian experience has been favourable. A "foreign" code has been adopted, virtually intact, and therefore bringing with it internal consistency, yet it is inevitably being interpreted with an eye to local particularities. For Canadians, reception of good law from external sources is hardly a new concept, and we commend it to others.

8. The Arbitration Bill and Equity Arbitrations in England

Art McInnis

Synopsis

This paper examines the concepts of amiable composition and arbitration ex aequo et bono and analyses how the judicial attitude towards equity arbitrations has developed in England toward recognition of the need for such extra-legal procedures in the Arbitration Bill.

Introduction

Clause 46(1)(b) of the new Arbitration Bill recognises for the first time under a proposed statute for parties to have their disputes decided in equity, or what is also termed under the Model Law and in other jurisdictions amiable composition or arbitration ex aequo et bono. This article is a preliminary look at this important change, the judicial steps that gave rise to it and what parties choosing this system should expect. It is also one view on some of the misconceptions that have arisen generally on the topic.

The English Framework

It is often assumed that English arbitrators have always had to state their award according to law. However, upon closer analysis, it can be argued that this was not always the case. Sir Michael Mustill: '[t]hree hundred years ago, there existed in England a system of voluntary arbitration which reflected very accurately the ideals of [transnational arbitration]...'.[1] The system operated independently of the courts and thus one must presume, at least initially, without the coercive powers of the court to see that awards were stated according to law. The point

---

[1] Sir Michael John Mustill, 'Transnational Arbitration in English Law', in *International Commercial and Maritime Arbitration*, F D Rose, Ed 15, at 17.

was not lost on Stewart Boyd QC who writes: 'There was indeed a time, before it came to be settled law that in the absence of express agreement an arbitrator had a duty to decide according to law, when judges themselves quite explicitly acknowledged that an arbitrator need not apply the law where it produced a harsh result';[2] Mr Boyd continued and also gave the following example, referring to the case of *Knox v Symmonds*, decided in 1791:[3] '...the arbitrator has a greater latitude than the court in order to do complete justice between the parties; for instance he may relieve against a right which bears hard upon one party, but which having been acquired legally and without fraud, could not be resisted in a court of justice'.[4] Over time that freedom of the English arbitrator and those powers were gradually eroded and eventually lost as the courts assumed a greater supervisory role to the point today where arbitrators are required to state their awards according to law.[5]

The recent English judicial attitude is perhaps best described simply as cautious, but while equity clauses have not unequivocally beenendorsed nor have they been ruled out either. Perhaps of more interest than ambivalent judicial attitudes in the caselaw is evidence of a more profound change in judicial attitudes seen in articles on the subject of equity clauses by leading jurists. This section will look at both some of this caselaw and these writings.

The modern English era regarding equity clauses perhaps begins with the Privy Council decision in *Roland v Cassidy*.[6] This case, which was a civil law appeal from what is the province of Quebec today, raised issues of construction surrounding a partnership agreement that contained an amiable composition clause.[7] Commenting on whether a distinction should be drawn between arbitration and amiable composition The Earl of Selbourne said that:

---

2   Stewart Boyd, '"Arbitrator not bound by the Law" Clauses', (1990) 6 *Arbitration International* 122, 128.

3   *Ibid*, 128.

4   *Knox v Symmonds* (1791) 1 Ves 369.

5   See for a full discussion of this evolution, Mustill, M.J. & Boyd, S., *The Law and Practice of Commercial Arbitration in England*, 2nd Edn, Butterworths, 1989, ch 29 'Judicial Control: a historical survey', pp 431-458; ('Mustill and Boyd').

6   [1888] 13 AC 770 (PC).

7   Article 1346 of the Code of Civil Procedure at the time provided for amiable composition.

'...*the distinction must have some reasonable effect given to it, and the least effect which can reasonably be given to the words [amiable composition] is, that they dispense with the strict observance of those rules of law the non-observance of which, as applied to awards, results in no more than irregularity.*'[8]

Thus, the case at least affirms that an amiable composition clause is distinct from that of an arbitration clause and that equity clauses will not be treated as nullities per se.

Various explanations could be given for judicial reticence toward equity clauses. Justice Andrew Rogers posits that it is the judges' function to ensure that all the subjects of the Sovereign live under the rule of law,[9] or more precisely under the rule of one uniform system of law.

Thus, in *Czarnikow v Roth, Schmidt & Co*,[10] where the Court of Appeal held an 'exclusion of jurisdiction' clause void for being contrary to public policy, Atkin LJ said:[11] 'If [judicial scrutiny] did not exist arbitration clauses making an award a condition precedent would leave lay arbitrators at liberty to adopt any principles of law they pleased...The policy of the law has given to the High Court large power over inferior Courts for the very purpose of maintaining a uniform standard of justice and one uniform system of law'.

A second case that may be referred to is *Orion Cia Espanola de Seguros v Belfort Maats*.[12] Here, the question concerned an arbitration clause that authorised the arbitrators to 'settle any dispute under [the] Agreement according to an equitable rather than a strictly legal interpretation of its terms'.

Megaw, J, after referring to *Czarnikow*, stated his opinion why he declined to give effect to the equity clause in question in these words:

---

[8]   *Ibid* 772-773
[9]   Justice Andrew Rogers, *The Determination of Insurance Disputes - The Letter or the Spirit?* (1990) BCL 84.
[10]   [1922] 2 KB 478.
[11]   *Ibid*, 491.
[12]   [1962] 2 Lloyd's Rep 257.

'The conclusion which I draw...is that it is the policy of the law in this country that, in the conduct of arbitrations, arbitrators must in general apply a fixed and recognisable system of law...and that they cannot be allowed to apply some different criterion such as the view of the individual arbitrator or umpire on abstract justice or equitable principles, which, of course, does not mean "equity" in the legal sense of the word at all.' [13]

Such a restrictive judicial attitude continued unchanged until it was eventually relaxed in the Court of Appeal decision in *Eagle Star Insurance Co Ltd v Yuval Insurance Co Ltd.*[14] In that case, an equity clause in substantially the same terms as that in *Orion* was considered. Lord Denning MR, with the agreement of Goff and Shaw LJJ, said:

'I must say that I cannot see anything in public policy to make this clause void...It only ousts technicalities and strict construction. That is what equity did in the old days. And it is what arbitrators may properly do today under such a clause as this.' [15]

The decision at first seemed important in that it suggested a change in judicial attitudes toward equity clauses. Viewed more closely, however, and owing to the narrow construction which was ultimately given to the equity clause in the case, the decision cannot be viewed as a milestone. The case confined equity clauses to the ousting of mere technicalities and strict constructions; in fact likely a narrower construction than was given to the amiable composition clause almost one hundred years earlier by the Privy Council in the *Roland v Cassidy*[16] case. In the latter case it was remarked:

'the least effect which can reasonably be given to the words [amiable compositeur] is, that they dispense with the strict observance of those rules of law the non-observance of which, as applied to awards, results in no more than irregularity.' [17]

---

[13]   *Ibid*, 264.
[14]   [1978] 1 Lloyd's Rep 357.
[15]   *Ibid*, 362.
[16]   [1888] 13 AC 770 (PC).
[17]   *Ibid*, 773.

A variation on the amiable composition clause can be seen in *Home Insurance Co v Administratia.*[18] The facts concerned a share reinsurance treaty between two foreign companies that stipulated it should be interpreted as an 'honourable engagement rather than a legal obligation'. Justice Parker rejected a submission that no agreement existed and said:[19] '[i]t is plain that it was the common intention that there should be an enforceable obligation to arbitrate and to abide by the award. All that was intended was to free the arbitrators to some extent from strict rules and this...is permissible'.

In *Deutsche Schatbau-und-Tiefbohrgesellschaft mbH v Ras Al Khaimah National Oil Co*[20] (*'DST v Rakoil'*) the first English milestone toward a truly more open approach toward equity clauses was reached. Here, the Court of Appeal gave effect to an agreement between the parties to the dispute which empowered the arbitrator to determine the applicable rules.

The facts in *DST v Rakoil* are complex and will be examined here only insofar as necessary to make the points intended. They entail both an outstanding arbitration award as well as a court judgment in which neither party participated in the other's proceedings. The arbitration took place pursuant to an International Chamber of Commerce ('ICC') arbitration clause. The clause provided for arbitration in Geneva according to a proper law adopted by the arbitrators. The arbitrators determined that the proper law was 'internationally accepted principles of law governing contractual relations'. It was submitted in opposition to this determination that it would be contrary to English public policy to enforce an award reached on the basis of some unspecified and possibly ill-defined principles of law. However, in response to the submission, Sir John Donaldson MR, with whom Woolf and Russell LJJ agreed, said:[21] 'I can see no basis for concluding that the arbitrators' choice of proper law, a common denominator of principles underlying the laws of the various nations governing contractual relations, is out with the scope of the choice which the parties left to the arbitrators'.

---

[18] [1983] 2 Lloyd's Rep 674
[19] *Ibid*, 677.
[20] [1987] 2 All ER 769
[21] [1987] 2 All ER 769, 779.

Despite this liberal attitude,[22] when compared to the traditional restrictive view, a heavy tinge of caution is still discernible in the judgment. Thus, Sir John Donaldson MR said he would approach the clause by asking himself three questions when the parties have agreed that their rights shall be governed by some system of law which is not that of England, another state or for that matter even a serious modification of such a law:

(1) Did the parties intend to create legally enforceable rights and obligations?

(2) Is the resulting agreement sufficiently certain to constitute a legally enforceable contract?

(3) Would it be contrary to public policy to enforce the award, using the coercive powers of the state?[23]

Depending upon the answers to these questions the court will decide whether to enforce the clause and if so how[24].

Stewart Boyd QC in looking at these three questions in detail, concludes with regard to the first and second questions respectively, that '[w]isely the courts have upheld the validity of the agreement despite the presence of an equity clause',[25] and 'the English court will not be too astute or subtle in finding defects in the agreement which would render it uncertain in the English legal sense, but will construe the arbitration agreement so far as it can in such a way as to give effect to it'.[26] Thus it is the third question, that pertaining to public policy, which seems most problematic. This can be seen in the leading case of *Home & Overseas Insurance v Mentor Insurance Co (UK) Ltd.*[27]

The *Home & Overseas Insurance* case too arose from an equity clause framed as an honourable engagement as in the earlier *Home Insurance* decision. The issue shortly concerned whether a stay of a summary judgment application would be granted in favour of arbitration on the strength of the honourable engagement clause. Both Parker and Lloyd

---

22 Justice Rogers *op cit* at 86 regards the decision as the highwater mark of the change in English attitude.

23 *Ibid*, 778-79.

24 This approach has been reiterated by Boyd, S *"Arbitrator not bound by the Law" Clauses'*, (1990) 6 Arb Intl 122, 126.

25 *Ibid*, 126.

26 *Ibid*, 126-27.

27 [1989] 1 Lloyd's Rep 473 (CA).

LJJ rejected arguments that such clauses are invalid without more. Justice Parker's views were the stricter of the two law Lords[28] but it is Justice Lloyd's holding implicitly acknowledging that such clause would be enforceable if given in England that is the more significant of the two. His lordship said:[29] 'If the English courts will enforce a foreign award where the contract is governed by a "system of law which is not that of England or any other state or is a serious modification of such a law," why should it not enforce an English award in like circumstances? And if it will enforce an English award, why should it not grant a stay'. This obiter comment stands in marked contrast to Justice Parker's statement that 'a clause which purported to free arbitrators without regard to the law and...according to what would be fair would not be a valid arbitration clause'.[30] However this statement has been strongly criticised by leading commentators and in view of more recent developments in English law should not be followed[31]. Stewart Boyd QC noting that Justice Parker's comment can be taken in a number of ways, puts it this way on one view, as 'questionable if what he had in mind was a clause authorising a decision in accordance with fairness and good conscience alone'.[32] After noting that in theory there is almost no rule of English contract which cannot be expressly or impliedly excluded, and that it is not a ground for refusal to enforce a foreign award per se which is contrary to ordinary principles of commercial law, Boyd writes: '[s]eeing that this is so, one is bound to question the proposition that a power to decide in accordance with equity and good conscience rather than English law, or the strict principles of English law, is antithetical to some fundamental concept of what an arbitration should be';[33] and then concludes: 'therefore...an arbitrator deciding in accordance with equity and good conscience is still conducting an arbitration and not some other procedure outside the Arbitration Acts'.[34]

---

[28] *Ibid*, 479.
[29] *Ibid*, 489.
[30] *Ibid*, 485.
[31] See the Right Hon Sir Michael Kerr, *"Equity" Arbitration in England*, [1991] 2 Am Rev Intl Arb 377, 394.
[32] Boyd, S., *"Arbitrator not bound by the Law" Clauses*, (1990) 6 Arb Intl 122, 128.
[33] *Ibid*, 128.
[34] *Ibid*, 129.

Another commentator, Lord Justice Steyn,[35] who has looked closely at the obiter remarks of Lord Justice Lloyd in the *Home and Overseas Insurance* case wrote: 'I share Lord Justice Lloyd's instinctive reaction. But it seems to me that we are dealing with a complex and fundamental problem which will require further analysis.[36] Lord Justice Steyn continued and raised several issues regarding equity clauses which he suggested there were no clear answers to and concluded by calling for 'reforming legislation'.[37]

Equally as interesting as Boyd's construction is the comment of Sir Michael Kerr who after noting as well that the passage should not be followed continues to note that 'this passage appears to contain the first recognition of the *lex mercatoria* in an English court'.[38] There has also been recent academic support for the enforceability of awards based on the lex mercatoria.[39] This subject of the lex mercatoria and the relationship of amiable composition to it will be returned to below.

Since these cases have been decided a number of other important decisions have been decided which have generally extended the boundaries of arbitration, in particular *Channel Tunnel Group Ltd and Anor v Balfour Beatty Construction Ltd*; *Harbour Assurance Co (UK) Ltd v Kansa General International Insurance Co Ltd and Ors*; and *SA Coppée Lavalin NV v Ken-Ren Chemicals and Fertilizers Ltd (in liquidation in Kenya)*[40] and may be noted for this reason although readers are referred elsewhere for comment on the cases.

In summary, the doctrine still appears ahead of the caselaw insofar as the effect that is given to equity clauses, and it is an open question whether this lead will be taken up by the judiciary in cases which

---

[35] Lord Justice of Appeal, and at the time then Chairman of the Departmental Advisory Committee on Arbitration Law.

[36] *England's Response to the UNCITRAL Model Law of Arbitration* (1994) 10 Arb Intl 1, at 15-16.

[37] *Ibid.*

[38] Kerr, *op cit*, 395. Since then further academic support has followed, see Rivkin, *Enforceability of Arbitral Awards Based on Lex Mercatoria'* (1993) 9 Arb Intl 67.

[39] See Rivkin, *op cit.*

[40] *Channel Tunnel Group Ltd and Anor v Balfour Beatty Construction Ltd* [1993] AC 334; *Harbour Assurance Co (UK) Ltd v Kansa General International Insurance Co Ltd and Ors* [1993] 3 WLR 42; and *SA Coppée Lavalin NV v Ken-Ren Chemicals and Fertilizers Ltd (in liquidation in Kenya)* [1994] 2 WLR 631.

present themselves in future or as a result of the further legislative support which may come with the passage of the Arbitration Bill.

Amiable Composition

The meaning of the term amiable composition is often said to be uncertain. Indeed English terminology often refers to 'equity clauses' rather than amiable composition[41] and even accepting this equation of the two concepts it must be conceded that there are significant difficulties which would lie behind it on a close historical analysis.[42] From a public international law point of view equity clauses have been common. In part this stems from their inclusion in a large number of submissions to arbitration beginning with the Jay Treaty in 1794.[43] Interest in equitable jurisdictions even reached such a high that in 1935 an International Equity Tribunal was proposed.[44] Equity clauses more recently at least, even if not amiable composition clauses expressly, are still quite common as can be remarked from the above cases in reinsurance contracts. Equity clauses per se though do not necessarily authorise the arbitrators to act as amiables compositeurs but rather release them from any obligation to strictly apply the law. The drafting of the equity clause itself may also lay down non-legal criteria that the parties wish taken into account in coming to a decision, eg 'ex aequo et bono', 'equity and good conscience', or 'usages and customs of the trade'.

The background to the use of equity clauses in England is set out in a very helpful article by Sir Michael Kerr entitled simply '"Equity" Arbitration in England'.[45] The author sets out four main reasons why the clauses still appear. In short, they may be particularly suitable for

---

[41] See eg the Rt Hon Sir Michael Kerr, *"Equity" Arbitration in England* [1991] 2 Am Rev Intl Arb 377.

[42] See eg V D Degan, *L'Équité et le Droit International*, The Hague (1970) at 14: 'Quant à la terminologie, l'équité est également nommée dans la littérature juridique - *ex aequo et bono*. Certains auteurs s'efforcent de trouver des différences dans la portée de ces deux termes. La doctrine n'a pas nettement délimité la notion d'équité avec celles d'amiable composition et de règlement d'intérêts.

[43] *Ibid.*

[44] See Dr Wolfgang Friedmann, *The Contribution of English Equity to the Idea of an International Equity Tribunal*, London, Constable (1935) with a preface by Sir William Holdsworth.

[45] Ibid.

long-term contractual relationships; to reduce unnecessary 'legalism'; to give greater freedom in some Continental jurisdictions to quantify compensation awards; and differing perceptions that the role of law plays in England versus on the Continent.[46]

Some of the problems and misunderstandings surrounding the concept of amiable composition may be illustrated by referring to an American Arbitration Association ('AAA') definition which is as follows:

> *"A French phrase for an arbitrator who has great freedom formulating the terms of his award. The concept of amiable compositeur is widely used in continental legal systems. It has been variously defined as conciliator, arbitrator de facto, or in the most extreme sense, an arbitrator under no obligation to observe the rule of law. An amiable compositeur is nevertheless subject to the rules of "natural justice" and must observe the fundamental rules governing judicial procedure and material law."*[47]

Firstly, it may be noted that the choice of emphasis in the first sentence is intriguing as it focuses our attention on the end result of an arbitration—namely the award—rather than the process by which it is arrived at and which conversely almost exclusively serves as the focus in academic writing on the subject. The point then, shortly put and without wanting to digress too far in this regard, is that the skilful arbitrator may well be able to arrive at whatever end he wishes, and whether bound by the law or not.[48] Returning to some of the misunderstandings, the reference to conciliation in the definition, is inaccurate. Occasionally one does see an amiable compositor described as a conciliator or mediator,[49] but this would only arise upon express authorisation and is rare. It would be unusual also as the amiable compositor acting solely in this capacity risks the enforcement of his award being turned down. Thus the starting position here would

---

46 See Sir Michael's reasons in full at 378. The reasons he puts forward were those that seemed to emerge from discussions at a London Court of International Arbitration Conference in Nice.

47 *The Dictionary of Arbitration*, the American Arbitration Association, New York, (1970) 14.

48 Craig, W.L., Park, W.W. Paulsson, J., *International Chamber of Commerce Arbitration*, ('Craig, Park & Paulsson') 2nd Edn, (1990) at 139 fn 14 and citing Lew, J.D.M., *Applicable Law in International Commercial Arbitration* (1978).

49 See eg ICC Case No 3938, 111 Clunet (1984).

seem to be that an arbitrator sitting as an amiable compositeur has no authority in the ordinary course to effect a compromise between the parties.[50]

Reference is made to the 'rule of law'—singular—and the fact that the amiable compositeur may be under no obligation to observe it.[51] However, he is nevertheless said to be subject to the rules of 'natural justice', which in some way implies that these rules are outside the 'rule of law' itself. Paradoxically, the amiable compositeur must yet observe 'the fundamental rules governing judicial procedure and material law'. It should immediately be apparent, even allowing for the different nuances which American and English legal systems may attach to these terms, that something is amiss. The last part of the definition weakly attempts to convey that there are still some limitations which govern amiable composition. It is true there are applicable limitations but not as expressed here rather they are routinely expressed as pertaining to arbitral procedure and ordre public, (which is used inaccurately but nevertheless interchangeably in English law with public policy). These limitations will be returned to again below.

While the AAA definition may be criticised it is still true to say that there is no generally accepted definition for either amiable composition or arbitration ex aequo et bono. It has also been remarked by English commentators that it would be almost impossible to frame a definition that would be accepted by all in any case.[52] The appreciation of this

---

[50]   See Goldman, (1970) *Rev Arb* 214.

[51]   The 'rule of law' versus 'rules of law' debate was central to the discussions of the Working Group drafting what became article 28 in the UNCITRAL Model Law. The traditional formulation has normally been singular—rule of law—both under domestic laws and was even embodied in the earlier UNCITRAL Arbitration Rules. However, the Model Law adopted the broader plural expression to further greater party autonomy in the choice of law and even the ability to designate different parts of different systems of law as applicable to the substance of their dispute. See Doc. A/CN.9/232, paras 158-162; Doc. A/CN.9.245, paras 93-94; and the discussion of the issue by Aron Broches, in *Commentary on the UNCITRAL Model Law on International Commercial Arbitration*, (1990) pp 141-146. The consensus view on allowing the parties the freedom to choose the 'rules of law' also indicates the parties may thereby choose the lex mercatoria: see eg Delaume, *Transnational Contracts*, §9.11; and Redfern, A. & Hunter, J.M.H, *Law and Practice of International Commercial Arbitration*, 2nd Edn, London, Sweet and Maxwell (1991), 121.

[52]   Redfern and Hunter, *Ibid*, at 36.

fact resulted in the drafters of the Model Law following the UNCITRAL Arbitration Rules precedent and not including definitions for either of the terms. However, while varying interpretations may be given to the terms in different legal systems, there is nevertheless a very strong common thread. The term should therefore best be understood by contrasting the mandate of an ordinary arbitrator with that of an amiable compositeur: while the former is obliged to apply strict rules of legal interpretation to the rights and obligations of the parties, the latter is entitled to have recourse to equitable principles of construction as well as notions of equity and justice to adjudicate the dispute. The premise is that the amiable compositeur should be able to avoid an inequitable result which might arise from a strict legalistic approach to the issues in dispute. The marriage of law and equity and how one fulfils the other should be taken as given. Notions of equity and how it may attenuate stricter aspects of the law in its application is familiar to both common law and civilian lawyers. Even without invoking the organisation of the system of courts in England prior to the Judicature Acts other allusions could be given. Recent writings of Judge Manfred Lachs, who formerly sat as the President of the International Court of Justice make the point convincingly even aside from amiable composition and with respect to both courts and arbitral tribunals.

Judge Lachs:

> '...I submit that it is important to bear in mind that the relationship between equity and law is not one between the legal system and a phenomenon exterior to it; equity is built into the legal system. In order to remove every possible misunderstanding and confusion on the issue it is important to emphasise that equity cannot be detached from law; it is inherent in it. Equity aims at proper application of law in a particular case in order to avoid decisions that are a reflection of abstract principles detached from the circumstances that a court or arbitration tribunal may face. Its function is to lead to an interpretation of a rule of law in the context of a concrete situation and to balance all the elements of the relationship between the parties concerned. Thus equity gives law vitality and makes it meet the requirements of the circumstances of each case. Equity provides a means by which rules of law, provisions of treaties or other sources of law may take a needed breath in order to meet the challenge of specific

situations arising between two or more states or in international relations in general. In sum, equity is the element to which Frederick William Maitland rightly referred when saying that it comes "not to destroy law but to fulfil it".[53]

Thus, the amiable compositeur is entitled to have recourse to equitable principles of construction as well as notions of equity and justice to adjudicate the dispute. This is very different from saying that an amiable compositeur has unlimited freedom to select the principles to be applied or that he decides simply according to the dictates of his own conscience. There is general agreement limitations will be applied in the exercise of his mandate by the amiable compositeur. The limits may derive from ordre public or any limitations which may be imposed under the applicable law or rules governing the arbitration; for instance article 28(4) of the Model Law stipulating that the amiable compositeur shall not only decide in accordance with the terms of the contract but shall also take into account the usages of the trade applicable to the transaction. For the time being then it is proposed that amiable composition maybe thought of as *permitting departure from the strict application of the rules of law when it would result in unfairness to the parties in the particular dispute.*[54]

---

[53] Judge Manfred Lachs, 'Equity in Arbitration and in Judicial Settlement of Disputes', in *The Flame Rekindled New Hopes for International Arbitration*, Muller, S. & Mijs, W. (Eds) Martinus Nijhoff, Dordrecht, (1994) 125, 127, and also referring to de Visscher, C., *De l'Équité dans le Règlement Arbitral ou Judiciaire des Litiges de Droit International Public* (1972); and Reuter, P., 'Quelques Réflections sur l'Équité en Droit International,' (1980) *Revue Belge de Droit International* 165. Later in the same article Judge Lachs added: 'principles and rules of law are not equitable in themselves, it is equity that confers upon them that quality' at p 128.

[54] There is significant support for this view, see eg Bernard, A., *L'arbitrage Volontaire en Droit Privé*, no 309; Robert, J., *Arbitrage Civil et Commercial*, 4th Edn (1967), no 161, p 202; Jarvin, S., 'The Sources and Limits of the Arbitrator's Powers', in *Contemporary Problems in International Arbitration*, Lew, J.D.M. (Ed) (1986) 50 at 70.

Arbitration Ex Aequo et Bono

The phrase ex aequo et bono often appears in tandem with amiable composition. The former may be translated as 'according to what is just and good'. This Latin phrase has an illustrious history. In Roman law, the power of decision comprised the notion of generous interpretation to attenuate the harsh results which often followed strict or literal interpretations given in the legis actio procedures.[55] The notion was expressed in a variety of forms in the Digest of Justinian, including *ex bono et aequo, aequm et bono* and *ius ars boni et aequii.*[56] In its broadest sense in the Roman law, it is the concept of justice and equality, or *'aequitas'.*[57]

The meaning and scope of the phrase today is equally as broad as these origins reveal. The genesis for the use of the phrase in a modern context can be traced to the inclusion of article 38(2) in the *Statute of the Permanent Court of International Justice.*[58] The authority to decide ex aequo et bono was incorporated in the statute so as to meet the suggestion that the court be permitted to apply the 'great principles of the law and justice' or the general principles of law recognised by civilised nations.[59] Later developments have made it clear though that

---

[55] See generally on the these procedures and the Roman law of obligations, Kaser, M., *Roman Private Law*, 3rd Edn Pretoria, University of South Africa Press, 1980; Kelly, J.M. *Studies in the Civil Judicature of the Roman Republic*, Oxford, Clarendon Press, 1976; and Watson, A., *The Law of Obligations in the Later Roman Republic*, Oxford, Clarendon Press, 1965.

[56] Buckland & McNair, *Roman Law and Common Law, A Comparison in Outline*, Cambridge, Cambridge University Press, 1965, 11, 'Law is the Art of Finding the Good and Equitable', referring to the Digest, D.1.1.1, p 17.

[57] See Brice, C.S. *Roman Aequitas and English Equity* (1913-14) 2 Georgetown Law Journal 16-24.

[58] See generally, de Visscher, C., *De L'Equite dans le Reglement Arbitral ou Judiciaire des Litiges de Droit International Public*, Paris, Pedone, 1972, ch 2 pp 21-27; Dr Max Habicht, 'Le pouvoir du juge international de statuer "ex aequo et bono"' *Receuil de Cours* 1934, vol 49, pp 281-369; this article is reproduced in 'The Power of the International Judge to Give a Decision "Ex Aequo et Bono"' London, Constable & Co, 1935, Series B, No 2.

[59] Scheuner, U., 'Decisions *ex aequo et bono* by International Courts and Arbitral Tribunals', in Sanders, P. (Ed) *International Arbitration: Liber Amicorum for Martin Domke*, The Hague, Nijhoff, 1967, 275. Among other views on the rationale for the inclusion is Fachiri's, *The Permanent Court of International Justice*, London, 1925, 94 who said it was to address issues of a political character which were unsuitable for decision on strictly legal grounds and a preference for

an authority to decide ex aequo et bono is distinct from the application of these general principles of law recognised by nations as forming a part of the international legal order. In fact, the attraction to and strength of the concept comes from its ability to exceed these principles and reach those fundamental standards and values which are in their most formative stages; for instance, United Nations resolutions, for guidance in adjudicating a dispute. The question that this position thus raises is how far beyond these principles is one then able to venture?

The answer to the question posed comes from an amalgam of academic sources.[60] These sources suggest that a body, acting ex aequo et bono, while not required to depart from the general principles of law referred to, is permitted to do so even overriding legal rights if a fair and just result calls for it. However, while fairness and justice would suggest complete freedom of action; in truth, arbitrators acting ex aequo et bono have routinely had this freedom of action referred to by academic commentators circumscribed in practice.

Even though the draft Arbitration Bill has eschewed the use of both Latin and French in the text, it is submitted that counsel should still be aware of the true meaning behind the provisions on the topic, the richness underlying it, and the guidance available in the civilian jurisprudence and doctrine as well as that of international tribunals including the International Court of Justice to assist in construing it.[61]

---

recourse to the Court moreover as an arbitral body than a Court with the strictures that implies.

[60] See P Fouchard, 'Amiable composition et appel', (1976) *Revue de l'Arbitrage* 18; J P Govare, 'L'amiable composition et les arbitrages anglais', (1955) *Revue de l'Arbitrage* 38; P Level, L'amiable composition dans le decret du 14 mai, 1980 relatif à l'arbitrage', (1980) *Revue de l'Arbitrage* 651; E Loquin, 'L'obligation pour l'amiable compositeur de motiver sa sentence', (1976) *Revue de l'Arbitrage* 223; F A Mann, 'Lex Facit Arbitrum', in P Sanders, Ed, *International Arbitration*, above, at 157; E Mezger, 'La distinction entre l'arbitre dispensé d'observer la loi et l'arbitre statuant sans appel', in P Sanders, Ed, *International Arbitration* above, at 184; I I Nestor, L'amiable compositeur et l'arbitre dispensé loi et l'arbitre statuant sans appel', in *Commercial Arbitration, Essays in Memoriam Eugenio Minoli*, Rome, Italian Arbitration Association, 1974, 341; L B Sohn, 'Arbitration of International Disputes *ex aequo et bono*', in P Sanders, Ed, *International Arbitration*, above, at 330.

[61] Some references have already been made regarding not only the difficulties in construction generally when discussing these concepts but also the extent to which they overlap, for instance with regard to arbitration ex aequo et bono. It may be noted that an overlap regarding the concept of equity and amiable composition has also been observed by numerous commentators including J C Witenberg,

Suggested Limits on the Amiable Compositeur

The amiable compositeur is subject to important limitations which may be given. The first and it would seem the most central limitation in this regard is that he is bound by any mandatory rules of law having a public policy character.[62] This phrase is perhaps more familiar to civilians whose legal systems often divide rules of law into three categories, that is: supplementary rules (lois supplétives); rules concerning public policy (lois d'ordre public); and imperative rules (lois impératives).[63] Supplementary rules apply only insofar as there is no contrary provision agreed by the parties; the rules concerning public policy may not be derogated from; while imperative rules may be waived by those for whose benefit the rules are intended to operate. One explanation put forward for the application of the mandatory rules is that the arbitrator is under a duty to seek to ensure that the award is enforceable.[64]

The amiable compositor may not modify the terms of the contract without more.[65] This situation, which may differ under individual national laws, is not uncontroversial as one may point to numerous exceptions in arbitration case reports where the opposite result has pertained.[66] However, it is submitted that if one accepts that the arbitrator is empowered only to decide a dispute then if he instead modifies the contracts under which the dispute has arisen he is no

---

L'Organisation judiciaire, la procedure et la sentence internationale, Paris, (1937) 341.

[62] Jarvin, S., *The Sources and Limits of the Arbitrator's Powers* (1986) 2 Arb Intl 140, 158 and citing comments by Derains to case 3267, (1980) *Journal du Droit International* 969. This article also appears in *Comtemporary Problems in International Arbitration*, Lew, J.D.M. (Ed) (1986) 50.

[63] See eg Simond, L., 'Amiable Compositeurs and their Reasoning' in Schmitthoff, C. (Ed) *International Commercial Arbitration, Collected Papers II* (1974-75) 130 at 137.

[64] Jarvin, S., 'The Sources and Limits of the Arbitrator's Powers' in *Comtemporary Problems in International Arbitration*, Lew, J.D.M. (Ed) (1986) 50, 71.

[65] Jarvin, S., *ibid* at 71 citing a Comment by Y Derains to ICC Case No 3267, 107 Clunet 969 (1980); Brown, H.J. & Marriott, A.L., *ADR Principles and Practice* Sweet & Maxwell London (1993) at 64 citing de Boisseson fn 34 at 345; Simond, L., 'Amiable Compositeurs and their Reasoning' *op cit* 130, 140-141.

[66] The issue itself has been said by René David to be 'one of the major subjects calling for attention in our times', *L'arbitrage dans le commerce international* at 37 quoted by Craig, Park & Paulsson at 143. The national law position of countries may be consulted in the *Yearbook on Commercial Arbitration*.

longer acting as an arbitrator and the award may no longer be enforceable.[67] An arguably stronger rationale for this proposition follows from the binding nature of the contract itself, which is often expressed in Latin as pacta sunt servanda which it can be argued is also of a public policy character in law and as such further reason against finding any power to modify the parties' agreement.[68] This is perhaps the strongest limitation which operates on the amiable compositeur as he is bound to enforce the contract which the parties have ultimately chosen as the governing law for their relationship.[69] Some obiter support for this proposition may also be found in Lord Justice Lloyd's remarks in the *Home and Overseas Insurance Co* case where at p 487 he stated: 'It is implicit in the decision of the Court of Appeal in *Eagle Star v Yuval* that arbitrators, appointed under a clause which entitles them to look to the general purpose of the contract, rather than the literal interpretation of the language, may properly reach a result which would not be the same, or not necessarily the same, as a Court would reach in the absence of the clause. *This does not mean that the arbitrators can re-write the contract,* or ignore the language altogether...' (emphasis added). The exceptional cases where a power to modify the contract has been found to exist seem to often involve price adjustment situations in long term contracting arrangements.

The amiable compositeur has a power to modify procedures. However the procedures that may be envisaged in this regard are those that are more properly confined to judicial procedure rather than the arbitral procedure which the parties have stipulated. Those procedures, for instance, where set out in the applicable rules of any arbitral institution or whether in a relevant civil code or otherwise, would only be derogated from at the amiable compositeur's peril.[70] The reason he is at risk here is that any one or more of the procedural rules may be characterised as a mandatory rule having a public policy character with the consequences this entails. A wealth of caselaw exists on these questions and the precise characterisation of those rules which do have

---

[67] Craig, Park & Paulsson, 143 citing Hnerner, L., *Internationella Handelskammarens forliknings - ochskiljedomsregler* 12-13 (1981) and Matray, L., 'National Report, Belgium' (1980) V *Yearbook of International Arbitration* 1, 6.

[68] See generally Simond, L., 'Amiable Compositeurs and their Reasoning' *op cit* who develops this argument.

[69] The principle of *pacta sunt servanda* would also appear to be part of the lex mercatoria.

[70] See Bernard, A., *L'Arbitrage Volontaire en Droit Privé* No 311; and Robert, J., *Arbitrage Civil et Commercial*, 4th Edn (1967) No 156.

a public policy character but without attempting to recite them all some conclusions may still be drawn from them. Thus the procedural rules that may not be derogated from will often pertain to the right to be heard, audi alteram partem;[71] basic rules of the defence;[72] 'due process in giving equality of treatment to the parties';[73] and the requirement for reasons where national law stipulates.[74] These limitations may broadly be analogised to discussions in the common law surrounding the grounds typically advanced for the setting aside of an award. On the basis of the research done for this paper, it can be said that the English common law in this bears a striking resemblence to much of the civilian caselaw which has ascribed limitations on the actions of the amiable compositeur. In short, an arbitrator may be said to have misconducted himself when he has:

- failed to conduct the reference in the manner expressly or impliedly prescribed by the submission;
- acted contrary to public policy;
- acted unfairly[75]
- breached minimum requirements notably the hearing of both sides, and abstention of receiving evidence or argument in the absence of one party.[76]

There is no reason to think that an amiable compositeur would not be sanctioned for acting in the same way.

The drafters of the Arbitration Bill have opted not to expressly make require the tribunal to take into account the 'usages of the trade' applicable to the transaction; reasoning that if the applicable law permits this to be done then such a provision is unnecessary, while if the law does not permit it then it could be said that such a direction

---

[71] See ICC Case No 3327, 109 Clunet 976 (1982).
[72] Robert, J., *Arbitrage Civil et Commercial*, 4th Edn (1967), No 160.
[73] Redfern & Hunter, *Law and Practice of International Commercial Arbitration*, 2nd Edn, London, (1991) 36.
[74] Robert, J., *Arbitrage Civil et Commercial*, 4th Edn (1967), Nos 160 and 219.
[75] Mustill & Boyd considers fairness not in relation to how it would be judged in a court but with regard to the identity of the parties, of the chosen arbitrator, and to the nature of the subject matter, p 551.
[76] Further detail on these points is given by Mustill and Boyd in chapter 22 of their text.

would override it and thus be incorrect.[77] It is submitted that the prevalence of trade usages and hence the arbitrator's duty to consider them in making his award is such as to be part of a lex mercatoria in any case and thus the provision was unnecessary.[78]

Eric Loquin in the leading treatise on the subject of amiable composition, *L'amiable composition en droit comparé et international,* expressly underlines the importance and the role that both good faith and collaboration play in amiable composition. He writes, at p 341: 'L'accord des parties sur son choix est le signe de la bonne foi qui devra imprégner leur relations futures. Elle indique que les contractants sont prêt à abandonner certaines de le leurs prérogatives pour faciliter leur collaboration'. In the construction context, readers will be aware of the concerted attention being given to encouraging more cooperation in the industry and the means whereby this may be achieved.[79] Thus, particularly in the context of and reference to long term contracting, equity clauses may be able to make a contribution to the promotion of these ends through their implicit expectation of good faith and collaboration in the parties' relations.

These notions have antecedents in relation to the topics under discussion here. In particular, with regard to and returning to article 38(2) of the *Statute of the Permanent Court of International Justice,* M.O.Hudson wrote: 'The provision in the Statute enables the Court under the condition set to go outside the realm of law to reach a solution of a problem presented; it relieves the Court altogether from the necessity of deciding according to law; it removes the limitations both of the existing law and of a law which might be made for future cases; it makes possible a solution based either on law or solely on

---

[77] Departmental Advisory Committee on Arbitration Law, *Report on the Arbitration Bill,* February (1996) 49.

[78] See Fouchard, P., 'Les usages, l'arbitre et le juge' in Fouchard, P. et al (Eds), *Le Droit des Relations Economiques Internationales, Etudes offertes a Berthold Goldman,* Paris (1982) 67, 74ff. It is interesting to note that the Working Group drafting the Model Law on this point originally deleted the reference to trade usage themselves as among other reasons it was thought to be redundant, see Fourth Working Group Report, A/CN.9/245, para 99. However the reference was reinstated by the Commission, see Commission Report A/40/17 para 241.

[79] See in particular Sir Michael Latham's report *Constructing the Team* (1994) and concepts such as 'partnering'.

considerations of fair dealing and good faith, which may be independent of and even contrary to law'.[80]

It is submitted that the role of good faith in the future will not only continue to grow in relation to commercial dispute resolution but in the law as a whole and whether through opportunities such as the proposed clause 46(1)(b) present in this respect or otherwise, and it is a role which is fully endorsed here. Further, the connection which is developed between the concepts below is intended in part to provide an additional entrée for good faith into the resolution of a dispute.[81]

Before leaving the limits on the amiable compositeur a word may be said about appeals. The DAC *Report on the Arbitration Bill* concludes that 'it is to be noted that in agreeing that a dispute shall be resolved in this way, the parties are in effect excluding any right to appeal to the Court (there being no "*question of law*" to appeal).[82] While this may be true in one sense it ignores the very real remedies which exist in civilian jurisdictions where amiable composition is more common. Thus, for instance in France, an action to annul the award may lie in cases where there has been procedural unfairness or a violation of public policy.[83] Civilians may also have other remedies including la requête civile, opposition a l'ordonnance d'exequatar, and the demande en annulation. Without descending into the details of these remedies or which jurisdictions continue to permit their use the point should be taken that appeals are *not* an exclusive remedy.[84] What is suggested is that in lieu of an appeal if grounds can be shown then one proper avenue of redress is that of judicial review in an English court. The procedure and basis is familiar and it would appear eminently suitable if a legitimate transgression could be shown.

---

[80] Hudson, M.O., *A Treatise on the Permanent Court of International Justice*, New York (1934), 530.

[81] See generally Goldman, B., 'The Applicable Law: General Principles of Law—the *lex mercatoria*', in *Contemporary Problems in International Arbitration*, Lew, J.D.M. (Ed) (1986) 113, 116.

[82] Departmental Advisory Committee, *Report on the Arbitration Bill*, February (1996) 49.

[83] Articles 1484, 1502 and 1504 French Code of Civil Procedure.

[84] See generally *Yearbook on Commercial Arbitration* for the national law position of civilian jurisdictions.

Amiable Composition and the Lex Mercatoria

No discussion of amiable composition would be complete without reference to lex mercatoria. It should be noted at the outset that there is still some debate about whether or not the lex mercatoria exists; however, the intention here is not to reproduce or comment on that debate, rather and for the purpose of the discussion here, to assume that it does exist and ask what are then the consequences given the use of equity clauses under the Arbitration Bill.

A serious objection has been raised regarding a credible relationship between the lex mercatoria and amiable composition by Lord Mustill. His Lordship has written: 'More difficult is the relationship between the two concepts. It has been said that an agreement to make the arbitrator an *amiable compositeur* enables, even if it does not require, the arbitrator to take note of the *lex mercatoria*. To an outsider this seems strange. The essence of amiable composition is to dispense the arbitrator from the duty of enforcing any system of law. Yet the *lex mercatoria* is a system of law. Why should an agreement to amiable composition summon up a reference to *lex mercatoria* any more than to any other developed system of commercial law? The literature gives no convincing answer'[85] (footnotes omitted).

The point is a good one but it is submitted that there are other points that may be made in reply to it. First of all the essence of the lex mercatoria bears such a strong resemblance to the objects of amiable composition that it would be imprudent for an arbitrator sitting in this capacity to simply disregard this 'system of law' without more. Naon refers to the essence of the lex mercatoria and concludes that 'consideration of the lex mercatoria concept leads to two central results: (a) it evinces the necessity of creating an *ad hoc* legal system for governing international economic relations in order to meet certain requirements of fairness and justice which may not be adequately achieved by a single national law and one provided with an appropriate choice-of-law methodology consistent with such ends; and (b) it emphasises the importance of customs, usages and practices in the

---

[85] The Rt Hon Lord Justice Mustill, *The New Lex Mercatoria: The First Twenty-five Years* (1988) 4 Arb Intl 85.

formation of such an *ad hoc* body of rules...' (footnotes omitted).[86]

A second reason may relate to the nature of the problems which typically arise when amiable composition clauses have been inserted in the agreements governing the parties' relationships. A survey of 35 cases involving ICC arbitrations with amiable composition clauses carried out by Loquin concluded almost all arose in contracts of long duration; such as transfer of technology, turnkey industrial plant contracts, raw materials purchase or production or latterly economic development contracts.[87] Hence it has been suggested that the 'very nature of long-term contracts, the lack of developed principles or precedents in many developing countries' national laws to deal with such complex agreements, and the economic interests at hand may commend an equitable solution to any dispute which may arise. *Amiable composition* is one method of securing such a resolution'.[88] It is submitted that the lex mercatoria would also appear to be relevant in this context.

Thirdly, the practice of amiable compositeurs. It would seem that they are naturally inquisitive and that they routinely refer to whatever legal principles are at hand. 'Indeed *amiable compositeurs* frequently prefer to investigate the underlying legal regime or regimes even when the contract is silent as to the applicability of any national law. As René David has put it: "In the vast majority of cases amiable compositeurs do not intend to work out a compromise, but they feel bound to decide as prescribed by the law; they see in the law a kind of ratio scripta and do not find any good reason for departing from its application in particular cases. The amiable compositeur is in fact a judge, but one who enjoys greater flexibility in adopting the solution which he regards as best, even though from a strictly legal point of view it may not be absolutely correct"'.[89] The point which it is submitted follows from this is then why not the lex mercatoria for the ratio scripta in such cases.

---

[86] Grigera Naon, H.A., *Choice-of-law Problems in International Commercial Arbitration*, (1992) 32-33.

[87] Craig, Park & Paulsson, above at 312 referring to Loquin, E., *L'amiable composition en droit comparé et international*, (1980) 145-154.

[88] Craig, Park & Paulsson, 312-313.

[89] Craig, Park & Paulsson, above, 313 and quoting David, R. in *Arbitration in International Trade* (1985) 355.

There may also be an express obligation imposed on the amiable to take into account or consider what are generally considered to be sources of the lex mercatoria.[90] Thus, for instance, under article 28(4) of the Model Law, the amiable compositeur must take into account the 'usages of the trade'. Similarly a case can be made that trade usage, either in this sense or independently, would include even conditions in the international standard forms of contract such as FIDIC.[91] The argument proceeds then that the amiable compositeur could thus be expected to take such matters into account under article 28(4) and may well wish to do so anyway.[92]

The observation may also be made that ultimately the right of amiable compositeurs to depart from the strict application of the law is not an obligation but a mere faculty.[93] Hence he is given the right to choose whether to attenuate the applicable law. Sigvard Jarvin has made the point this way. 'The power of amiable compositeur does not relieve the arbitrator from deciding which law applies to the contract, unless it is the parties' intention to exclude the application of a particular law. Having decided an applicable law on which to base his decision on the merits, the arbitrator attenuates its effect by applying his amiable compositeur powers[94] (footnotes omitted).

Lastly, Berthold Goldman[95] has written on this question: '...certain contractual classes may be construed as implying a reference to the lex

---

[90] Once again it is conceded that the sources that comprise any lex mercatoria is open to debate and thus, for the purpose of this discussion, sources including custom and trade usage and, as will be noted below, international standard forms of contract are all assumed to be sources in this regard.

[91] See in particular Boggiano, A., *International Standard Contracts, The Price of Fairness*, Dordrecht, (1991) 2-3; and Schmitthoff, C.M., 'Nature and Evolution of the Transnational Law of Commercial Transactions' in Horn, N. and Schmitthoff, C.M. (Eds), *The Transnational Law of International Commercial Transactions*, Deventer, (1982) 19, 29-30.

[92] See again Craig, Park & Paulsson, above, 313 and quoting Rene David in *Arbitration in International Trade* (1985) 355.

[93] Robert, J., *Arbitrage Civil et Commercial*, 4th Edn (1967) No 161, p 202.

[94] Jarvin, S., 'The Sources and Limits of the Arbitrator's Powers', in *Contemporary Problems in International Arbitration*, Lew, J.D.M. (Ed) (1986) 50, 71.

[95] The author puts forward a 'narrower' view of the conception of the lex mercatoria, in contrast to others such as Clive M Schmitthoff, whom the author suggests has a 'wide' view of the conception, see Goldman, B., 'The Applicable Law: General Principles of Law - the *lex mercatoria*', in *Contemporary Problems in International Arbitration*, Lew, J.D.M. (Ed) (1986) 113.

mercatoria, for example, the amiable composition clause, which empowers the arbitrator to decide ex aequo et bono. In my opinion, the lex mercatoria is not just "equity" (in the civil law sense) since it is, on the contrary, a set of rules of law. However, while being authorised to decide without applying such rules, the amiable compositeur is of course not prevented from referring to them; and when so doing, he might rightly construe the "amiable composition" clause as implicitly directed to the lex mercatoria'.[96] Thus, in effect the amiable composition clause is being treated as a choice of law clause.[97]

In summary, it is submitted that a case can be made for a credible relationship between amiable composition and the lex mercatoria. Much has changed since the point raised above was first made not the least the prospect of legislation which endorses equity clauses in themselves. It could thus be asked will the connection thus now not be taken to the logical conclusion which these authorities would suggest. Before leaving this question though there is another perspective that deserves mention. That is, the view not that the amiable compositeur either resorts to the lex mercatoria in some instances but that amiable composition itself is *part of* the lex mercatoria. Based upon what are often held out as the sources of the lex mercatoria, the UNCITRAL Model Law, the UNCITRAL Arbitration Rules, ICC Rules, and a small but significant number of other institutional rules, the concept of the amiable compositeur has become a substantive rule of international private law. In this regard, and as the concept thus can be said to stand apart from either domestic substantive or procedural law, further support is given to the concept as part of the lex mercatoria rather than simply one separate from it. If there are consequences which follow from this for those resorting to the use of equity clauses in the new Bill they must be that the arbitrator deciding in equity has a greater freedom of action and possibly more sources of inspiration in the resolution of the dispute than thought possible before.

---

[96] Goldman, B., 'The Applicable Law: General Principles of Law - the *lex mercatoria*', in *Contemporary Problems in International Arbitration*, Lew, J.D.M. (Ed) (1986) 113, 117.

[97] Others share this view, see eg Bockstiegel, K.-H., 'States in the International Arbitral Process', (1986) *Arbitration International* 22, 28.

Conclusion

In conclusion it may be appropriate to close with a comment from V V Veeder QC who spoke recently at the London Court of International Arbitration Centenary Conference.[98] In his address he set out the background to and the reasons behind the failure of Unidroit's Draft Uniform Law of Arbitration, 1936[99] to achieve international recognition. While there are numerous reasons mentioned, he dwells on the objections of four national committees to an ICC Congress which considered the Draft; of the two principal objections noted one pertained to the powers of amiable compositeurs. The objection was based upon a misunderstanding of their true role. It took Unidroit 20 years to appreciate the basis of the misunderstanding and at which time and as a result of which it added an amendment to the Draft in an attempt to clarify the matter.[100] However, the damage had been done much earlier and the amendment came much too late. It was this missed opportunity that Mr Veeder laments. He writes:[101]

'And so what are the lessons to be learnt today from the failure of the Rome Draft, particularly for the UK? Owing to a series of possible misunderstandings a great opportunity was lost in 1936 which could have advanced the "internationalisation" of commercial arbitration by 50 years [the time when it caught up with the adoption of the UNCITRAL Model Law]. By 1936, the day was long past when UK merchants could impose English law and English arbitration by raw commercial strength. There was no cause in London for legal isolationism; and the enormous experience of English commercial arbitration could have been better applied to produce truly "international" commercial arbitration. There is perhaps a more basic

---

[98] Veeder, V.V. 'Two Arbitral Butterflies: Bramwell and David',*The Internationalisation of International Arbitration*, The LCIA Centenary Conference, Hunter, M., Marriott, A. & Veeder, V.V. (Eds) Graham & Trotman/Martinus Nijhoff, London, 1995, 15.

[99] 'Comité d'étude pour l'arbitrage en droit privé: Rapport sur le project d'une loi uniforme sur l'arbitrage', Rome, September 1936; SdN - UDP 1936 - Etudes III - Arbitrage - Doc 24.

[100] The Draft of a Uniform Law on Arbitration in respect of International Relations of Private Law and Explanatory Report; Unidroit, 1954, Rome.

[101] Veeder, V.V., 'Two Arbitral Butterflies: Bramwell and David',*The Internationalisation of International Arbitration*, The LCIA Centenary Conference, Hunter, M., Marriott, A. & Veeder, V.V. (Eds) Graham & Trotman/Martinus Nijhoff, London, 1995, 15 at 23.

lesson. For all the expertise and experience now accumulated in the field of international commercial arbitration, there is something more intractable than the difficulties of comparative law. It is comparative perceptions, or misperceptions, which often lie at the heart of disagreements over international commercial arbitration'.[102]

---

[102] Mr Veeder, has also argued in favour of recognising equity clauses generally in the British Insurance Arbitration Lecture (1992). On the subject of equity clauses per se even former antagonists may change their view toward them. In the final footnote of his compelling article, Sir Michael Kerr writes:

"*The author must confess that the views expressed in this article stem from a gradual change of heart and mind. He had reservations about the Arbitration Act 1979 when its contents were under discussion, and later on he fully agreed with the Mustill Committee's rejection of the UNCITRAL Model Law. But his cumulative experience over recent years, and the opportunities of seeing the perspective of English arbitration from abroad, have led to a firm Pauline conversion in favour or radical change. (Better late than never!)*", "'Equity" Arbitration in England' (1991) 2 *Amercian Review of International Arbitration* 377, 401 fn 72.

9. Arbitration, the use of user-specific procedures

Pamela Kirby Johnson

Synopsis

This paper examines how the GAFTA rules operate in the international grain and feedstuffs industry.

Introduction

The two tier GAFTA arbitration system has evolved over a century or more from a simple start in the 19th century London coffee houses to the well regulated system in place now, which has to be acceptable to the world's trade in grain, animal feedstuffs and other commodities. Originally it was intended to provide the emerging international trading houses in London with a speedy and cheap means of dispute settlement, avoiding the use of lawyers, and utilising trade expertise.

Until the 1960's much of this expertise was needed for what is often referred to as *"look/sniff arbitration"*, which was the means to resolve quality and condition disputes arising from the way in which grain and feed was then traded. These goods would leave the country of origin, and upon receipt by the buyer at destination, if he was of the opinion that he had received inferior goods to that contracted, or that which was available generally from the harvest in that region, for that season's shipments, arbitrators would examine the goods and decide by visual examination and smell whether the goods were of *"fair average quality" (faq)*. If not, they would award an allowance off the contract price.

Trade in the latter part of the 20th century is markedly different. Quality certificates, issued in the countries of origin, are now final as regards to the quality aspects of the goods and the shipment tonnages have increased from about 2,000 tons to anything upto 120,000 tonnes, panamex vessel size.

All these materials are shipped around the world, from production to end use, under the terms of one of the 80 standard contract forms issued by

GAFTA. With very few exceptions the disputes which now arise are the result of market price fluctuations, failure to perform under the contract, natural or trade disasters, and legislative or government interference in trade. Only in about 3% of the cases is there a need to examine samples.

Standard Clauses

The two GAFTA contract clauses, the arbitration and domicile clauses, are standard throughout the entire range of contracts. The domicile clause provides that the buyer and seller agree for the purpose of legal proceedings or arbitration that the contract shall be deemed to have been made in England, and to be performed there, and that the courts or arbitrators appointed have jurisdiction over all disputes which arise out of the contract, and that these disputes shall be determined according to English law.

The arbitration standard clause provides that the written agreement between the parties that in the event of a dispute they agree that arbitration shall be carried out in accordance with the association's rules, form 125. Form No.125 arbitration rules set out in detail what a party needs to know when they wish to go to arbitration. The rules state that arbitrations will be held in London, or elsewhere if agreed by the parties. Often they don't agree and most are held in GAFTA's offices in London. A good number have however been held in the Netherlands, Switzerland and Germany.

For the very few quality arbitrations which might arise, the association still maintains the facilities for the examination of samples and receives from many countries of origin samples of their materials harvested for that season for comparison against delivered goods. Although there is no restriction on the place of arbitration, and we try to encourage our members world-wide to take a more active role as arbitrators, "London" arbitrators are still the most sought after and still carry a certain respect.

It makes sense to have an established law backing arbitration facilities, and although GAFTA has more members outside than in the UK, they still allow English law to apply to their trade and for the arbitration acts 1950, 1975 and 1979 to apply to all GAFTA contracts. The acts have been modified by the GAFTA rules where we are able to do so by special provisions to suit the trade. It is hoped that a new act will be adopted to replace these three arbitration acts, and on the basis of the current draft bill, we are confident that it will be incorporated into the arbitration rules.

Procedural Devices Implicit to GAFTA Rules

The international grain trade requires a well administered and regulated system in place, leaving the minimum of issues to be decided by the parties after the dispute has arisen. The GAFTA rules attempt to meet the needs of the users by reference to custom and practice in the industry. The following procedures are catered for thus:

Time limits

The trading world is very keen on time limits, and one often hears that *"time is of the essence"*. Consequently the arbitration rules contain time limits for claiming arbitration and when to appoint an arbitrator, separated into sections for time limits for technical and quality arbitrations, relating to the appropriate contracts. A technical dispute is intended to cover any dispute arising out of a contract other than that involving the quality and/or condition of the commodity. The technical time limit varies from 90 days for a c.i.f. contract, to 21 days from receipt of analysis certificate. When the quality or condition of the goods is in dispute parties must notify the other party of their claim within very strict shorter time limits. If any notice is late, then the arbitration claim will be time barred and the claim waived.

Arbitrators have discretion to extend the time limits, but this is not something that they undertake lightly bearing in mind for example, the quality or condition of the goods and that the samples may deteriorate and not be representative of the goods discharged. This section of the rules also ensures that once a quality arbitration is claimed the arbitrators must proceed within a specified time. Usually arbitrators would be expected to have a quality arbitration completed 6-8 weeks from the claim.

Although the parties are encouraged to settle their disputes amicably, the clock still keeps ticking during any negotiations towards a settlement, so that a vast number of arbitrations are claimed which never come before the arbitrators. It is an acceptable practice in the trade to claim arbitration *"lightly"* without ill will or any loss of customer relationship. These claims are made as a safeguard and withdrawn at a later stage if the parties are able to reach an agreement. This is a very important point to bear in mind in light of the recent debate on whether arbitration is litigation. In the grain and feed trade if a settlement is not achieved, the parties often resort to arbitration to avoid having a personal, litigious, emotional dispute between their two companies' employees, preferring instead to leave the resolution to a third party so that they may continue trading with one another.

This is pure arbitration on a consensual basis and not litigation. Some companies may well take the view that referring its problems or difficulties to arbitration, is a sensible alternative to having an in-house department dealing with those specialist aspects which can be handled by arbitrators. Many an arbitrator working on laytime statements feels he is being employed in the place of accountants. Of course, often parties feel strongly about the issues in dispute, but the association takes the view that on these occasions it is the duty of the arbitrators to take the heat out of the problem by shedding some light.

Lapse of claim

A special trade rule, refers to lapse of claim. If someone claims arbitration, perhaps as a safeguard, and then does nothing thereafter, the claim is still outstanding and provision may have to be made by the respondents in their accounts. This rule provides that the claimant has to renew his claim every year in order to keep it alive. Failure to do so means the claim is deemed to have lapsed.

The arbitrator(s)

To be in line with the recommendation of our members overseas the arbitration rules provide for determination by an uneven number of arbitrators, one or three.

This means there will be either a sole arbitrator or a tribunal of three from the outset. In accordance with the rules, no later than 7 days after the last day for claiming arbitration the claimant must appoint an arbitrator. They must appoint someone from the membership of GAFTA, and who has no interest in the transaction. Alternatively, they may apply to GAFTA to appoint an arbitrator for them. The other party can agree to accept the claimant's appointed arbitrator to act as a sole arbitrator, or they can appoint someone else. If they fail to do so, again GAFTA will appoint the arbitrator. In the majority of cases, although the number of sole arbitrators is increasing, there will usually be a tribunal of three. On the next review of our rules we will change the emphasis to having a sole arbitrator appointed wherever possible, rather than being someone who is of the claimant's choice. This can be agreed by the parties or he may be appointed by GAFTA.

Since not all claims proceed, a practical rule has been included that the third arbitrator is appointed only after the first set of documents is submitted by the claimant. The association then takes it that the case has started and it will appoint the third arbitrator, who will be the chairman of the tribunal.

There should never by any direct communication between the arbitrator and the party appointing him, other than the party asking if the arbitrator will act and the arbitrator's acceptance. The association will handle the administration and the chairman will progress the case and see to the proceedings at the hearing. If there are any delays in proceeding, then the association is entitled to set down a date for a hearing and/or set down a timetable for the submission of documents.

Arbitration hearing (first tier).

Parties do not often attend the first tier arbitration hearing. These arbitrations are usually carried out by examination of documents and the parties' own statement of events and evidence. Parties may wish to be represented by agents engaged in the trade, or attend the hearing personally, they may not be legally represented by solicitors or counsel in private practice. The reason for this is that it is the view that commercial arbitration is best dealt with by commercial men, who are familiar in their own business, with the contract and the commodity. It is also intended to be speedier and less complicated.

The rules lay down the procedure for submitting documentation to the association and what happens at the arbitration hearing. Any documents relating to the dispute are submitted to GAFTA and the other party prior to the arbitration. The parties provide each other with submissions and documents as well as to the arbitrators, via GAFTA. Both parties should have ample opportunity to examine all the documents and evidence, and the chairman has a duty to see that this is done.

String arbitrations (consolidation or concurrent hearings)

This is a special rule for the grain and feed trade which relates only to quality and condition disputes. If several buyers and sellers, of the same commodity have bought and sold on identical terms, except price, then the arbitration may be held between the first seller in the string and the last buyer, with all the other buyers and sellers being shown on the one award as *"intervening principals"*. This procedure has worked efficiently for many years and as only one award is given it is a great saving on costs to the parties. It is not something we are able to do on technical arbitrations as this would be considered to be a consolidation of disputes, which is not yet provided in the acts. Wherever possible however for a group of similar arbitration cases in a string of contracts, to save costs they are heard together, but separate awards issued.

Preliminary issues (jurisdiction)

Arbitrators are not entitled to decide on their own jurisdiction, but this may shortly be changed by a new act. At present, however, this is something that can be dealt with to an extent under GAFTA rules when there is a defence that there is no jurisdiction as there is a no agreed GAFTA contract or arbitration rules in place. A rather complex, but effective, rule has been drawn up so that the arbitrators may decide whether or not there is a contract between the parties. If they find that there is and it incorporates the arbitration agreement referring to GAFTA rules, then they will take the view that it follows that they have jurisdiction to enter into the reference and proceed with the case.

Appeal (second tier).

GAFTA has a two tier arbitration system. Within 30 days from the date of the first award of arbitration the parties have the right to lodge an appeal against it.

When the association receives notice of the appeal, a five man board of appeal will be elected to hear the case. (we are currently considering reducing this to three). The election is by postal ballot from a committee established for that specific purpose comprised of people from all sectors of the trade.

The procedure for hearing an appeal is far more formal than at the first tier arbitration. The association sets down a date for a hearing. Again the parties may be represented by an agent engaged in the trade; they may appear personally or present their case in writing; they cannot be legally represented unless they first obtain special leave from the board of appeal. Usually parties will ask a member of GAFTA, familiar with arbitration matters, to present their case for them at the hearing. Appeal boards will probably allow legal representation when the case involves complicated issues and questions of law, and when both parties ask for solicitors/counsel to be present. In which event the board itself may decide to appoint a legal assessor to interpret the law for them and to draft their award.

At the hearing the appellants will present their case to the board on the basis that the board has no prior knowledge of it and that it is a completely fresh hearing. The respondents will then reply and may also bring in fresh arguments to which the appellants will have the right of reply. The parties should in advance of the hearing submit the documents on which they intend to rely, to the association to issue to the board prior to the hearing so that the board has some background information.

Reasons

GAFTA has for some time maintained that arbitrators should always give reasons when they make their awards of arbitration, mainly to demonstrate to the parties why they were successful or otherwise, and perhaps to enable them to avoid the same problem in the future. Also it is because some countries' laws require that, in the interest of natural justice, reasons should be given for the enforcement of the award.

Judicial review

When a final appeal award is published by GAFTA it should be settled forthwith. The parties may apply to the courts for a review and the GAFTA rules need not make any reference to this procedure for a judicial review as it is contained in the act and established by the courts.

Although in fact the rules do remind the parties that in the event that they may wish to have a judicial review they have to ask the board at the hearing to give a reasoned award. If they do not do so they may lose their rights to apply for the review.

Enforcement

Once the board has dated and published an award it becomes final and binding on the parties. With very few exceptions GAFTA has a good record of awards of arbitration being enforced throughout the world. It is rare that an award of GAFTA is not paid by a defaulting party. However, should a party fail to comply with a final award, the association's council may inform all its members of that fact and publish to them the name of the company involved. This is a drastic measure and one which it is hoped is to be avoided.

The Way Ahead — Form 126

For those disputes which require only an answer to a simple problem, from 1 March 1994 GAFTA introduced a new set of rules, form 126. This set of rules can be agreed upon by the parties only after a dispute has arisen. The agreement to arbitrate is attached to the rules and provides that GAFTA will appoint a sole arbitrator, there is a fixed timetable in the rules for the presentation of the case and the publication of the award. GAFTA's council will decide on a set fee each year for these arbitrations. By entering into this arbitration agreement the parties have effectively contracted out of form 125 and, also by doing so, have agreed to a one tier arbitration system, without the possibility of an appeal to GAFTA or to the courts.

10. The Predictability Factor in International Arbitration

John Uff

Synopsis

This paper examines the relationship between the aspirations of the individual parties when submitting to a procedural regime and the unpredictability of the institutional rules which seek to control the procedures.

Introduction

One purpose of this collection of papers is to bring together contrasting experiences from different commercial areas, from different forms of dispute resolution and from different jurisdictions. These contrasts are found in sharp focus in international arbitration where there is often an additional element to be found in the cultural differences between the participants—not simply the parties themselves but also their lawyers and other representatives, as well as the arbitral tribunal. On occasions, the differences which have generated the arbitration seem less significant than the fundamental differences of approach to the dispute resolution process.

The forms of procedure which are generated and demanded by such situations may suggest conclusions as to best practices for dispute resolution generally. They also underline the paramount need for flexibility of approach and highlight the palpable advantages of arbitration through its adaptability. However, an even more desirable facet than these is predictability. The parties ought to know in advance the type of arbitration to which they are committed. In most cases, all that commercial parties know is that they have contracted for arbitration, usually in accordance with identified institutional rules and with a specified or at least predictable "seat" and governing law. In practice, this still leaves a vast range of possibilities as to the way the arbitration will actually be run. This paper addresses the need for greater predictability.

The popular notion is that arbitrations are 'run' by rules and directions from administrative institutions, while being guided in more fundamental respects by the applicable procedural law. This paper demonstrates that these organs of control represent only the loosest framework within which arbitrators exercise a vast and largely uncontrolled discretion. In most cases it is a matter of pure chance whether the parties to an international arbitration end up with what might objectively be called a 'good' resolution of their dispute or alternatively whether the case turns into a costly procedural nightmare.[1] It is suggested that, while procedural rules have many advantages, they fail totally to address this uncertainty factor. The writer agrees with Professor Reymond [2] that the introduction of rules to achieve uniformity is undesirable but it is considered essential that means are found to determine certain basic questions in advance of the arbitration so that the conduct of the proceedings is rendered at least reasonably predictable. It is suggested that such choices should generally be made at the contract stage.

A second and particular aspect of predictability, which is largely determined by detailed procedural issues, is the overall length of the proceedings. Yet in terms of efficiency and cost effectiveness this factor subsumes all others. To put the point more directly, even apart from the commercial benefits of speedy resolution, an arbitration which is concluded in 6 months is going to be much cheaper than one which runs for years. Few would disagree with the notion that, assuming at least one of the parties so wishes, an international (or any other) arbitration ought to be concluded within the shortest reasonable timescale. This is often found reflected in applicable rules and sometimes in municipal laws. But such rules are complied with in only the very rarest of cases and it is worthwhile considering whether they have any serious part to play in the predictability of arbitration.

A third aspect of predictability which is a direct function of the forms of procedure and the time element, is the cost of the arbitration. This is, curiously, probably the least often considered element of arbitration, perhaps because it is difficult to see any academic or theoretical side to

---

[1] Refer to the infamous "Macau sardine" case at 3 Arbit Int 79 which, although claimed by the author to be wholly fictitious has generated much serious comment.

[2] Paper 18, *infra* p. 263.

it.[3] Yet it must be the second most important factor to the parties, after the question of the outcome of the arbitration. The cost to the individual parties, being compounded from the unpredictability of the procedure and of the time element, as well as being subject itself to unpredictable rules in terms of recovery, is probably the least predictable of all the factors—probably less predictable than the outcome of the arbitration itself. This factor merits serious consideration.

General approach to procedure

The classic English authorities deal with the concept of 'procedural law' in distinction to the substantive law, and to other laws which affect different aspects of an arbitration.[4] In practice, however, it would be a mistake to conclude that any arbitration is 'governed' by a particular procedural law, other than in regard to specific and limited issues. Professor Böckstiegel[5] has drawn attention to the trend towards limiting mandatory legal provisions to the absolutely necessary minimum, leaving questions of procedure to the parties and the arbitrators; and to the importance of the predictability of the procedure adopted, where not specifically agreed. He was referring, however, to the need for the arbitrators to decide upon matters of procedure at an early stage so that the parties can prepare themselves to present their cases effectively. The point which is made here is that the likely course of an arbitration ought to be predictable before the parties are even committed to arbitrate, so that they know, at least in broad terms, the consequences of the course which they may be advised to pursue.

Very little guidance is to be found on how a case will actually be conducted, even under a particular set of rules or procedural law. Redfern & Hunter, after quoting the requirement of the ICC rules for the arbitrator to establish the facts "by all appropriate means" comment that this "can scarcely be described as a comprehensive guide to the

---

3   But see now O'Reilly, *Costs in Arbitration Proceedings*, LLP, London, 1995.
4   *Black Clawson v Papierwerke Waldhof AG* [1981] 2 Lloyds Rep 446; *Naviera Amazonica v Cie International* [1988] i Lloyds Rep 116
5   Hunter, M., Marriott, A. & Veeder, V.V., *The Internationalisation of International Arbitration, The LCIA Centenary Conference*, Graham & Trotman, London 1995, p. 79

parties (or indeed the arbitral tribunal itself) as to the actual procedures which should be followed in the conduct of an arbitration". They point out that what tends to happen in practice, is that the parties and the tribunal work out for themselves the details and the procedure to be followed.[6] What actually happens is that a form of procedure is evolved, sometimes after lengthy debate, which satisfies (or fails to satisfy) in roughly equal measure the expectations of those involved. This means, however, not so much the parties, who will often have no relevant expectation at all as to these matters, but the lawyers involved and the arbitrators themselves. As already pointed out, a particular feature of international arbitration is the wide cultural and other differences which are frequently found between the people involved in it. All this adds to the unpredictability. The individual factors which will eventually determine the procedure adopted are themselves unpredictable until they all come together, for example, at a Terms of Reference meeting. Only then can the process of defining the procedure even begin.

Lawyers from different jurisdictions will naturally tend towards adopting their own established and familiar domestic procedures. Is there, nevertheless, any recognised international approach to procedure in international arbitration? At the recent LCIA centenary conference on "The Internationalisation of International Arbitration", many speakers addressed the importance of procedure. The late Dr Gillis Wetter emphasised the importance of cost-effectiveness, stating that "it must be recognised that international arbitration is subject to the same economic laws as other endeavours in a free market and will not subsist (and certainly not thrive) unless it responds adequately and flexibly to the demands of users".[7] Professor Lalive[8] referred to the increasing "processualisation" of arbitration, meaning the increasing tendency to adopt the national judicial process. Jan Paullson characterised this factor as an indication of cost effectiveness being "menaced by the beast of US-style litigation methods, lurching towards Bethlehem"[9]. While there may be an "international" approach in terms of very broad principle, individual procedures based on particular jurisdictions

---

[6] Redfern, A. & Hunter, J.M.H.H., *Law and Practice of International Arbitration*, 2nd ed. Sweet & Maxwell, London, 1991, pp. 66-67

[7] *Ibid*, p. 103

[8] *Ibid*, p. 74

[9] *Ibid* p. 61, and see W B Yeats

remain likely to dominate the procedure—to what extent this occurs is at the heart of the predictability factor.

Is the position different under the ICC rules, which require the applicable procedural rules to be specified in Terms of Reference?[10] In practice, ICC arbitrators, in drawing up Terms of Reference, often simply repeat the relevant rule in terms such as:

> *"The rules governing the arbitration shall be those resulting from the ICC Rules of conciliation and Arbitration and, where these rules are silent, any rules which the parties (or the arbitrators) may settle, providing that the arbitrators shall respect any mandatory procedural rules applicable to the reference."*

Such drafting effectively leaves the arbitrators with the widest possible discretion and also means that every procedural dispute must be approached in two stages: first, to establish the relevant rule and secondly to apply it to the facts in issue. In practice, in long-running and multi-stage arbitrations typified by construction disputes, ICC arbitrators tend to build up a series of procedural rulings whereby the applicable procedure is progressively defined. But it remains the position that the detailed procedure is unpredictable before the arbitration commences, and this includes major questions such as production of documents, the form of proceedings, the introduction of expert evidence and many other detailed matters.

In the following sections consideration is given to some of these procedural issues where a wide variety of practices exists internationally. Many of these issues are discussed specifically as between the civil law and common law systems by Professor Reymond.

Production of documents

This is probably the most fundamental aspect of procedure in terms of its effect on the preparation and conduct of a case. The production of documents has a major impact on timing of the arbitration, both in terms of the length of the proceedings and, even more fundamentally,

---

[10]   ICC Rules, Article 13.1(g) and Article 11

on the preparation necessary before the hearing. It also has a major impact on the costs of preparation for and conduct of the hearing.

In broad terms, there are three possible approaches to the production of documents. First, the English system, generally known as 'discovery', requires each party to produce to the other in advance of the hearing all documents falling within a broad test of relevance, including particularly those potentially damaging to the party's own case. The process of discovery is no longer formally applicable to arbitration governed by English procedural law, but it remains optionally available if ordered by the arbitrators, and is still frequently employed, at least in English domestic arbitration. Secondly, the US system whereby the search for documents is assisted by the taking of depositions from potential witnesses, produces an even greater volume of potential trial documents. Thirdly, the civil law approach allows a party to choose those documents it wishes to bring forward. The opposing party has a right to request production of specific documents but there is generally no obligation to produce a document potentially damaging to a party's case.

Apart from the enormous disparity in terms of costs and time which these systems represent, they have fundamentally different effects in the way in which an arbitration proceeds. In the case of civil law procedure, the absence of any significant subsequent documentary process allows a party to present his full written case at the outset, including evidence and documents. The application of English documentary procedures makes this impossible, since a party cannot fully prepare its case in the absence of documents from the other party which may have an important bearing on the issues. The application of US procedures has an even more fundamental effect in that presentation of the case may be preceded by extensive deposition hearings before the parties can be in a position to prepare the actual case for trial. These differences are well known and international lawyers are practised in working within and around them. The vital question which subsumes all detailed issues, however, is which system should apply. In practical terms, arbitrators must furnish an answer in terms of formulating procedural orders. The answer arrived at will be an amalgam of many factors including the previous experience of the arbitrators and the representatives of the parties. It is unsatisfactory that the resolution of such an important issue should be so uncertain. None of the available sets of arbitration rules descends to such level of detail that the parties could, at the contract stage, stipulate the form of disclosure to be given in the event of a dispute. There is, however, no reason why this, and other procedural issues, should not be dealt with in this manner before disputes have arisen.

Orality of proceedings

This is a second major factor which determines the form and length of proceedings, and to some extent, their cost. There are at least two aspects to the issue: first whether a case is to be presented in a relatively complete written form prior to any oral hearing; and secondly, the procedure adopted at the oral hearing. The two issues largely go hand in hand in that the civil law tradition of presenting a fully prepared written case presupposes limited oral proceedings, dealing principally with matters arising as a result of the latest submissions of the parties. Again, the possibility of conducting an arbitration in this way depends upon the parties' acceptance of limited cross examination of opposing witnesses and the limited availability of documents damaging to (rather than supportive of) the parties' cases. The alternative common law approach can be characterised as seeking to prove the case by damaging the case of the opponent. Under English procedure the requirements as to oral proof are now largely superseded by the general acceptance of written evidence. But a substantial part of the role of the common lawyer is still seen as advancing his case by disproving the case of the opposition.

Which system is to be adopted in a particular case? The answer again depends upon a variety of factors and will be determined only at the stage of settling Terms of Reference or giving procedural directions in the arbitration. Again, none of the available sets of arbitration rules permits an effective choice at the contract stage. Often, the use of English or US lawyers or arbitrators will result in a degree of orality commensurate with their professional skills and expectations, while the engagement of civil lawyers is more likely to result in written procedures with limited orality. It could be said that the choice should be the other way round: the lawyers should be selected to fit the type of dispute resolution procedure which the parties have agreed upon at the contract stage.

The role of experts

There is an alarmingly wide range of approaches to the introduction of expertise relating to the matters in dispute. The civil law approach appears to be well-established and perfectly logical. The parties set out their full cases in writing including evidence and submissions on technical issues. The only 'expert' appointed, however, is appointed to investigate and advise the tribunal. By contrast, the common law tradition is for the parties to introduce their own experts, often in addition to a tribunal appointed expert. This gives rise, in addition to excessive costs, to real confusion as to the role of these various experts, all of whom are notionally 'independent', although some more than others.

A further point of difference under the common law system is that arbitrators are often technically qualified, and where this is so, will be able to bring their own expertise to bear on the issues. This has given rise to a so-far unresolved debate as to the limits upon the arbitrator's use of his own expertise and a further debate as to when, if at all, an arbitrator who is himself technically qualified can refuse to hear technical evidence which he regards as unnecessary. The position becomes more complex when, as is usually the case under the civil law system, three arbitrators are appointed, who may have different areas of expertise.

A related issue upon which views differ internationally is the selection of experts. The English tradition is firmly in favour of avoiding any distinction between or grading of experts, whose only distinguishing feature, usually, is that they give evidence of opinion rather than fact. The civil law tradition, by contrast, is to appoint only 'established' or recognised experts; and in the US an expert has to be 'admitted' as such and may be challenged as to his qualification so to act.

None of the available sets of rules offers guidance but most permit virtually any procedure which does not infringe mandatory requirements of the applicable law. As in other areas, the result is unpredictability and a necessarily *ad hoc* solution based largely on the experience of the arbitrators and the representatives of the parties. Again, it is suggested that it would be appropriate that matters of such importance should be dealt with at contract stage.

Effect of institutional rules

It is thus seen that in a number of important instances the course of an arbitration can be a lottery in the sense that it is determined by factors not directly within the control of the parties and often having little to do with their commercial needs. How is the situation affected by recognised arbitration rules? The choice of procedural law under the ICC rules has already been mentioned. In terms of the conduct and control of the proceedings, the various sets of rules all tend to speak in the same vague language. Thus the ICC Rules provide by article 14:

> "14.1 *The arbitrators shall proceed within as short a time as possible to establish the facts of the case by all appropriate means. After study of the written submissions of the parties and of all document relied upon, the arbitrators shall hear the parties together in person if one of them so requests; and failing such a request he of his own motion decide to hear them.*
>
> *In addition, the arbitrator may decide to hear any other person in the presence of the parties or in their absence provided they have been duly summoned.*"

The LCIA rules, article 5 provide:

> "5.1 *the parties may agree on the arbitral procedure, and are encouraged to do so*
>
> 5.2 *in the absence of procedure agreed by the parties or contained herein, the Tribunal shall have the widest discretion allowed under such law as may be applicable to ensure the just, economical, and final determination of the dispute.*"

The UNCITRAL rules, article 15 provides as follows:

> "15.1 *Subject to these Rules the arbitral tribunal may conduct the arbitration in such manner as it considers appropriate, provided that the parties are treated with*

> *equality and that at any stage of the proceedings each party is given a full opportunity of presenting his case.*

15.2   *If either party so requests at any stage of the proceedings, the arbitral tribunal shall hold hearings for the presentation of evidence by witnesses, including expert witnesses, or for oral argument. In the absence of such a request, the arbitral tribunal shall decide whether to hold such hearings or whether proceedings shall be conducted on the basis of documents and other materials."*

Thus, as anticipated above, it can be seen that the institutional rules give no guidance on the early choice of procedural rules. These rules may be compared to the UNCITRAL Model Law and to the new English Arbitration Act, based on the Model Law in part. These provisions may have a somewhat different effect. Article 19 of the Model Law provides:

> "19 (1) *Subject to the provisions of this Law, the parties are free to agree on the procedure to be followed by the arbitral tribunal in conducting the proceedings.*
>
> (2) *Failing such agreement, the arbitral tribunal may, subject to the provisions of this Law, conduct the arbitration in such manner as it considers appropriate. The power conferred upon the arbitral tribunal includes the power to determine the admissibility, relevance, materiality and weight of any evidence."*

These provisions were substantially adopted in early drafts of the Bill. In the final form, however, as a result of specific debate as to the extent to which procedure should be controlled by the Tribunal or the parties, the following form emerged:

> "34 (1) *It shall be for the tribunal to decide all procedural and evidential matters, subject to the right of the parties to agree any matter.*
>
> (2) *Procedural and evidential matters include -"*

Section 34 (2) then sets out a substantial list of matter to be decided either by the tribunal or by the parties. The key to this section, however, is in the word "agree". Section 5(1) of the Act states:

> "5 (1) *The provisions of this Part apply only where the arbitration agreement is in writing, and any other agreement between the parties as to any matter is effective for the purposes of this Part only if in writing.*
>
> *The expressions "agreement", "agree" and "agreed" shall be construed accordingly.*

Thus the parties must express their agreement on detailed procedural matters in writing and this means effectively that they must be part of the arbitration agreement, rather than mere matters of oral agreement between the parties' representatives as the case goes along.

Both the Model Law and the new English Act can therefore be seen as inviting the parties to determine at least the major elements of procedure as part of their initial agreement to arbitrate, as opposed to leaving such matters to the unpredictable decision of the arbitrators. While such agreement can be made after the dispute has arisen, experience shows that this is the stage where parties are least likely to be able to reach sensible agreements as to the form and details of dispute resolution procedure. The most favourable time for seeking agreement is at the contract stage where discussions may be conducted against the background of mutual interest and good-will, the reverse of the situation which obtains when a dispute arises.

Examples of procedural choice

It is unrealistic to expect the parties, having negotiated an international contract, then to proceed to negotiate also an international arbitration procedure, against the possibility of a dispute arising. However, it is common-place for negotiation to include questions of perceived importance such as whether to incorporate an arbitration clause at all, the incorporation of institutional rules and, particularly, the means of appointing the tribunal and the venue of the arbitration. Parties often hold and express strong views on these latter issues.

There is no reason why parties should not, either in the arbitration agreement or through incorporated rules, make further agreements in order to render the course of any future arbitration proceedings more predictable in regard to the crucial questions considered above. By far the best vehicle for this is in theory institutional rules, but the need is for much more specific measures than those presently promulgated to cover any type of dispute. For example, both the ICE and the JCT have produced domestic rules specific to construction disputes. Similarly detailed rules need to be available in the international context for adoption and amendment if necessary when using international forms such as the FIDIC contract form. These should deal specifically with the procedural rules to be adopted in the instances noted above. For example, they could allow parties to "contract in" to the right to demand disclosure of documents, with a fall-back provision giving the right only to demand specific documents. In similarly vein, the parties could contract in to the right to call independent expert witnesses, in default of which any expert needed would be tribunal-appointed.

The time factor

How long should an international arbitration last? The ICC rules are quite specific. Article 18 provides:

> "(1) *The time-limit within which the arbitrator must render his Award is fixed at six months. Once the terms of Article 9(4) have been satisfied [payment of the advance on costs], such time-limit shall start to run from the date of the last signature by the arbitrator or the parties of the document mentioned in Article 13 [Terms of Reference] or from the expiry of the time-limit granted to a party by virtue of Article 13 (2) [if Terms of Reference not signed] or from the date that the Secretary General of the International Court of Arbitration notifies the arbitrator that the advance of costs is paid in full, if such notification occurs later.*

> (2) *The court may, pursuant to a reasonable request from the arbitrator or if need be on its own initiative, extend this time-limit if it decides it is necessary to do so.*

(3) *Where no such extension is granted and, if appropriate, after application of the provisions of Article 2(11) [Replacement of Arbitrator who does not proceed] the court shall determine the manner in which the dispute is to be resolved."*

These are impressive and potentially powerful rules. Unfortunately, as is well known, the time-limit is enforced in only the rarest of cases, if ever. There is a ready acceptance on all sides that in anything but the simplest case, the six months time-limit must be extended and this is invariably done as a matter of course by the ICC Secretariat, whether or not a reasoned request is received from the arbitrator. In effect, the timing of the arbitration is determined by the procedural factors discussed above. It is simply not part of the function of the ICC or of any other administrative body to seek to control the procedure being used in the arbitration, in order to facilitate compliance with the time-limit. Such an approach would, of course, be fundamentally inconsistent *inter alia* with Article 19 of the Model Law. Time-limits can also exist under the applicable municipal law. For example, in the State of Bahrain a six month time-limit is applicable, but this may be extended by agreement.

One advantage of time-limits, even where not observed, is that they may be regarded as providing a target, putting the parties on notice that they should be proceeding more rapidly. But in practice the time taken by any arbitration is determined by a number of major factors, beginning with the procedure adopted and the form in which the parties are to present their cases, and including questions of availability of lawyers and arbitrators, most of whom tend to work to busy and tight schedules. The result is unpredictability, not only at the date of the commencement of the arbitration but continuing thereafter.

There are two possible approaches to predictability of the time factor in international arbitration. First, by reducing the procedural uncertainties, the programme would automatically be rendered more certain and reliable. Secondly, adopting a more or less fixed programme for the arbitration, by agreement of the parties or by direction of the arbitrators, will necessarily impose limits and checks on the procedures which can be employed within the available time. Often it is desirable and necessary to employ both methods before the timing begins to acquire a reasonable degree of certainty. Greater control over time-limits by the institutions, including the ICC, would be a welcome step. But it is recognised that such control without a detailed knowledge of the issues is extremely difficult; and the institutions must always respect the wishes of the parties.

Costs of the arbitration

Reference has already been made to the need for cost effectiveness and that this is largely a function of procedure and programme. The question examined here is whether, by exercising control over either the expenditure or the recovery of costs, advantage might accrue in terms of procedure, programming and predictability. In terms of English domestic arbitration, the question of recoverable costs was debated in the context of section 18(3) of the Arbitration Act 1950, which provided

> "(3) *Any provision in an arbitration agreement to the effect that the parties or any party thereto shall in any event pay their or his own costs of the reference reward or any part thereof shall be void, and this Part of this Act shall, in the case of an arbitration agreement containing any such provision, have effect as if that provision were not contained therein:*
>
> *Provided that nothing in this sub-section shall invalidate such a provision when it is part of an agreement to submit to arbitration a dispute which has arisen before the making of that agreement*

According to Mustill & Boyd, the sub-section dates from the Act of 1934. Contrary to appearances, its purpose is not to bar any restriction on payment of lawyers' fees but rather to avoid arbitration agreements which would have the effect of preventing or discouraging a less pecunious party from employing proper legal representation. That particular debate resulted in a decision to re-enact the section in the new English Arbitration Act (section 60), albeit expressed in simpler terms. The Act does contain, however, a far-reaching provision which has the potential for establishing a degree of control over procedure:

> "65 (1) *Unless otherwise agreed by the parties, the tribunal may direct that the recoverable costs of the arbitration, or any*

part of the arbitral proceedings, shall be limited to a specified amount.

(2) *Any direction may be made or varied at any stage, but this must be done sufficiently in advance of the incurring of costs to which it relates, or the taking of any steps in the proceedings which may be affected by it, for the limit to be taken into account.*"

This power will thus be available unless the parties agree in writing to exclude it. The reference to the timing of any direction being done sufficiently in advance "for the limit to be taken into account" clearly contemplates the parties being on notice that the incurring of costs or further costs will be at their client's expense in any event. It is thus plainly intended to result in the adoption of procedures or other measures consistent with the limit being imposed. This is a major and most welcome step in relation to English procedure which will apply equally to domestic or international arbitration.

There is some experience of the effect of cost limitations on procedure through existing arbitration rules. One example under the ICE Arbitration Procedure (1983) Part F(short procedure) and Part G (special procedure for experts). Both of these procedures (which have to be agreed after the dispute has arisen) provide that unless the parties otherwise agree, the arbitrator has no power to award costs, so that the parties pay their own costs irrespective of the outcome and share the costs of the arbitrator. In practice, this has usually had a major effect on the timing and procedure, resulting in the rapid disposal of complex and potentially costly issues. In the absence of written agreement between the parties (either in applicable rules or subsequently) arbitrators will now be able to impose such limits without the need for the parties to "contract in".

One reason why one rarely finds provisions dealing with the recoverability of costs outside England and the Commonwealth, is that there is no automatic expectation of cost recovery. This is indeed one of the major factors of unpredictability in any international arbitration, which is often overlooked totally by the parties: how will the arbitrators deal with the award of the parties' costs. The disparity of practice is highlighted by reference to Craig Park and Paulsson on ICC arbitration, where one finds extensive discussion of the issue of payment of the administrative costs of the arbitration, including the arbitrators' fees as fixed by the ICC, apparently on the assumption that the parties' own legal costs are comparatively insignificant. Article 20 of the ICC rules does encompass the "normal legal costs incurred by the parties" but Craig Park and Paullson comment on this section as follows:

> *"Article 20 of the Rules gives the arbitrator the power not only to allocate the burden of costs of arbitration and arbitrators' fees between the parities, but also to award an amount on account of fees for the prevailing parties' counsel. This is common practice in certain countries, unlike the United States where each party is generally required to bear its own attorney's fees"*. [11]

The unfortunate experience of many common lawyers is that the parties' own legal costs are usually not only significant in relation to the administrative costs and the arbitrators' fees, but they are usually also significant in relation to the sums in issue, and therefore directly relevant to the question of cost-effectiveness. To put the matter more directly, practically all common lawyers will have the experienced of seeing a major arbitration in which the total costs of the parties equal or exceed the sums in issue. Such a situation, save in comparatively trivial cases, is rare in civil law arbitration. It is this huge disparity between the common law tradition, the US tradition and the civil law tradition, which constitutes one of the major elements affecting the predictability factor in international arbitration.

Conclusions

This paper has examined particular features of international arbitration in relation to the control of procedure. The general conclusion is that there is a substantial measure of unpredictability stemming from the late stage at which fundamental decisions are taken regarding procedure. The degree of uncertainty could be substantially reduced by bringing forward certain fundamental decisions to the contract stage. This would render the proceeding more predictable and ease the task of

---

[11] 2nd edition, p147

predicting the costs and likely duration of the proceedings. Programme and cost recovery are particular elements of unpredictability which are in part derivative of procedural uncertainties but also operate as individual factors.

Procedure in arbitration is subject to the rules of natural justice, or due process, which require that the parties each know the case of the other, have an opportunity to formulate their own cases and to address the arbitrators. As with procedural law and rules, these basic requirements do not dictate the actual procedure to be adopted. Given the general acceptance of cost effectiveness and the potential for any large scale arbitration to generate huge costs and delay, it is suggested that in any international arbitration the following matters should be addressed at the earliest opportunity:

- the parties and their representatives should know the procedure to be adopted in detail;

- a time-table for the arbitration should be established with the intention that it be adhered to by all parties;

- the extent of possible cost-recovery must be known.

By these means the parties with their lawyers should be enabled to make decisions about the resources to be deployed, so that cost effectiveness is achieved having regard to the possible level of cost recovery. The programme for the arbitration itself and for any hearings must allow for unavoidable adjustment, and should therefore contain elements of "float" or contingency time which can be used when necessary. What cannot be tolerated is any semblance of "timeless" litigation, as is still found in the courts of most common law countries. The ability to programme an arbitration is dependent on knowledge of the procedure and particularly of those aspects which crucially affect the manner in which an arbitration is prepared and presented.

For parties contemplating the major expenditure involved in a substantial international arbitration, it is vital for them to know on what basis the arbitrators will deal with the award of costs: will they be awarded on the basis of the outcome of the arbitration, and if so will the quantification of costs be based on substantial compensation or on some other measure of assessment? It is essential for these questions to be raised and determined, so far as possible, before the costs are expended.

No useful view can be offered on whether greater predictability in international arbitration would cause the process to be viewed more favourably or, conversely, whether greater fore-knowledge of it would lead the parties to opt for conciliation or to avoid disputes altogether. It is suggested, however, that predictability is a basic entitlement of any party to arbitration, particularly in the light of the huge areas of uncertainty which exist in other facets of international arbitration.

Part III

ADR and Fast-Track Procedures

11. The Influence of Commerce on the Changing Face of Dispute Resolution

Martin Odams

Synopsis

This paper examines the relationship between the expectations of commerce and the development of alternative dispute resolution mechanisms.

Introduction

It has been said that 'one of the most powerful influences on human activity is the driving force of trade'.[1] Whether this a universal truism is of course open to debate. What, however, is abundantly clear is that trade is omnipotent, possesses great force and is inherently dynamic. Indeed the mores and customs of, in tandem with trade usage within, the commercial world augmented the development of commercial law; thus, the body of legal rules now known as the generic 'commercial law' evolved. One has, therefore, inevitably to refer to the now less fashionable concept of *lex mercatoria*.[2] There is no doubt that *lex mercatoria* has had a profound and irrevocable effect on the development of arbitration law,[3] the current conundrum is whether it should continue to so do.[4]

In this brief paper, which forms part of a wider research project, I seek to examine how dispute resolution mechanisms are affected by the requirements of commerce and how change and developments are sought to be, and have been, achieved in the common law world.

---

[1]   Goode, R., *Commercial Law 2nd Edition*, Penguin Law, London, 1995, p.3.
[2]   For an explanation as to the application and effect of *lex mercatoria* see Burdick, F.M., *What is the Law Merchant?* (1902) 2 Columbia LR 470.
[3]   Tudsbery, F.C.T., *Law Merchant and the Common Law* (1918) 34 LQR 392.
[4]   On the one hand see Mustill, M.J. *'The New Lex Mercatoria'* in Bos, M. & Brownlie, I. (Eds) *Liber Amicorum for Lord Wilberforce*, Oxford, republished as (1988) 4 Arb Intl 86, and on the other see Lowenfeld, A.F., *Lex Mercatoria: An Arbitrator's View* (1990) 6 Arb Intl 133 and Lando, O., *The Lex Mercatoria in International Commercial Arbitration* (1985) 34 ICLQ 747 for the civilian counterpoint.

Towards a new law

The debate as to modernisation or alternatively codification, the vehicle by which swingeing changes seem more readily to be achieved than an overt drive towards modernisation, has brought a number of issues to the fore. It was evident from the debate that until the situation was regularised, England would continue to cede a high proportion of international arbitration instructions to a more user-friendly environment.

In this context, 'user-friendly' implies a more pro-active stance to the requirements of commerce and does not simply mean aficionados gazing into their crystal balls divining a system that might in the future adapt to the needs of commerce, but that the fundaments of commerce are intimately understood and that the framework of a competent system is in place before it is required.[5]

Model Laws

In 1985 the United Nations Commission on International Trade Law published their Model Law on Arbitration. The 'Model law' is clear, precise and uncomplicated, indeed on these counts alone it embodies the essential requirements of commerce: pro-activity in action. The Model law has so far been adopted by 18 states,[6] 8 jurisdictions within the United States[7] and Scotland. Such adoption is not always done simply by giving direct effect to the Model law, it may be tailored to suit in respect of the particular needs of the jurisdiction or so as to be fitted in with less controversy. The latter applies more commonly to common law jurisdictions.[8] After a long and tortuous debate[9] finally the Arbitration Act of 1996 includes the spirit and principle of the Model law. There is a residual concern that in this form the clarity of the model law is not preserved, nevertheless the adoption in itself goes a long way to ameliorating if not fully satisfying commercial concerns.

---

[5] Wetter, J.G., *'The Internationalisation of International Arbitration: Looking Ahead to the Next Ten Years'* in Hunter, M., Marriott, A. & Veeder, V.V., *The Internationalisation of International Arbitration, The LCIA Centenary Conference*, Graham & Trotman, London, 1995.

[6] Australia, Bahrain, Bermuda, Bulgaria, Canada, Republic of Cyprus, Egypt, Hong Kong, Hungary, Mexico, Nigeria, Peru, Russian Federation, Singapore, Slovenia, Tunisia, Ukraine.

[7] California, Conneticut, Florida, Georgia, North Carolina, Ohio, Oregon and Texas.

[8] Paterson, R.K., *Implementing the UNCITRAL Model Law, The Canadian Experience* (1993) 12 Jnl Intl Arb Vol 2 p. 29.

[9] Uff, J. & Keating, D., *Should England Reconsider the UNCITRAL Model law or not?* (1994) 10 Arb Intl 179.

In the common law world, Canada has embraced the Model law with considerable enthusiasm. UNCITRAL was implemented at Federal level in 1985,[10] subsequently the implementation process was fully ratified by it being implemented at local level, in the case of Ontario as late as 1991.[11] The express reasoning behind the enactment was that as Canada was set to become a multilateral trading entity, as well as having strong bilateral trade and investment ties to the United States, the provision of certainty in the commercial dispute settlement arena was of paramount importance. The lessons are self-evident, Canada has enjoyed stable and sustained economic growth in recent years. However, the inherent dynamism and great force of international trade law has lead to domestic legislation being somewhat bulldozed in the process.[12] Notwithstanding that Canada's legal topography may benefit by being relieved of the rigours of particular legislative remedies and sanctions, the fact that domestic law has ceded to an external force may cause even the confirmed modernist to raise an eyebrow. But this is a real risk and one that must be addressed: legislative reform in a jurisdictional vacuum is anathema.

Harmonisation

One of the most significant obstacles to English law is the fact that try as it may harmonisation in the framework of the European Union is complex, convoluted and menacing. In the same way that domestic legislation loses it bite when faced with the onslaught of commerce, the rigours of sovereign law are continually challenged by the law of the supranational Union. It makes sense, therefore, to be one step ahead of the tide by drafting legislation that is in harmony with the rest.[13] This is not an appropriate forum to stoke the harmonisation debate, save for to observe that the new English Act, whilst a resolute step in the right direction, may not be all things to all men.[14] This said, the drafters are to be commended for producing a coherent Act.

---

[10] *Commercial Arbitration Act* (Canada), RSC 1985, c 17 (2nd Supplement)

[11] *Arbitration Act* 1991, SO 1991, c.17.

[12] See Paper 7 *Commercial Arbitration in Canada: A " Model" Law for Others? supra* p. 93.

[13] On this subject see the excellent paper by Professor Boodman entitled '*The Nature of Harmonisation of Laws*' in Odams, A.M. (Ed), *Comparative Studies in Construction Law: The Sweet Lectures*, Construction Law Press, London, 1995.

[14] The passage of the Bill was impeded by considerations as to domestic consumer arbitrations.

Alternative Dispute Resolution

There is a current trend in the common law world to embrace and develop techniques known collectively as Alternative Dispute Resolution (ADR). The range of techniques is wide and extensive, but they seem neatly to fall into two discrete categories; on the one hand those subsidiary to the judicial process and from which they derive their power, court-annexed mediation in Canada and court-appointed referees in Australia being cases in point, and, on the other hand, those alternative to the litigation process, such as arbitration, mini-trials, Dispute Review Boards in America and Building Disputes Tribunals in Australia. Generally speaking the ADR techniques deployed as an alternative to litigation are a response to the needs of commerce, although the distinction is becoming blurred with time.

'Subsidiary' ADR

It is interesting to observe the relationship between developments in ADR and other aspects of court reform such as the creation of a commercial court in Ontario[15] and the implemetation of a two-year alternative dispute resolution pilot project in Toronto.[16] The ADR pilot project is court-annexed. It envisages that the prospective litigants undergo a voluntary pre-trial mediation session at which the presence of clients is mandatory; this in turn can be supplemented by neutral evaluation or by a mini-trial, in cases where a long trial is envisaged. The pilot project is to be deployed in virtually every area of litigation, save for personal injury claims and family law matters, and is not meant to discourage the parties from using a privately appointed mediator or from referring the dispute to arbitration. The Attorney-General, Mr Charles Harnick, has given the pilot project his full support 'The judicial system can no longer afford to have cases lingering on the courthouse steps. The courts must become the adjudicator of last resort ...' [17] The Attorney-General expanded the scheme province-wide and made it mandatory. Current opinion is that even if the mediation fails the parties will be persuaded to refer the dispute to arbitration and that given the current

---

[15] The Ontario Commercial List was modelled in part on the English Commercial Court and commenced in 1991.

[16] See the *Practice Direction Concerning the Alternative Dispute Resolution Project in the Ontario Court (General Division)* September 6, 1995, 24 O.R. (3d) 161.

[17] *Ontario to streamline justice*, Makin, K., The Globe and Mail, Toronto Friday January 26, 1996.

judicial sentiment the incidence of commercial arbitration will rise dramatically. As Richard Potter demonstrates in his paper[18] the Ontarian arbitration legislation has come of age and is now eminently capable of meeting the challenge.

In the Australian construction sector, the combination of dissatisfaction with the cost and efficiency of commercial arbitration has impelled the participants to seek alternative means to resolve disputes. Unlike in Canada, it is notable that the Australian movement towards the introduction of ADR has been driven by commerce, rather than by the judiciary. From time to time standard form contract draftsmen seek to introduce clauses which attempt to stay arbitration or litigation in favour of conciliation or mediation, or another hybrid mode of ADR.[19] This can, however, lead to judicial jealousy. In Australia this judicial jealousy has been to the extent that courts have held that such clauses, upon proper construction, are mere agreements to negotiate and therefore unenforceable.[20] The judiciary has gone further and responded to the draftsman's initiative by controlling the reference procedure,[21] such that the court appoints an expert, where necessary, according to the Rules of the Court, which were revised to embrace such a procedure.[22] It is submitted that commerce can draw valuable experience from this situation and seek not to develop alternative solutions within a contractual or jurisdictional vacuum.

'Alternative' ADR[23]

In the same jurisdiction, New South Wales, a mechanism which has become known as a 'Building Disputes Tribunal', or BDT, has proved durable as an alternative to litigation or arbitration as a means of

---

[18]   *Commercial Arbitration in Canada: A "Model" Law for Others?* p. 93.

[19]   See Taylor, R.G. & Hinkle, B., *How to Use ADR Clauses with Standard Form Construction Industry Contracts* in *The Construction Lawyer* p.42 April 1995 for an interesting discussion as to the problems encountered in the United States.

[20]   *Coalcliff Colleries Pty Limited v. Sijehama Limited* (1992) 24 NSWLR 1 and *Walford v. Miles* [1992] 2 WLR 174.

[21]   The legal and practical implication of which are analysed by Ian Bailey in his paper *Court Appointed References in Australia*, infra p.   .

[22]   See for example, Part 72C of the New South Wales Supreme Court Rules (1970); Order 50.07 of the General Rules of Procedure in Civil Proceedings 1986 of the Supreme Court Rules of Victoria.

[23]   Although arbitration is of course of form of ADR it is not included under this head. I am here concerned with the innovative, more transient, methods.

resolving building disputes.[24] The BDT as an institution is closely linked to the Consumer Claims Tribunal (CCT), a creature of statute empowered by the Consumer Claims Tribunal Act 1987 (NSW), but unlike the CCT the BDT has no underpinning statutory framework from which it can derive support. The BDT provides a fast-track procedure unencumbered by legal obstacles such as joinder, consolidation or legal complexities such as, for example, rules of evidence or discovery. Awards from the BDT are final. Appeals can, however, be made to the Supreme Court on very limited grounds: jurisdiction or breach of natural justice. The BDT has enjoyed great success in New South Wales and is to being considered for adoption in other jurisdictions.[25]

In United States' construction practice, the discovery of a 'new' alternative methods of dispute resolution is commonplace. The current initiative is the Dispute Review Board (DRB).[26] The DRB has the advantage that is is sympathetic to construction practice and seeks to convene periodically on the jobsite to review progress and the problems in hand and attempt to find a solution which is the least expensive in terms of time and programme, essentially a technical advisory board. The decisions of the DRB are generally non-binding, but can be made so on the parties by being a condition precedent to arbitration, for example.[27] Whilst DRB's have been welcomed by project engineers, they are held in scant regard by lawyers.

The success of the BDT in Australia may be unique. It is a truly alternative method which has the support of the courts, albeit tacitly in that they seem markedly reluctant to intervene in the process.[28] As with the majority of 'alternative' initiatives, the durability of the DRB is difficult to predict. Whilst it appears to be a good idea on the one hand, on the other it perhaps does not incorporate fully the essential legal

---

[24] This is dealt with in more detail by Philip Davenport in his paper *Fast Track Disputes Procedures for Construction, infra* p.175.

[25] See Schwarz, L. & Guymer, L., *New Rules for the Domestic Building Industry* Law Institute Journal (Aust) p.1244 December 1995, which examines the provisions of the proposed Victorian Domestic Building Contracts and Tribunal Act 1995 and the statutory implementation of the BDT.

[26] Kohnke, J.R. *Dispute Review Boards - Rising Star of Construction ADR Arbitration Journal* p.53 June (1993).

[27] See Myers, J.J. *Resolving Disputes in Worldwide Infrastructure Projects* [1995] 12 ICLR 429.

[28] Davenport, *op cit*, p.191.

principles required to ensure judicial support.[29] It is very difficult to predict whether the judiciary will support this procedure, if at all. However, procedural reforms, such as these, whether 'subsidiary' or 'alternative', or attempts at modernisation by the judiciary,[30] greatly favour the needs of commerce.[31] Perhaps one should, therefore, not be too sceptical at the outset as to the durability or fortitude of developments, and simply allow initiatives which afford a wider range of litigants greater access to justice to be put to the acid test. Thus, if the method works, does not deprive the parties of perceived justice, and does not trangress fundamental legal principles, it has a fair chance of passing the test; and if it contines to so do, durability may follow.

What price procedural efficiency?

Given the nature by which arbitration has developed in England over the past 100 or so years and has become a credible alternative to litigation, particularly for international commercial disputes, it would be easy to assume that arbitration has always been sensitive to the requirements of commerce. Whereas this may be the case, it drastically oversimplifies the situation. The latter part of the nineteenth century saw a concerted and sustained effort between lawyers and merchants jointly to develop arbitration and arbitral integrity.[32] This initiative has not been sustained. It is true to say that, over the years, there have been some momentous and dramatic judicial U-turns made in an attempt to keep arbitration on the perceived 'right track'. This, however, raises questions as to motive. For example, the 1979 Arbitration Act was enacted to reverse the decision in *Halfdan Grieg*[33] and thereby reverse the 'Case Stated' procedure.[34] The

---

[29] For example the members of the dispute review board, such as the project engineer, may later have to exercise a quasi-judicial function in the matter of a arbitration and in this case he will substantially have heard the evidence and passed an opinion on it at the DRB.

[30] In England I cite the 'Woolf Report' *Access to Justice: Interim Report to the Lord Chancellor on the Civil Justice System in England and Wales*, HMSO, London, June 1995. For an in depth discussion of this and other proposals see Marriott, A.L. *The 1995 Freshfields Lecture* reproduced at (1996) 12 Arb Intl 1

[31] ADR has the added benefit of actively reducing the court's load, which in turn reduces fiscal burden.

[32] Veeder, V.V. *'Two Arbitral Butterflies: Bramwell and David'* in Hunter, M., Marriott, A. & Veeder, V.V. (Eds), *The Internationalisation of International Arbitration, The LCIA Centenary Conference*, Graham & Trotman, London, 1995.

[33] *Halfdan Grieg & Co. v. Sterling Coal & Navigation Corp. 'The Lysland'* [1973] 1 QB 843.

1979 Act came about primarily because London was losing prominence as an international arbitration situs, not because commerce was necessarily unhappy with the procedure.[35] Following the enactment of the 1979 Act, judicial review of arbitration was further limited by the House of Lords decisions in *The Nema*.[36]

What then is then meant by procedural efficiency in commercial arbitration? In his paper [37] Dr. Towson considers that privacy and autonomy of the proceedings, confidentiality of the documents and finality of the award are the most important elements to commerce. To this list may be added predictability and neutrality of the forum. The scope of this paper does not permit me to examine the twin towers of predictability and neutrality.[38] I therefore propose to limit this paper to the list identified by Dr Towson, but will deal separately with the issues affecting party autonomy, in order to sharpen the focus on the principles involved.

Autonomy of Proceedings

This could better be framed as a question, thus: should the court be able to intervene in the arbitral process? The (typically legal) answer has to be: it depends on the circumstances. If, for example, fraud was an issue in the formation of contract then the proceedings would be void;[39] if fraud was present in the reference, procedural autonomy

---

[34] Prior to the 1979 Act the case stated procedure was contained in s. 21 of the Arbitration Act 1950. This section re-enacted the provisions of the Common Law Procedure Act of 1854 which empowered arbitrators to state their awards in the form of a special case for the opinion of the courts. And see Kerr, Sir Michael, *The Arbitration Act 1979* (1980) 43 MLR 45.

[35] *'The main object of this bill is to attract arbitration to London' per* Lord Lloyd of Kilgerran 398 Parl Deb HL (5th Ser) 536 (1979).

[36] *Pioneer Shipping Ltd v. BTP Tioxide Ltd* [1982] AC 724.

[37] *Sanctity Revisited: The Efficacy of Commercial Arbitration in Australia* paper 7, *supra* p. 77.

[38] See Davis, M., *'Choice of Law Rules and International Construction Contracts'* in Odams, A.M. (Ed) *Comparative Studies in Construction Law: The Sweet Lectures*, Construction Law Press, London, 1995; Uff, J., *The Predictability Factor in International Arbitration* Paper 10 *supra* p 143 and generally Park, W.W., *International Forum Selection*, Kluwer, Deventer, 1995.

[39] In the case of an illegal contract the maxim *ex dolo malo non oritur actio* (no right of action can have its origin in fraud) would apply.

similarly would not be appropriate.[40] But to the extent that the arbitrator has not behaved so as to be held to have misconducted himself,[41] in some way acted *ultra vires*,[42] or breached the rules of Natural Justice[43] arbitral proceedings certainly should enjoy autonomy from the courts.

The new English Arbitration Act now sets out explicitly how and when the court may intervene in the procedure of the tribunal. Such intervention is limited to enforcing and support for tribunal orders,[44] securing the attendance of witnesses,[45] and determining preliminary points of law.[46]

The robust drafting of this Act mirrors the common law sentiment as to judicial intervention in arbitral procedure. In Australia, and in the face of statutory provisions to remit for reconsideration,[47] judicial intervention is limited to breach of natural justice.[48] In Canada legislative policy actively dicourages intervention, 'where parties have agreed by contract [to arbitration] ... the parties should be held to [this]'.[49] The civilian attitude to judicial intervention is similarly robust; simply put, the court will support and reinforce the arbitration and such support does not constitute a breach of the contract to arbitrate.[50]

The collection and administration of evidence presents special difficulties and is an exception to the above principle. Unless otherwise

---

[40] For a detailed analysis of the problem see Eriksson, M. *Arbitration and Contracts Involving Corrupt Practices: The Arbitrator's Dilemma* (1993) 4 Am Rev Intl Arb.

[41] For a definition of misconduct see *Williams v. Wallis and Cox* [1914] 2 KB 478 "*Such a mishandling of the arbitration as is likely to amount to some substantial miscarriage of justice.*" *per* Atkin J at 485.

[42] For example adducing his own evidence: *Fox v. P.G.Wellfair* [1981] 2 Lloyd's Rep 514.

[43] For example *London Export Corporation Ltd. v. Jubilee Coffee Roasting Company Ltd* [1958] Lloyd's Rep 197.

[44] Sections 39, 41 and 42

[45] Section 40

[46] Section 43

[47] For example section 43 of the Commercial Arbitration Act (NSW) 1984

[48] *Nauru Phosphate Royalties Trust v. Matthew Hall Mechanical and Electrical Engineers Pty Limited* [1994] 2 VR 386, and see p. 81.

[49] *Boart Sweden AB et al v. NYA Stromnes AB et al* (1988) 41 BLR 295 (Ont HCJ), 302; and see pp. 98-99.

[50] Cass Com 3 juil 1951, Dalloz 1951, p.701, and see p. 258.

agreed, arbitrators are bound by the same rules of evidence that apply to the courts.[51]

Privacy of Proceedings

Procedural privacy ensures that external parties do not affect the proceedings and that equally one's dirty washing is not laundered in public. English law offers support to this notion as of right.[52] However, in the case of *Esso v. Plowman*[53] the High Court of Australia has held that confidentiality is not an essential attribute of arbitration; that arbitration does not impose an obligation on each party not to disclose the proceedings or documents and information provided in and for the purposes of the arbitration.[54]

The *Esso/BHP* arbitrations arose from contracts for the supply of gas and electricity in the state of Victoria. If the companies won then the price of gas and electricity would inevitably rise. Considerable public interest therefore surrounded the outcome of this case. Not surprisingly the arbitration award and documents which engendered public interest were sought to be made available to interested parties. The court faced a residual problem: how to square the inherent right to privacy with the public interest, on which point Mason CJ said:

> " ... the efficacy of a private arbitration will be damaged, even defeated, if proceedings in the arbitration are made public by the disclosure of documents relating to the arbitration."[55]

In the majority judgment, delivered by Mason CJ, it was made clear that the decision, which undermines the very essence of arbitration, only applies to Australia. Privacy can, however, still be achieved if the parties expressly agree to it prior to commencement of proceedings.

---

[51] *Re Enoch and Zaretzky, Bock & Co* [1910] 1 KB 327.

[52] *Oxford Shipping Co Ltd v. Nippon Yusen Kaisha 'The Eastern Saga'* [1994] 2 Lloyd's Rep 373.

[53] *Esso Australia Resources Limited & Others v Plowman (Minister for Energy and Minerals) & Others*(1995) 128 ALR 391

[54] The facts of this case were dicussed in depth by Sir Patrick Neill in his 1995 Bernstein Lecture entitled *Confidentiality in Arbitration*, shortly to be published in *Arbitration* the Journal of the Chartered Institute of Arbitrators and *Arbitration International*, the experts reports prepared for the case are reproduced together with further commentary in Volume 11, number 3 (1995).

[55] *Esso Australia Resources Limited & Others v Plowman (Minister for Energy and Minerals) & Others*(1995) 128 ALR 391, 399.

There is no doubt that following this decision Australia as a situs for international commerical arbitration has become less attractive.[56] However, as was demonstrated in England by the remarkably short consultation process from presentation of the draft Bill in July 1995 to promulgation, the legislature can work fast to overcome economically damaging conflict between law and commerce. It is somewhat ironic to note that events are similar to those which hastened the 1979 Bill on to the statute book.

Confidentiality of documents

Confidentiality in documents is regarded to be an incident of privacy.[57] However, following the *Esso* decision, the basis of such confidentiality has been challenged. In Australia, third parties are not now under an obligation of confidence[58] and may disclose their evidence or a report of the proceedings to interested parties.

There are two species of documents that are generated by an arbitral tribunal, those arising from the procedure and those which relate to the award. Arbitral awards have officially been published in England[59] and publication is regarded as a matter for agreement between the parties and the tribunal, diametrically opposed to the situation in Australia. When the report is sought to be used as precedent, a residual issue may revolve around the weight that the tribunal may attach to it.[60]

Documents prepared for the tribunal or arising from the tribunal may be of great use in other related arbitrations. For example, in the construction industry much of the work is subcontracted and if disputes arise it may be desirable that documents prepared for one arbitration, say between the main contractor and employer, be used in another, say between the main contractor and a subcontractor. Apart from the obvious reductions in cost and time, it is also presumed that

---

[56] See for example Park, W.W., *Neutrality, Predictability and Economic Co-operation* (1995) 12 Jnl Int Arb No 4, p.99.

[57] *Oxford Shipping Co Ltd v. Nippon Yusen Kaisha 'The Eastern Saga'* [1994] 2 Lloyd's Rep 373.

[58] *Ibid*, 400.

[59] Uff, J. & Furst, S, *Construction Law Yearbook 1994*, Wiley Chancery, London 1994.

[60] See for example *Ventouris v. Mountain (No 2)*[1992] 1 WLR 887
   "... *The modern tendency in civil proceedings is to admit all evidence,and the Judge should be trusted to give only proper weight to evidence which is not the best evidence.*" *per* Balcombe LJ at 899.

this practice will ensure consistency in judgments. The Court of Appeal in *Dolling-Baker v. Merrett & Another*[61] proposed that the parties are under an 'implied obligation':

> "*... not to disclose or use for any other purpose any documents prepared for and used in the arbitration, or disclosed or produced in the course of the arbitration ... save with the consent of the other party, or pursuant to an order or leave of the court.*"[62]

Thus, on the one hand, if the parties at the outset consent to make such documents available then they can be used. On the other hand (the more likely situation is where the parties do not consent) an order seeking discovery will have to be obtained from the court to overcome the privilege. In *Dolling-Baker* it was held that discovery will not be granted unless the documents sought were relevant to the proposed action. Following the logic of *BHP/Esso* it would seem that this process is to be left to the parties, on whom it is encumbent to decide whether documents are or are not the subject of privilege, irrespective of their content or importance. I submit that the reckless diminution of judicial control on such documents will inevitably lead abuse, necessitating some form of reconsideration by the judiciary. As with the attack on privacy examined above, I await the developments in Australia with interest.

Finality

Section 58 of the Arbitration Act 1996 provides that:

> " (1) *Unless otherwise agreed by the parties, an award made by the tribunal pursuant to an arbitration agreement is final and binding both on the parties and on any other persons claiming through or under them.*
>
> (2) *This deos not affect the right of a person to challenge the award by any available arbitral process of appeal or review or in accordance with the provisions of this Part*"

---

[61]   [1990] 1 WLR 1205

[62]   *Ibid* 1213, *per* Parker LJ.

This provision seeks to limit the court's power of review to questions of substantive jurisdiction (s.67), serious irregularity (s.68) or points of law (s.69). Sections 67 and 68 are procedural safeguards. The backbone of the drafting is section 69, which codifies *The Nema*[63] guidelines. This provision gives much needed legislative support to the finality of the award.

In his paper[64] Dr Towson reviews the situation in Australia, where the current judicial trend is to allow the court to intervene, despite legislation which adopts the provisions of the English Arbitration Act 1979.[65] Although this intervention is echoed in Canada inspite of the fact that *The Nema* guidelines have partially been adopted, unlike Australia such intervention is perceived incapable of having "a significantly dampening effect on the flowering of [arbitration] in Canada".[66] Given the fortitude of the new Canadian legislation, this should be the case, but I would rather be sure, and therefore support the English initiative.

Conclusion

The above examples have demostrated, albeit briefly, that commerce can react to ensure that its needs are met. The debate as to whether or not *lex mercatoria* prevails, or is to be recognised as an alternative to an integrated framework of legal principles, seems somewhat subsidiary to events. This is evidenced by the dynamic manner in which commerce meets its current objectives, namely expedient and just dispute resolution. On this note, I leave the final comment to the late Dr Gillis Wetter:

> "... *international arbitration is subject to the same economic laws as other endeavours in free markets and wi᾽ not subsist (and certainly not thrive) unless it responds adequately and flexibly to the demands of users.*"[67]

---

[63] *Pioneer Shipping Ltd. et al. v. B.T.P. Dioxide Ltd.* [1982] AC 724.

[64] *The Efficacy of Commercial Arbitration in Australia, supra* p.77 at 87.

[65] The situation in Australia regarding *The Nema* guidelines is that universally they are neither adopted nor fully approved of, and see *ibid* pp.88-91 as to the developments.

[66] Potter, R.B., *Commercial Arbitration in Canada: A Model Law for Others?* paper 7 *supra* p.93 at 106.

[67] 'Looking Ahead to the Next Ten Years' in Hunter, M., Marriott, A. & Veeder, V.V. (Eds), *The Internationalisation of International Arbitration, The LCIA Centenary Conference*, Graham & Trotman, London, 1995, p. 103.

12. Fast Track Disputes Procedures for Construction

Philip Davenport

Synopsis

This paper describes the Building Disputes Tribunal of New South Wales. It examines how, and what, actions may be commenced, and the range of orders available to the parties. Conclusions are made as to how the Tribunal may develop in the future.

Introduction

The Building Disputes Tribunal of New South Wales (BDT) evolved from the Consumer Claims Tribunal (CCT), itself a creature of statute and consumer demand. The initiative for the BDT resulted from consumer dissatisfaction with the existing regime—indeed severe criticism was directed at arbitration. The BDT brings, for the first time to building disputes, speed and economy long recognised as a feature of the CCT. The BDT as an institution commenced in 1991 and now receives about 1000 claims annually.[1]

Under the Consumer Claims Tribunals Act 1987, the tribunal has jurisdiction to hear claims by consumers against builders and vice versa arising out of residential building work. The BDT is equally available to licensed contractors and subcontractors to pursue claims against owners or even against one other. CCT's continue under the Act, side by side with the BDT, sharing the same premises, the same registry and some of the same Referees.[2]

---

[1] The Building Disputes Tribunal commenced with a jurisdiction limited to $10,000. This has been increased to $25,000 in respect of claims lodged on or after 7 March 1994.

[2] Because the Building Disputes Tribunal grew out of the Consumer Claims Tribunal, there is no separate Act covering the Building Disputes Tribunal. The Building Disputes Tribunal is created by the Consumer Claims Tribunals Act 1987 NSW. Because the Building Disputes Tribunal was created by amending an existing Act, the legislation is particularly convoluted and difficult to follow. But

Commencing an action

A person residing anywhere in Australia can bring a claim in the Building Disputes Tribunal against a builder located anywhere in Australia who performed building work in NSW or contracted to perform building work in NSW, even though the contract was made outside NSW or the builder is resident outside NSW or both. Corporate entities, such as builders and subcontractors can also bring actions, the only limitation on claimants who are the recipients of goods or services is legal capacity. However, where the claimant is the supplier of the goods or services, the claimant can only make a building claim in the Building Disputes Tribunal when both:

- the claimant holds a licence enabling the claimant to contract to supply the relevant goods or services; and
- the relevant goods or services cannot lawfully be supplied without such a licence.

Where the claimant sues in the capacity of a supplier of building goods or services, not only must the claimant have had a licence authorising the entering of the contract for the supply of those goods or services, but the claim must arise from the supply of goods or services covered by the licence or under a contract that is collateral to a contract for the supply of goods or services covered by the licence.

Builders

A builder can be both a supplier to the owner and a purchaser or recipient of building goods or services from a wholesaler, a retailer, a consultant or a subcontractor. As a respondent to a claim, the builder can have rights to claim which would not exist if the builder initiated the claim.

Section 4 of the Building Services Corporation Act 1989 provides:

> *A person must not contract to do:*
> *(a) any residential building work: or*
> *(b) any specialist work,*

---

using existing legislation had the advantage that there was already a body of case law on the interpretation of provisions of the Act.

except as or on behalf of an individual, partnership or corporation that is the holder of a licence authorising its holder to contract to do that work.

The fact that a claimant who contracts in breach of section 4 of the Building Services Corporation Act 1989 cannot bring a claim in the Building Disputes Tribunal does not necessarily mean that the claimant cannot bring a claim in a court or raise a crossclaim in the Building Disputes Tribunal. If the Tribunal finds in favour of a builder on the builder's crossclaim, the Tribunal can order the owner to pay moneys to the builder even though the builder is unlicensed and could not have initiated such a claim in the Tribunal except by way of crossclaim.

Section 12 of the Building Services Corporation Act 1989 NSW provides:

An individual must not do any residential building work, or specialist work, except:

(a) as, or as a member of a partnership or an officer of a corporation that is, the holder of a licence authorising its holder to contract to do that work; or
(b) as the holder of an owner-builder permit authorising its holder to do that work; or
(c) as an employee of the holder of such a licence or permit.

The only claim which an unlicensed builder could validly initiate in the Tribunal—except by way of crossclaim—is one against a supplier or subcontractor to the builder. In those circumstances, the builder would be the recipient not the supplier of the goods or services. *Unlicensed* refers to the time when the contract for the supply of goods or services was made, that is the point of time which is relevant to give jurisdiction to the Building Disputes Tribunal. The fact that the license lapsed before the work was completed or before the claim was lodged, does not go to the question of jurisdiction.

The fact that a builder does not have a contract in writing signed by the owner does not preclude the builder from lodging a claim. Section 6(1) of the Building Services Corporation Act 1989 provides:

(1) A contract under which the holder of a licence undertakes:

(a) to do, in person or by others, any residential building work or specialist work; or
(b) to vary any residential building work or specialist work or the way in which any such work is to be done,

is not enforceable against the other party to the contract unless the contract is in writing signed by or on behalf of each of the parties to it and sufficiently describes the work the subject of the contract.

The absence of a written contract where required means that the builder cannot enforce the contract. However, the owner can enforce the contract. While the builder cannot enforce an unwritten contract, a builder may be able to obtain an order for restitution on the basis of the doctrine of unjust enrichment. Such orders are made almost every day in the Building Disputes Tribunal.

Subsequent purchasers and others

In *Bryan v Maloney* [3] the Australian High Court recognised the right of a subsequent purchaser to sue a builder in tort for economic loss arising from the builder's negligence in the construction of a house. The builder constructed the house in 1979. The then owner sold it to another person who subsequently sold it to the claimant in 1986. Six months later cracks appeared. The house suffered substantial damage. The problem was traced to inadequate footings. The owner sued the builder in tort for negligence. The Court held that in constructing the house, the builder owed a duty of care not only to the client but also to subsequent purchasers.

As to whether a subsequent purchaser of a house can sue the builder in tort in the Building Disputes Tribunal, the answer would appear to be "yes". Of course, the time limit in section 10 of the Consumer Claims Tribunals Act 1987 [3 years] will mean that many claims in tort by subsequent owners cannot be brought in the Building Disputes Tribunal. But there will be many instances where a house has been sold within 3 years after construction. The jurisdiction of the tribunal to

---

[3]   [1995] 128 ALR 163

entertain claims in tort was established in *Fairey Australasia Pty. Ltd. v. Joyce.*[4]

The interesting possibility arises of claims in the Building Disputes Tribunal by neighbours or persons living close to the premises where residential building work is being carried out. This would be of particular concern to developers who in the course of constructing residential unit blocks may cause nuisance to many neighbours. The nuisance may take the form of dust, vibrations, noise, or pollution. The fact that for a fee of $100 or less a neighbour might recover damages of up to $25,000 might induce disgruntled neighbours to sue. Prior to the creation of the Building Disputes Tribunal, a major deterrent to such an action was the cost of pursuing a claim in the courts and the risk that if the claim was lost the claimant would have to pay the developer's costs.

There is no limit upon the amount which a party can claim. However the tribunal cannot award more than $25,000[5] to any party. If the tribunal makes several orders against a party, for example to perform work and to pay damages, the combined value of the orders must not exceed $25,000. Sometimes, because of the attractive nature of the fast track procedures of the tribunal, a claimant will bring a claim exceeding $25,000 in full knowledge that he will not be able to recover in excess of the statutory limit.

Who can be sued

Actions can be brought against builders, licensed or otherwise. The limitation on unlicensed builders initiating action does not prevent them being sued. Licensed builders regularly use the Tribunal to recover debts and licensed subcontractors regularly sue contractors and vice versa.

The Tribunal has a wide power to join as claimant or respondent any person who, in the opinion of the Referee has sufficient interest in the resolution of the dispute. This power is not one open to arbitrators or courts generally. For example, the owner may have relied upon the

---

4   [1981] 2 NSWLR 314

5   At the time of writing Aus $ 2 = £1

advice of a supplier, the manufacturer, that certain bricks would be suitable. Assume that the owner specifies those bricks in the building contract and that the builder purchases the bricks from the manufacturer and lays them. Assume that the unlicensed builder is not in breach of contract to the owner. The owner could nevertheless initiate a building claim against the manufacturer directly or, if the owner sued the builder, the Referee could order that the manufacturer be made a party to the proceedings. The liability of the manufacturer could be in tort or breach of statute.[6]

The following table is a brief overview. It omits many qualifications, in particular, that to succeed in a claim, the claimant must demonstrate a legal right; a debt, breach of contract, tort, breach of statute or right to restitution. The fact that an owner can initiate a building claim against a subcontractor does not of itself overcome the problem of privity of contract. The owner must still demonstrate a right, for example in tort.

Claimant	Owner	Contractor licensed or unlicensed	Supplier	Subcontractor licensed or unlicensed	Prior owner-builder
Owner	N/A	Yes	Yes †	Yes	Yes
Licensed contractor	Yes	No	Yes	Yes	No
Unlicensed contractor	No	No	Yes	Yes	No
Licensed subcontractor	Yes	Yes, main	Yes	N/A	No
Unlicensed subcontractor	No	No	Yes	N/A	No

† but if the supply is made to him directly, the action has to come before the Consumer Claims Tribunal not the Building Disputes Tribunal

Note that other claims made by the owner may be consumer claims not building claims. This includes ostensibly building claims against the following:

- a supplier;
- the architect;
- a consultant;
- the engineer.

---

6 For example, the Fair Trading Act 1987 NSW

Consumer claims which are not building claims can be made by the consumer in the Consumer Claims Tribunal which can award up to $25,000. But claims by:

- consultants, including architects, engineers, building consultants for their fee;
- manufacturers and suppliers only of goods,

are neither building claims nor consumer claims and can only be pursued in the courts or arbitration.

Claims procedure

Section 13(1) of the Consumer Claims Tribunals Act 1987 provides:

(1)   A consumer who wishes to have a consumer claim heard and determined by a tribunal must lodge at the registry or at a Local Court a claim in the prescribed form, together with the prescribed fee.

(2)   It is the duty of staff of the registry or of a Local Court to help a consumer who requests assistance in completing the prescribed form.

To make a building claim, the claimant must complete a claim form. The claimant lodges the completed form and the prescribed fee which can be as little as $2 and no more than $100. The fee varies depending upon the amount of the claim and whether the claimant is a pensioner or full time student. There is provision for the waiver of the fee in the case of genuine hardship. As soon as practical after a claim has been lodged, the Registrar must set the matter down for hearing and serve on the parties notice of the claim and of the hearing date and time. The hearing usually takes place about two months after lodging of the claim.

Joinder

There can be several claimants and several respondents but the claim must arise out of the same supply of goods or services. For example two subcontractors who have separately contracted with the one contractor cannot join in making the one claim. Each must bring a separate claim because each provided separate services under a separate contract. Similarly, the builder cannot join the owner and a subcontractor as respondents to the one action. The claim against the owner arises out of the supply of services from the builder to the owner. The claim against the subcontractor arises from the supply of services from the subcontractor to the builder. They are quite separate claims. There is power in section 17(2) of the Consumer Claims Tribunals Act 1987 for a referee to hear and determine together two or more consumer claims if they are "related".

Section 14(2) of the Consumer Claims Tribunals Act 1987 empowers a referee, whether constituted as a tribunal or not, to make an order directing the joinder of another person as claimant or as respondent. The referee must first form the opinion that that person "has sufficient interest in resolving the dispute to which the consumer claim relates". A third party can only be joined where an order could be made by the Tribunal against the third party. The Referee has no power to make an order against the third party in favour of the respondent. Hence, if the claimant does not want the third party joined, then irrespective of the wishes of the respondent, the third party must not be joined.

In a claim by an owner against a contractor in respect of defective work performed by a subcontractor, a Referee could join the subcontractor but before the Referee could make an order that the subcontractor must pay money to the owner, the Referee would have to find a legal liability on the part of the subcontractor to the owner. There being no contract between the owner and the subcontractor, this would be difficult. The Referee could not make an order that one respondent, the subcontractor must pay an amount to another respondent, the builder, and that the builder must pay the same amount to the owner. Thus, if a builder respondent wants an order against a subcontractor respondent, the builder must commence a separate claim against the subcontractor. The claim could be heard with the owner's claim against the builder.

Concurrent arbitration or litigation

Section 11 of the Consumer Claims Tribunals Act 1987 deals with the situation where a claim is commenced in a court or an arbitration before or after a claim involving the same issues is lodged in the Building Disputes Tribunal. In essence, the action commenced first prevails.

Taking the case where a claim is first commenced in the Building Disputes Tribunal, thereafter no other tribunal, court, arbitrator, expert or person can validly hear or determine an issue which is before the Building Disputes Tribunal, unless the Building Disputes Tribunal or the Supreme Court dismisses the Building Disputes Tribunal claim for want of jurisdiction or the claim in the Building Disputes Tribunal is withdrawn.

That means that even though a building contract includes an arbitration clause, either party can avoid arbitration by commencing a claim in the Building Disputes Tribunal before the other party commences an arbitration. Section 39 of the Consumer Claims Tribunals Act 1987 provides:

> *(1)   This Act has effect despite any stipulation to the contrary in any contract, agreement, arrangement or understanding.*

> *(2)   No contract, agreement, arrangement or understanding made or entered into either before or after the commencement of this Act has the effect of nullifying or excluding any of the provisions of this Act.*

If, part way through an arbitration, an arbitrator discovers that a claim involving the same issues as those before the arbitrator was lodged in the Building Disputes Tribunal before the arbitration commenced, the arbitrator must immediately cease the arbitration of that claim. The arbitration of that claim would have been a nullity since the beginning.

Section 53 of the Commercial Arbitration Act 1984 NSW will be of no avail to stop proceedings before the Tribunal. Section 53 provides that if a party to an arbitration agreement commences proceedings in a court against another party to the arbitration agreement, the other party can apply to the Supreme Court to stay the proceedings. A stay of the proceedings in the Building Disputes Tribunal would not mean that an arbitrator had jurisdiction. Section 11 of the Consumer Claims Tribunals Act 1987 deprives the arbitrator of jurisdiction.

On the other hand, assume that a party has already instigated proceedings in a court or an arbitration has commenced before a claim involving the same issues is lodged with the Building Disputes

Tribunal. The Building Disputes Tribunal now has no jurisdiction unless the other proceedings are withdrawn or dismissed by the court, arbitrator or other person having the conduct of the proceedings.

Limitation of action

If a claim is in respect of defective building work, the claim must be commenced in the Building Disputes Tribunal by lodging a claim within three years after the defective work was done. If the claim relates to work not performed, the claim must be lodged within three years after the date by which the contractor agreed to perform the work. The time limit on commencing a claim in the courts is usually 6 years. If a claimant misses the time limit for commencing an action in the Tribunal, the claimant is not thereby precluded from suing in the court.

The Hearing

A date for hearing is usually set down approximately two months after the claim is lodged. Hearings are not as formal as in a court. The Referee is alone with the parties and their witnesses and has no transcript writer, clerk or usher present. The Referee has control of the procedure. Some Referees insist on more formality than others. The hearing is private but confidentiality does not attach to any documents produced in the hearing or any evidence given in the hearing. There is no restriction upon anyone disclosing what happened during the hearing except for any statement or admission made in the course of attempts at reconciliation.

The Referee is not bound to follow the rules or practice of evidence. Evidence can be given by affidavit. In fact, a party may present the party's whole case by affidavit and not attend the hearing. The Referee has no power to subpoena anyone. In the course of proceedings a Referee may require witnesses to wait outside until called to give evidence. Of course, none of the parties must be excluded from the hearing at any time, as an overriding requirement of the tribunal is that its procedural integrity must conform with the principles of natural justice.

Some Referees follow the adversarial system, some follow the investigative system. The former ask few questions and leave it to the parties to present their respective cases and refute the case of the other. The latter enquire of the parties the cause of the complaint and may cross-examine them. Some Referees adopt a combination of the adversarial and the investigative processes. Again, the overriding requirement is that the parties are accorded natural justice.

Referees' Orders

Prior to the making of an order the Referee will have to keep in mind the provisions of section 29(1) of the Consumer Claims Tribunals Act 1987, which provides:

> *A tribunal must not make an order in respect of a consumer claim that is before it unless it has brought, or used its best endeavours to bring, the parties to the claim to a settlement acceptable to all of them.*

If a settlement is reached, the Referee must make an order which gives effect to the settlement to the extent permitted by the Act. In giving effect to a settlement, the Referee can only make an order which the Referee could make in the absence of a settlement. At all times the Referee has to keep in mind the jurisdiction of the tribunal. For example, the order made on settlement could not exceed $25,000 in value. If a settlement agreement is for more than $25,000, the Referee should make no order. An order for $25,000 would not give effect to a settlement agreement for $30,000.

The settlement agreement is one thing. The Referee's order is another. The settlement agreement may contain matters which are not in the order, but not vice versa. The settlement agreement may result in an accord and satisfaction that will extinguish rights beyond those which the order may extinguish.

Decisions

Usually a Referee orally gives a decision, with reasons, at the end of the hearing. The Referee tells the parties what the order is and, after the hearing, the Referee writes out the order and reasons and places them on file. Sometimes the Referee will reserve the decision and deliver it in writing at a later date. This is more common when issues of jurisdiction are raised. The reasons of some Referees rarely exceed a page of handwriting. Others type out pages of reasons.

Section 31(1) of the Consumer Claims Tribunals Act 1987 provides:

> *When making an order or orders under section 30, a tribunal must make such orders as, in its opinion, will be fair and equitable to all the parties to the claim.*

This provision does not authorise a Referee to decide issues otherwise than according to the general law. The Tribunal does not administer "palm tree justice". This term was used by Yeldham J in *Fairey Australasia Pty. Ltd. v Joyce.*[7] It has since been used on a number of occasions to reflect the fact that the Tribunal must decide issues according to law and not according to some general notion of fair play.

The term was used in *Jet 60 Minute Cleaners Pty Ltd v Brownette,*[8] In describing the obligation of the Referee to act in accordance with and apply the general law in determining a claim, Hunt J said:

> *"The Consumer Claims Tribunal is required to make such order as is, in its opinion, fair and equitable to all the parties to the proceeding before it. That obligation, however, in its context relates to the nature of the order to be made; it does not give the tribunal freedom to act otherwise than in accordance with the general law in determining whether the claim before it has been made out. ..."*

Orders available

The orders which can be made against either a claimant or a respondent, in abbreviated form are:

---

[7]   [1981] 2 NSWLR 314 at 321

[8]   Unreported, Supreme Court of NSW, Hunt J, 24 February 1981, the case went on appeal, [1991] 2 NSWLR 314, but the appeal was dismissed on other grounds.

- a party must pay the other an amount up to $25,000;[9]
- a party must perform specified work;
- a party must supply specified services;
- a declaration that a specified amount of money is not owed by one party to another;
- a party must deliver goods of a specified description;
- a party must return specified goods;
- a party must replace goods;
- the claim is dismissed in whole or in part.

Before making the order, the Referee must also ensure that the respondent has raised a crossclaim. Without formal pleadings, this will not always be obvious. The respondent might be able to recover an amount in excess of $25,000 if the respondent sued in a court rather than raising a crossclaim in the Building Disputes Tribunal. By submitting to an order in the Building Disputes Tribunal on the crossclaim, the respondent cannot recover more than $25,000 and, by virtue of the doctrine of issue estoppel, the respondent is precluded from pursuing the claim elsewhere.

When making an order a Referee has to have in mind that, save for an order dismissing a claim, the order must have been sought by the party in whose favour the order is made and the nature of the order sought must have been clearly communicated to the other party. Sometimes this will involve an amendment of the claim. For example, in the claim form a claimant may have sought an order for work to be done. The Referee might consider a work order inappropriate but be inclined to make a money order instead. The Referee could not validly do so unless the claimant amended the claim and the respondent had notice of the amendment and an opportunity to make submissions with respect to the amended claim.

In cases where there are two respondents, for example a contractor and a subcontractor, the Referee cannot make an order that one respondent pay the other respondent, or does not owe money to the other

---

9   Section 32 of the Consumer Claims Tribunals Act 1987 limits the Referee to making an order not exceeding $25,000 in value, whether it is money or the value of the work to be performed or goods to be supplied. Similarly, the Referee cannot make a declaration that an amount in excess of $25,000 is not owing.

respondent, or must provide goods or services to the other respondent. The Consumer Claims Tribunals Act 1987 only permits an order in favour of a claimant to be made against a respondent or an order in favour of a respondent to be made against a claimant. Provided that a party has requested multiple orders and the orders would not be inconsistent, the Referee can make multiple orders, for example. for a payment of money, for specified work to be done and for specified goods to be supplied. An order may require the owner to pay the builder an amount of money and the builder to do work within a specified time.

The order should include a time within which money must be paid or work performed or goods supplied. The only occasions when a time for compliance is not required is when the order is one dismissing the claim or making a declaration that an amount is not owed.

Section 27 empowers a Referee to dismiss a claim which the Referee considers frivolous, vexatious, misconceived or lacking in substance. The Referee can also dismiss a claim when for any other reason the Referee considers that the claim should not be dealt with. Since such a dismissal is not necessarily a decision on the merits, the dismissal would not necessarily be a bar to the claimant bringing another claim either in the Tribunal or in a court.

Interim Orders

The Referee can make an interim order. An interim order might relate to the preservation of property pending a final order, or the delivery up of property to a party who unarguably owns that property. Without the consent of all parties, the Referee must be careful before making an interim order which may have to be reversed or changed in the final order. The claimant can withdraw a claim without leave and at any time prior to the Referee commencing to make a decision on the claim. If the claimant withdrew after the Referee made an interim order, the Referee could not then make a final order reversing the interim order.

Interest

In the Consumer Claims Tribunals Act 1987 there is no power given to the Tribunal to award interest. Nevertheless, the Tribunal's order can include a component for interest which is part of a debt or damages.

There are two categories. The first is interest which a party has contracted to pay. That interest is part of the debt owed. When the Tribunal orders that the debt be paid, the debt will include that interest component. It is not the Tribunal which is creating the liability for interest. The parties have themselves agreed it. The second category is a component of damages. In Australia it is commonly called *Hungerfords interest* or *Hungerfords damages*. Such damages are interest incurred or interest forgone as a foreseeable consequence of the breach of contract or wrong in respect of which the Tribunal is making the order.

The terms *Hungerfords interest* and *Hungerfords damages* are used interchangeably. They derive from the name of the case in which the Australian High Court recognised that damages could include interest paid or interest forgone: *Hungerfords v Walker*.[10] Strictly speaking, *Hungerfords interest* is not interest. It is damages just like any other damages.

Hungerfords, accountants, were negligent in preparing tax returns. As a consequence the clients overpaid tax which was not recoverable. The clients sued for and were awarded the amounts overpaid plus compound interest at 20% p.a., the rate at which they were borrowing money to finance their business. The High Court drew a distinction between interest on damages [which a Referee cannot award] and an actual award of damages which represents compensation for the foreseeable loss actually incurred by the claimant. The negligence of the accountants meant that money which the clients would have used to reduce their overdraft were lost to them. As a direct and foreseeable consequence, the clients incurred a large interest bill which they would not otherwise have incurred. This was damage caused by the accountants' negligence.

Costs

Section 28 of the Consumer Claims Tribunals Act 1987 provides:

> *A tribunal has no power to award costs to or against a party to a consumer claim.*

---

[10]   [1989] 171 CLR 125

In this context costs refer to costs incurred in preparing and presenting the claim. It refers to the fee for lodging the claim, legal expenses and witnesses expenses. It refers to the salary or wages lost while attending the Tribunal and the costs of travelling to and from the Tribunal. It is those expenses which would not have been incurred had the dispute been resolved without recourse to the Tribunal. The cost of photographs to be used in evidence and expert reports to be presented at the hearing are part of the costs which the Tribunal cannot award.

When a defect is discovered, it may be necessary to engage an expert to advise on what is the cause and what should be done to rectify the defect. If the cost of the expert is a necessary expense whether or not the matter goes to litigation or arbitration, then it is probably part of the damage recoverable from the builder. The Tribunal could award that cost. The additional cost of having the expert prepare a report for the Tribunal or give evidence would be a cost which the Tribunal could not award.

Enforcement of orders

If an order is for payment of an amount of money, the time for payment stated in the Referee's order has expired and the payment has not been made, the party to whom the money is payable can make a request to the Building Disputes Tribunal registry for a certified copy of the Referee's order. The party can then file the certified copy of the order in a Local Court. No fee is payable for filing the order in the Local Court but to file the order the applicant must file with it an affidavit specifying the amount then unpaid under the order. The order is then deemed to be an unsatisfied judgment of the Local Court for the amount specified in the affidavit as being unpaid.

If an order, other than a money order, for example. an order to rectify work, is not complied with, the matter can be relisted before the Referee and a money order substituted for the unsatisfied order.

Grounds for appeal

There are no appeals from the Tribunal. Section 34 of the Consumer Claims Tribunals Act 1987 provides:

An order of a tribunal is final and binding on all parties to a consumer claim that is heard and determined by the tribunal and no appeal lies in respect of an order of the tribunal.

There are, however, four grounds upon which a Tribunal order can be challenged in the Supreme Court. These grounds are that:

- the Tribunal had no jurisdiction;
- a party disputed the Tribunal's jurisdiction and the Tribunal failed or refused to give a ruling as required by section 26 of the Consumer Claims Tribunals Act 1987;
- the Tribunal gave an erroneous ruling on jurisdiction; or
- a party to the claim was denied natural justice.

It goes without saying that only a valid order of the tribunal is final and binding. If an order of the Tribunal is clearly *ultra vires*, the Supreme Court may grant an injunction and declare the purported order of the Tribunal to be void. If the Referee had jurisdiction and accorded the parties natural justice, the fact that the Referee made an error of law or fact, no matter how obvious, or made a decision which the Supreme Court considers unjust, would not represent grounds for setting aside the Referee's order. Section 17 of the Consumer Claims Tribunals Act 1987 provides that a Tribunal has control of and responsibility for its own procedures but "must conform to the rules of natural justice".

The Supreme Court can alternatively grant relief if, after a party has disputed the jurisdiction of the Tribunal, the Tribunal fails or refuses to give a ruling under section 26 on its jurisdiction or gives a ruling that is erroneous. Section 26(1) of the Consumer Claims Tribunals Act 1987 provides:

If, before a tribunal has determined a consumer claim, the jurisdiction of the tribunal to hear and determine the claim is disputed by a party to the claim, the tribunal must not proceed to determine the claim without first giving a ruling as to whether or not it has that jurisdiction.

A party to a claim can dispute jurisdiction orally or in writing. It is not necessary to dispute jurisdiction on oath or even by appearing in person before the Tribunal. Jurisdiction could be disputed by a letter or perhaps even by a telephone call to the Registry.

Section 26 provides that after giving the ruling, the Referee must not determine the claim earlier than the 15th day after the ruling was given. If proceedings are instituted in the Supreme Court in respect of the ruling on jurisdiction, the Referee must not decide the claim until the Court proceedings have been concluded. The Referee can nevertheless proceed to hear the claim without waiting the prescribed 14 days. It is only the final order which must be adjourned.

Conclusion

The track record of the BDT in New South Wales in the expedient and cost-effective resolution of building disputes is exemplary. The greatest drawback of the regime is that the BDT only has jurisdiction in claims arising from residential work. Even if parties to a commercial building dispute wished to voluntarily submit to the jurisdiction of the BDT, it could not entertain the dispute: the jurisdiction of the tribunal cannot be expanded except by legislation. The BDT's successful track record is seen by some sections of the legal community as a threat to established systems of dispute resolution. Any attempt to expand the jurisdiction would inevitably lead to strong lobbying.

It would be quite feasible, without the need for enacting legislation, to establish an independent commercial tribunal run along the same lines. As with arbitration, the tribunal's jurisdiction would be dependant upon voluntary submission of the parties to enter into this type of dispute settlement. The total adminstrative costs per dispute under the BDT system is $630, inclusive of referee's fees and rents. To render an independent commercial tribunal viable, it may be necessary to have a sliding scale of fees calculated according to the amount of the claim. Such is commercial demand that the proposed tribunal could be very profitable to both those who agree to submit to its jurisdiction and those managing its adminstration.

13. Court Appointed References in Australia

Ian H Bailey

Synopsis

This paper examines the legal and procedural implications of the Court appointed referee system in New South Wales and its effect on resolution of commercial construction disputes in Australia as a whole.

Introduction

In New South Wales there has been developed an ex-curial procedure for determination of proceedings by the appointment of Referees to inquire and report on the whole of proceedings or on any question arising in proceedings. Similar procedures are prescribed in each State and Territory. They are, however, by no means consistent and have not been used to the same extent as in New South Wales. The procedure in New South Wales is, in effect, compulsory and subject to very limited rights of review.

References out of Court

All State and Territory Courts have rules and procedures for the use of court-appointed referees and arbitrators to determine proceedings or specific issues in proceedings before the Court by a process of inquiry and report to the Court. While the concept is consistent, the actual rules and procedures differ markedly among the States. Since 1984, New South Wales has led in this field primarily because the judges of the Commercial Division of the Supreme Court are prepared to adopt 'innovative" approaches to dispute resolution. Generally the system of court referrals has provided cheap and speedy determinations, but sometimes there are surprising results.[1]

---

1   *Najjar v. Haines* (1991) 25 NSWLR 224 overturning (1991) 7 BCL 145; and *Hughes Bros. Pty Ltd v. The Minister for Public Works* (unreported Supreme Court of NSW, 17 & 31 August 1994, Rolfe J).

The system of Court referrals was incorporated in earlier legislation[2] but was not used extensively, partly as a result of rulings to the effect that the review by the Court of a report or award of a Court-appointed referee or arbitrator was to be made on the same basis as the Court's consideration of a consensual award from an arbitration. The High Court decision in *Buckley v. Bennell Design & Constructions Pty Limited* [3] held that the applicable principles for an award by an arbitrator appointed by the Court under s. 15 of the Arbitration Act 1902 (NSW) were not the same as those applicable to a consensual award. The Court reviewed the history of references out of Court, identifying the long-standing powers in this respect in the Courts of Chancery in England and the creation of official referees and the powers provided to Common Law Courts under the Supreme Court of Judicature Acts of 1873 and 1884 (UK).

The recent development of the Court-appointed referee system in New South Wales was part of the reforms associated with the development of Australia-wide Uniform Commercial Arbitration Acts. Amendment to the Supreme Court Act 1970 (NSW) separated Court-appointed arbitrations from consensual arbitrations. The Commercial Arbitration Act 1984 (NSW) allowed consensual arbitrations to proceed independently of the Courts. Section 124(2) of the Supreme Court Act 1970 (NSW)[4] enabled the Court to make the rules under which referees or arbitrators could be appointed to assist the Court by inquiry and report—part 72 of the Supreme Court Rules (NSW) prescribes the process.[5] A later rule change removed the term "arbitrator" from the collective term of "referees or arbitrators" because of the possibility of confusion with "arbitrators" under the Commercial Arbitration Act 1984 (NSW), and in recognition of the different procedures for review applicable to the decisions or findings made. The District Court of New South Wales adopted a similar process incorporated in the District Court Rules (NSW).[6] Whilst based on historic English provisions, and being to some extent similar to the references contemplated or possible under O.36 r.10 of the rules of the Supreme Court (UK), the process of

---

2   For example, the Arbitration Act 1902 (NSW) ss. 15-17.
3   (1978) 140 CLR 1.
4   Extracts of which are included in Appendix A of this paper.
5   Extracts of which are included in Appendix B of this paper.
6   Part 28B, District Court Rules.

determination of proceedings under Pt 72 includes a number of interesting aspects which have attracted considerable judicial attention.

In addition to the introduction of Pt 72 of the Supreme Court Rules (NSW), Pt 14A of those rules established a Construction List to be administered by the judges in the Commercial Division of the Supreme Court of New South Wales. The rules under Pt 14A and Practice Note 58 - Construction List set out the requirements for entry in the List, the conduct of Directions Hearings, the setting of timetables and making of directions for preparation of matters for hearing. The usual procedure involves a number of Directions Hearings at which a timetable is set for the completion of pleadings, the filing and service of Statements of Evidence and Experts' Reports upon which the parties wish to rely, and to deal with interlocutory applications. The originating Summons is required to identify the issues which the plaintiff considers appropriate for reference.

When the matter is ready for hearing, a determination is made, either by agreement or by the Court, of the issues which are appropriate for reference to a referee and an Order for Reference in terms of the Usual Order in the Practice Note (see Appendix C) is made. Initially there was a tendency to refer out the whole proceedings, but experience has led to the narrower definition of issues and the selection of referees for specific technical questions. The case management procedures in Part 14A of the Rules and in Practice Note 58 along with the manner of their application by the Judges of the Commercial Division of the NSW Supreme Court has created an extremely efficient and expeditious process of commercial construction dispute resolution. A most important ingredient in that process is the Part 72 reference procedure.

Power to Order Reference

Under Pt 72, a reference may be ordered without the consent of one party[7] or over the objection of both parties.[8] Rule 3(1) of Part 72 provides that any person may be appointed as a referee. The referee is

---

7   *Super Pty Ltd v. SJP Formwork (Aust) Pty Ltd* (1992) 29 NSWLR 549 at 556E-F and *Najjar v. Haines* (*op cit.*) at 245.

8   *Park Rail Developments Pty Ltd v. R J Pearce Assoc. Pty Ltd* (1987) 8 NSWLR 123.

not an officer of the Court.[9] He has, however, an immunity even where the reference fails due to error by the referee. References are made to a wide range of nominees, including retired judges, senior counsel, architects, engineers and builders. In construction matters involving some complexity, the Court may order joint appointments including a retired judge or senior counsel sitting with a technically qualified person. Part 72 references are not confined to the Construction List and in many Commercial Division matters references are made, including references of limited matters such as assessment of damages.[10]

The Order for Reference

Apart from identifying the specific issues or questions to be reported upon, the Court gives directions as to the payment of the fees of the referee and the dates for commencement of the reference and the date by which the referee is to report.

In most cases the evidence in chief in the proceedings is completed by the filing of written statements prior to the reference out. The referee has power to permit amendment and addition to the matters referred and to the evidence filed in the proceedings. The Court may also order that the referee proceed in the absence of legal representatives.[11] A referee, it would seem, does not have the power to exclude legal representatives.[12]

Conduct of Reference

Part 72 r. 8, is second only to r. 13, the most difficult and contentious provision. Under r. 8 the Court may give directions as to the conduct of the proceedings, including directions that the matter proceed on the evidence as filed and that the referee not permit the tendering of any further evidence in chief.[13] The discretion granted to the referee under sub-rule 2(a) is in the same terms as s. 14 of the Uniform Commercial

---

9 *Najjar v. Haines (supra)*. In Victoria see s 27B of the Supreme Court Act.

10 *Telecomputing PCS Pty Ltd v. Bridge Wholesale Acceptance Corp. Aust Ltd* (1991) 24 NSWLR 513.

11 *Triden Properties Ltd v. Capita Financial Group Ltd* (1993) 30 NSWLR 403.

12 *Argyle Lane Corp. Ltd v. Tower Holdings Pty Ltd* (unreported, Supreme Court of NSW, 3 September 1993, O'Keefe J).

13 Where there has been repeated failure to comply with directions to file evidence.

Arbitration Acts. Sub-rule 2(b) permits the referee to be informed "in relation to any matter in such manner as the referee thinks fit". The equivalent provision in the Commercial Arbitration Acts is s. 19(3).

Early authorities[14] held that a referee should conduct the reference as if it were a trial before a court, but in appropriate circumstances dispensing with the strict rules of evidence.[15] In *Xuereb v. Viola* [16] Cole J held that in the face of r. 8 "it is not correct that a referee should conduct his inquiry as if it were a trial by a judge"; Rogers CJ in *Beveridge v. Dontan Pty Limited* [17] agreed. The Court of Appeal in New South Wales in *Super Pty Limited v. SJP Formwork (Aust) Pty Limited* [18] has held that:

> *"Part 72, r 8 is of importance. It provides that, subject to any contrary directions given by the court, the referee may conduct the proceedings in such manner as the referee thinks fit and is not bound by the rules of evidence, but may inform himself or herself in relation to any matter in such manner as the referee sees fit. Although evidence may be given orally or in writing in the same manner as evidence is given before a court, that is by no means necessarily the way in which referees conduct proceedings before them. The circumstance that referees are not bound by the rules of evidence, and may inform themselves in such a manner as they see fit, is in turn related to what is often a major part of the objective in appointing a referee. ... No doubt part of the object in appointing an architect as referee in relation to a building dispute is often that the architect may, if appropriate, bring personal knowledge and experience to bear. Referees do not operate under the same constraints as judges in relation to the limitations upon the use they make of personal knowledge."* [19]

14 *Pimas Constructions Pty Ltd v. Metropolitan Waste Disposal Authority* (1988) 17 ACLR 68.
15 *Clark Equipment Credit of Australia Ltd v. Como Factors Pty Ltd* (1988) 14 NSWLR 552.
16 (1989) 18 NSWLR 453 at 466.
17 (1991) 23 NSWLR 13.
18 (1992) 29 NSWLR 529
19 *Ibid.* at 557 C-E.

Notwithstanding the power of a referee "to inform himself or herself ... in such manner as the referee thinks fit", the referee must still observe the concepts of natural justice in the conduct of a reference:

> "... *What may be required by natural justice may vary with the particular circumstances of the particular question upon which the referee is asked to report. ... However, it is clear, in my judgment, that concepts of natural justice must be observed in the conduct of a reference. This is so notwithstanding that the referee is not an officer of the Court, a delegate of the Court, is not conducting a trial, is not making a finding of fact or law and is not determining any issue.*" [20]

The Court has recognised the necessity for flexibility and accepts that informality of procedure may be appropriate and acceptable if each party is given a fair opportunity to put its case and point of view.[21] Whilst a referee is at liberty to proceed on the basis of his own knowledge and experience, he is nevertheless required to draw to the parties' attention his intention to rely upon the same.[22] It is difficult to prove that the referee has proceeded on the basis of his own undisclosed knowledge and experience rather than on the evidence. Referees ought to reach their decision on the basis of logically probative evidence, and to elicit that reliance in their report.

In certain limited circumstances a referee may be permitted to delegate some of the tasks referred. This is probably limited to accounting and calculation procedures or the preparation of documents forming part of the report.[23]

---

20 *Xuereb v. Viola* (1989) 18 NSWLR 453 *per* Cole J at 467B.
21 *Beveridge v. Dontan Pty Ltd* (1990) 23 NSWLR 13.
22 *Thiess Watkins White Constructions Ltd (R & M Appted) (in liq) v. Commonwealth of Australia* (unreported, Supreme Court of NSW, 23 April 1992, Giles J) applying, inter alia, *Fox v. P G Wellfair Ltd (in liq)* [1981] 2 Lloyds Reports 514.
23 *Telecomputing PCS Pty Ltd v. Bridge Wholesale Acceptance Corp. Aust Ltd* (1991) 24 NSWLR 513.

The Report

Part 72 r. 11 requires that the report annex the parties' statements under r. 8(5) and should state the referee's opinion and his reasons for the opinion. In *Hughes Bros. Pty Limited v. The Minister for Public Works*,[24] substantial parts of a referee's report were rejected as a result of the inadequate or completely absent explanation of the reasons for the conclusions made. Ultimately the entire report was rejected and the Court refused to remit the matter to the referee. It has been said[25] that whilst detailed reasons are not necessary, they are important so as to permit the Court to properly exercise its function under Pt 72 r. 13, and so that the parties and the disinterested observer can know that the opinion of the referee is not arbitrary, or influenced by improper considerations. The reasons should disclose sufficiently the process whereby the referee arrived at the conclusion stated.[26]

Proceedings on the Report

After some tentative and conflicting statements[27] as to the correct procedure to be adopted by the Court under Pt 72 r.13, the Court of Appeal in *Super Pty Limited v. SJP Formwork (Aust) Pty Limited* [28] held that a party who is dissatisfied with a referee's report is not entitled as of right to require the judge acting under Pt 72 r. 13 to reconsider and determine afresh all issues, whether of fact or law, which that party desires to contest before the judge:

> *"What is involved in an application under Pt 72, r 13 is not an appeal, whether by way of a hearing de novo or a more limited re-hearing. This is consistent with the right of the referee to conduct the reference as the referee thinks fit and unconstrained by the rules of evidence. Rather, the judge, in reviewing the report and deciding whether to adopt, vary or reject it, has a judicial discretion to exercise in a manner that is consistent both with the*

---

24 (1994) (unreported, Supreme Court of NSW, 17 and 13 August 1994, Rolfe J).
25 *Sundin's Building Co. Pty Ltd v. Winrobe Pty Ltd* (unreported, Supreme Court of NSW, 18 July 1991, Giles J).
26 *Silo-Wand GmbH v. Crontec Manufacturing Pty Ltd* (unreported, Supreme Court of NSW, 14 July 1994, O'Keefe J).
27 See, for example, *Hoogerdyk v. Condon* (1990) 22 NSWLR 171.
28 (1992) 29 NSWLR 549.

object and purpose of the rules and with the wider setting in which they take their place.

That wider setting is a system for the administration of justice according to law. In so far as the subject matter of dissatisfaction with a referee's report is a question of law, or the application of legal standards to established facts, then a proper exercise of discretion would require a judge to consider and determine that matter afresh. That was decided by this Court in Homebush Abattoir Corporation v. Bermria Pty Ltd (1991) 22 NSWLR 605: *see also,* Cape v. Maidment (1991) 98 ACTR 1 *at 4. That conclusion is entirely consistent with the history of the rules and the reasoning of the High Court in Buckley which, although the case related to different provisions is also instructive as to the present provisions.* "[29]

The Court of Appeal agreed with the approach taken by Cole J in *Chloride Batteries Australia Limited v. Glendale Chemical Products Pty Limited* [30] when dealing with an application for the rejection of a report by one party. Cole J referred to the wide power under Pt 72 r. 13, the scope of which meant that the Court should not automatically adopt a report received. However, the requirement that consideration be given to an expert referee's report before its acceptance or rejection did not necessarily involve the Court in conducting a re-hearing of the technical issue the subject of the report and the Court then reaching its own conclusion in relation to that technical issue. The width of power and flexibility conferred under r. 13 paras (a) to (d) do not permit the delineation of the proper approach for a Court to take to each or any particular report. Each instance must be separately considered:

"This does not mean that certain considerations will not be present when the Court considers each application. The Court will have regard to the futility of a process of re-litigating an issue determined by the referee in circumstances where parties have had an opportunity to place before the referee such matters as they desire. It will also have regard to cost. If the report shows a thorough, analytical, and scientific approach to the assessment of the subject matter of inquiry, the Court will have a disposition

---

29 *Ibid.* at 563D-F *per* Gleeson CJ.
30 (1988) 17 NSWLR 60.

towards acceptance of the report, for to do otherwise would be to negate the purpose of and the facility of referring complex technical issues to independent experts for inquiry and report. This disposition may be enhanced in circumstances where the parties, as a consequence of the operation of r 8, have had the opportunity to place before the referee such evidence and technical reports as they may wish. The Court may be more hesitant in its disposition if the report is provided by the expert in the absence of the parties having been given such an opportunity. The disposition must always yield to the requirements of justice, if it becomes apparent for any reason that to adopt the report would result in an injustice or unfairness to a party. These matters reinforce the view that each matter requires its own consideration." [31]

Cole J referred to and accepted statements of principle in the Victorian cases *Nicholls v. Stamer* [32] and *Integer Computing Pty Limited v. Facom Australia Limited* [33] and said:

"The circumstance that r 13 does not include the expression 'the interests of justice' does not affect the weight to be attached to the statement of principle (i.e. that justice must be served). The decision to adopt, reject or vary a report must always be determined in accordance with perceived justice." [34]

The Court has shown a marked reluctance to permit the tender and review of the evidence before the referee when hearing an application under r. 13. The evidence before the referee does not become evidence in the Court on the proceedings under r. 13 unless it is tendered and admitted by the Court. In Skinner and *Edwards v. Australian Telecommunications Corporation* [35] Cole J held:

"It may become evidence in the action or on the motion for adoption or variation of the referee's report only if it is tendered and admitted into evidence by the court.

---

31 *Ibid.* at 67.
32 [1980] VR 479
33 Unreported, Supreme Court of Victoria, 10 April 1987, Marks J.
34 *Chloride Batteries op cit.* at 69D.
35 (1992) 27 NSWLR 564.

However, the scheme of Pt 72 is for the court to receive the report of the referee with exposed reasons for his opinion. Initially it does not receive the evidence upon which he reached his opinion.

Adopting the opinion of the referee on a question of fact (or law) constitutes that opinion the opinion of the court and thus its judgment on that fact. The court may properly act upon the opinion of the referee expressed in his report without specific or detailed regard to the primary evidence led before him, for it does not initially receive that evidence. If a reading of the report satisfied the court that the reasons given by the referee for his opinion logically and cohesively lead to the opinion of fact or law, such report and its constituent opinion may be adopted without reference to the evidence. Such adoption may result in ultimate judgment in the action, or other appropriate order." [36]

Where the report is by a referee who is a technical expert and the matters relate to technical issues, the Court has a pre-disposition to accept the referee's report.[37]

An appeal does lie to the Court of Appeal from the decision of the judge at first instance to exercise his discretion in favour of adopting a referee's report. The only ground, however, upon which an appeal will lie is that the judge has made an appealable error in the exercise of his discretion.[38] The Court of Appeal will not review the decision of the referee, but will restrict consideration to whether the judge has made an error on a question of law, an error in the exercise of discretion as to the adoption of the report, or if the judge has made decisions of fact, an error of fact.

Provisions in Other States

In Victoria a new Order 50 of the General Rules of Procedure in Civil Proceedings 1986 was introduced in 1992. The procedure echoes that

---

36 *Ibid.* at 575.
37 *Chloride Batteries (op cit.)* re credibility of witnesses etc. and *Everyready Cranes Pty Ltd v. Archer Hydraulics* (unreported, Supreme Court of NSW, 3 March 1995, Bainton J).
38 *Nine Network Pty Ltd v. Kennedy Miller Television Pty Ltd* (unreported, NSW Court of Appeal, 8 June 1994).

under Pt 72 (NSW), however the flexibility provided by Pt 72 r. 8(2)(a) and (b) is not included. Nevertheless under r. 50.02 the Court may make directions as to procedure. The Court has shown a reluctance to refer without consent[39] and as a result the procedure has not been widely used.

In South Australia the Supreme Court Act 1935 (SA) ss. 65-67 provide for Inquiries and Trials by Referees and Arbitrators. A limitation in the system is the requirement under Rule 76 of the Supreme Court Rules that Special Referees be legal practitioners of six years standing. The procedure also requires the consent of the parties. The report or award under s. 67 is the "equivalent to the verdict of a jury" though this may not mean what it says.[40] Another restriction on the process is that Court-sponsored arbitrations under Supreme Court Rule 49 are conducted in accordance with and subject to the Commercial Arbitration Act 1986 (SA).

In Queensland the approach of the Supreme Court to reference out to Assessors, Special Referees and Arbitrators made possible under Order 39 r. 7 and rr. 40-50 has been to apply a general rule that the parties are entitled to a judicial determination, and without consent of all parties, a reference out will not be made.[41] In Western Australia there is a power to refer to Assessors and Referees,[42] but again it is not used without consent.

The Federal Court of Australia has power under Order 72 of its Rules to order reference to an arbitrator. The power is rarely used, probably due to the entitlement of parties, subject to a costs order, to terminate the process at any time.[43]

---

39 *AT & N R Taylor & Sons Pty Ltd v. Brival Pty Ltd* [1982] VR 762.
40 *Leighton Contractors (SA) Pty Ltd v. Hazama Corp. (Aust) Pty Ltd* (1991) 56 SASR 47.
41 *Tropeano v. Monogram Pty Ltd* [1992] 2 Qd R 324 and *Everingham v. Clarke* [1994] 1 Qd R 34.
42 Supreme Court Act 1935 (WA) ss. 50-55 and Order 34 of the Supreme Court Rules.
43 Order 72 r 10.

The Northern Territory[44] has similar rules to Victoria, as does the Australian Capital Territory,[45] where the reference is conducted as if it were an arbitration under the Commercial Arbitration Act 1986 (ACT).

Conclusion

In New South Wales the ex-curial procedure described above is compulsary. As to whether this procedure is universally to be embraced as the panacea for expedient and cost effective dispute resolution for the construction sector I make no further comment than to say let the users decide.

---

44 Order 50 - Rules of the Supreme Court.
45 Order 83 - Rules of the Supreme Court.

APPENDIX A

Section 124(2) of the Supreme Court Act 1970 (NSW)

(2)   The rules may make provision for or with respect to -

(a)   the cases in which the whole of any proceedings or any question or issue arising in any proceedings may be referred by the Court to an arbitrator or referee for determination or for inquiry and report;

(b)   the appointment of a Judge, master, registrar or other officer of the Court or other person as an arbitrator or referee;

(c)   the fees to be paid to such an arbitrator or referee;

(d)   the persons by whom the whole or any part of any such fees are payable;

(e)   the consequences of a determination or report by an arbitrator or referee;

(f)   the manner in which such a determination or report may be called in question;

(g)   whether or not, or to what extent, a determination or report may be called in question on a matter of fact or law;

(h)   the provision of the services of officers of the Court and the provision of court rooms and other facilities for the purpose of a reference of any proceedings or any question or issue arising in any proceedings to an arbitrator or referee; and

(i)   any other matters associated with such a reference.

APPENDIX B

Part 72 of the Supreme Court Rules (1970) New South Wales

Interpretation
1.   In this Part, unless the context or subject-matter otherwise indicates or requires, "question" includes any question or issue arising in any proceedings, whether of fact or law or both and whether raised by pleadings, agreement of parties or otherwise.

Order Referring
2.   (1)   The Court may, in any proceedings in the Court, subject to this rule, at any stage of the proceedings, on application by a party or of its own motion, make orders for reference to a referee appointed by the Court for inquiry and report by the referee on the whole of the proceedings or any question or questions arising in the proceedings.

(2)   The Court shall not make an order under subrule (1) in respect of a question to be tried with a jury.

(3)   In respect of a question which may, under section 86 of the Act, be tried with a jury, the Court shall not, before the expiry of the time prescribed by Part 34 rule 3 (which relates to a requisition for trial with a jury), make an order under subrule (1), unless the Court also makes an order under section 89(1) of the Act (which section relates to trial without a jury).

Appointees
3.   (1)   Subject to this rule, the Court may appoint any person as a referee.

(2)   A Judge, master, registrar or other officer of the Court may not act as referee otherwise than with the concurrence of the Chief Justice.

Two or more Referees
4.   (1)   Where the Court appoints two referees and a decision to be made in the course of proceedings under the reference is not agreed, the decision -

        (a)   where a Judge or Master is a referee - of the Judge or Master; and

        (b)   in any other case - of the referee appointed by the Court to be senior referee,

        shall be binding.

(2)   Where the Court appoints three or more referees, any decision to be made in the course of proceedings, under the reference may be made by a majority of the referees and, failing a majority, the decision -

        (a)   where a Judge or Master is a referee - of the Judge or Master; and

        (b)   in any other case - of the referee appointed by the Court to be senior referee,

    shall be binding

Inquiry and report

5.   (1)   Where the Court makes orders under rule 2 the Court may, at any time and from time to time -

        (a)   authorise the referee to inquire into and report upon any facts relevant to the inquiry and report on the matter referred;

        (b)   direct the referee to make a further or supplemental report or inquiry and report;

        (c)   give such instructions as the Court thinks fit relating to the inquiry or report.

    (2)   Instructions pursuant to subrule (1)(c) may include provision concerning any experiment or test for the purposes of any inquiry or report of a referee.

Remuneration of referee

6.   (1)   The Court may -

        (a)   determine the amount of the fees to be paid to a referee;

        (b)   direct how, when and by whom the whole or any part of any such fees are to be payable;

        (c)   determine the consequences of failure to comply with a direction under paragraph (b);

    (2)   Subrule (1) does not affect the powers of the Court as to costs.

Court rooms, etc.

7.   The Court may give directions for the provision -
       (a)   of services of officers of the Court; and
       (b)   of court rooms and other facilities,
       for the purpose of any reference under rule 2.

Conduct of proceedings under the reference

8.   (1)   Where the court makes an order under rule 2, the Court may give directions with respect to the conduct of proceedings under the reference.

       (2)   Subject to any direction under subrule (1) -
               (a)   the referee may conduct the proceedings under the reference in such manner as the referee thinks fit;
               (b)   the referee, in conducting proceedings under the reference, is not bound by rules of evidence but may inform himself or herself in relation to any matter in such manner as the referee thinks fit.

       (3)   Evidence before the referee -
               (i)   may be given orally or in writing; and
               (ii)   shall, if the referee so requires, be given on oath or affirmation or by affidavit.

       (4)   A referee may take the examination of any person.

       (5)   Each party shall, within a time fixed by the referee but in any event before the conclusion of evidence on the inquiry, give to the referee and each other party a brief statement of the findings of fact and law for which the party contends.

       (6)   The parties shall at all times do all things which the referee requires to enable a just opinion to be reached and no party shall wilfully do or cause to be done any act to delay or prevent an opinion being reached.

Interlocutory directions

9.   The Court may, at any time and from time to time, on motion of the referee or of a party, give directions with respect to any matter arising in proceedings under the reference.

Setting aside or variation of reference

10. (1) The Court may, of its own motion or on application by a referee or a party set aside or vary any order made under rule 2.

    (2) Nothing in this rule affects any other power of the Court to set aside or vary an order made under rule 2.

Report

11. The referee shall, unless the Court otherwise orders, make a report to the Court, in writing, on the matter referred to the referee annexing the statements given under rule 8(5) and stating -

    (a) the referee's opinion on the matter; and
    (b) the reasons for the opinion.

Service of report

12. On receipt of the report, the Court shall serve it on the parties.

Proceedings on the report

13. (1) Where a report is made, the Court may, of its own motion, after notice to the parties, or on application by any party, on a matter of fact or law or both -

    (a) adopt, vary or reject the report in whole or in part;
    (b) require an explanation by way of report from the referee;
    (c) on any ground, remit for further consideration by the referee the whole or any part of the matter referred for a further report;
    (d) decide any matter on the evidence taken before the referee, with or without additional evidence.
    and shall given such judgment or make such order as the Court thinks fit.

    (2) Evidence additional to the evidence taken before the referee may not be adduced before the Court except with the leave of the Court.

APPENDIX C

Annexure 3 to Practice Note 58 - Construction List (Supreme Court Rules 1970 (NSW))

USUAL ORDER FOR REFERENCE

1. Pursuant to Pt 72 r2(1)(a) refer to [state name of referee] for inquiry and report the matter in the Schedule hereto.

2. Direct that (without affecting the powers of the Court as to costs) the parties namely [state relevant parties] be jointly and severally liable to the referee for the fees payable to him.

3. Direct that the parties deliver to the referee forthwith a copy of this order together with a copy of Pt 72 of the Rules.

4. Direct that -
    (a) subject to paras (b) and (c) hereof the provisions of Pt 72 r 8 shall apply to the conduct of proceedings under the reference;
    (b) the reference will commence on [date] unless otherwise ordered by the referee;
    (c) the referee consider and implement such manner of conducting proceedings under the reference as will without undue formality or delay enable a just determination to be made including if the referee sees fit the making of enquiries by telephone, site inspection, inspection of plant and equipment and communication with experts retained on behalf of the parties;
    (d) any evidence in chief before the referee shall unless the referee otherwise permits be by way of written statement signed by the maker of the statement;
    (e) the referee submit the report to the Court in accordance with Pt 72 r 11 addressed to the Commercial Division Deputy Registrar on or before .... 19....

5. The referee shall have power to permit such amendments or additions to the matter in the Schedule as the referee sees fit in order to dispose of the true issues between the parties.

6. Grant liberty to the referee or any party to seek directions with respect to any matter arising in proceedings under the reference upon application made on twenty-four hours' notice or such less notice as to the Court seems fit through the Associate to the Judge for the time being administering the Construction List.

7. Reserve costs of the proceedings.

8. Stand the proceedings over for further directions on .... 19..

SCHEDULE

The whole of the proceedings; or
The following questions arising in the proceedings, namely [state the questions]

14. The Role and Development of Alternative Dispute Resolution in The United States

Charles B. Molineaux

Synopsis

After a brief yet incisive examination of the Latham report recommendations this paper reviews the range of ADR methods available in the United States and examines how some methods have successfully reacted to the needs of construction.

Introduction

Construction is quite different from other types of commercial enterprises for reasons which are fairly obvious. Every construction project is unique. It is one of a kind, on a particular site (in itself unique) and produced over time, thus there is a certain inevitability to disputes in construction. Construction projects are typically carried out in a more-or-less free enterprise economic system, pursuant to contract documents which set out the obligations and rights of independent parties. In theory, if the perfect construction-contract could be formulated by engineers, and if contractors were angels and not men, there would be no disputes.

In his paper,[1] Sir Alastair Morton refers to original sin. Because of original sin and human imperfection, at best we all make mistakes; even the best-intentioned engineers will make design errors or draft ambiguous specifications, owners will ill-advisedly attempt to save money during the site investigation phase or fail to make the site fully available, and contractors will try to achieve minimal contract compliance with the least costly construction methods and materials. In short, only God is perfect and there will be construction disputes.

In many quarters of the construction industry lawyers are seen the harbingers of doom, alternatively and less charitably as bearers of the

---

[1]   *The Channel Tunnel Contract: Conflicts and Interests, supra* p. 7.

pox, and at best a necessary evil. If you will, we would have to note that the very inclusion of an arbitration clause in a construction contract is but recognition that disputes will occur under the best-drafted contracts. The question, for men of good will and some sense of wanting to make the construction procurement system work well for society in general, is: How can the process of dispute resolution, including arbitration, be achieved in a manner that is fair and efficient.

The Latham Report

The post-Latham year has been one of great and varied debate. In this paper it is impossible to set out a comprehensive American reaction to all of the 130-page Report, particularly since some aspects are directed to uniquely British situations. But observations can be made. Thus, from the perceived safety of the other side of the Atlantic, I will make a few comments on the *Latham Report.*[2] Sir Michael in his interim report, one will recall, considered 'Trust' and 'Money' to be the cornerstones of a healthy construction industry. In the Foreword to the final report, Sir Michael speaks of the goal of helping clients obtain quality projects, the need for better performance in construction, contractual fairness, enhanced teamwork and for enhanced dispute resolution mechanisms as a response to commercial requirements. So far, so good. But then the Report begins the slide into "happy talk." Instead of the voguish expression, "Seeking win-win solutions," which is *a fortiori* illogical, Sir Michael goes further; he prefers what he calls the immortal words of the Dodo in *Alice in Wonderland:* "Everybody has won and all must have prizes."[3] Frankly, the Latham Report and its reception suggest another literary reference: *The Emperor's New Clothes* by Hans Christian Andersen. In that story, you will recall, all courtiers were intimidated into polite silence when the Emperor appeared in the buff. Similarly enough, we have the initial and favourable reaction to the Report, for the moment everyone politely, finding it most constructive indeed, even though Sir Michael himself admits that the issues discussed provoke profound disagreement and some radical recommendations.

---

[2]   Latham, Sir Michael, *Constructing the Team, A Joint Review of Procurement and Contractual Arrangements in the United Kingdom Construction Industry*, HMSO, London, 1994.

[3]   *Ibid*, Foreword, p.4.

Sir Michael recommends change has to begin with clients, who are, he states, at the 'core of the process'. The initial focus is on public work. Briefly put, privatisation has had the effect of freeing UK Government offices "to make their own arrangements."*Constructing the Team* nods to the subsidiarity principle and then qualifies the nod with this comment:

> *"The delegation of authority within the public sector to those best placed to assess local needs was a sensible and welcome move. But it is greatly in the interests of such clients to have the best advice and robust guidelines which will assist them to obtain value for money."* (Emphasis added.)

The term "robust guidelines" suggests mandatory government contracting procedures;[4] Latham had also earlier said that he does not recommend the reintroduction of a central procurement agency. In short, the study recommends that the public clients take the lead, specifically the Department of the Environment, more specifically its Construction Sponsorship Directorate. But Latham also suggests that there should also be an organisation for private sector owners to participate as the UK pursues better construction practice. Nevertheless some recommendations are useful, but others are plain naïve. For example:

> *"Subcontractors should undertake that, in the spirit of teamwork, they will co-ordinate their activities effectively with each other [sic], and thereby assist the achievement of the main contractor's overall programme."*[5]

This in itself contradicts the reasoning behind free market principles.

In another piece of unsatisfactory discussion, the Report notes that it is 32 percent less costly to construct an office building in North Carolina than at Heathrow Airport and, further, that McDonald's Restaurants

---

[4] Perhaps like the US Federal Acquisition Regulation which in itself is a complex area, and one which is undergoing a radical rethink. See Jones, J.S. "Federal Aquisition Regulations: Principle and Procedure" in Odams, A.M. (Ed.) *Comparative Studies in Construction Law: The Sweet Lectures*, Construction Law Press, London, 1995, p.197.

[5] *Constructing the Team, op cit*, § 6.41 note 6.

Ltd. uses "a great deal of off-site prefabrication".[6] The point of these rather thin examples, says Sir Michael, is that they may show that British construction performance is below that of competitors', and that some clients are introducing new techniques.

Contract forms

A key paragraph of the Report,[7] sets forth 13 points that the author recommends for a most effective form of contract. Again, disappointingly, many belabour the elementary; fair dealing among parties, teamwork to achieve "win-win" solutions, interrelated documents packaging, comprehensible language, separate roles for lead manager and adjudicator, clear risk allocation, pre-pricing of changes, speedy dispute resolution. There is nothing innovative here and some points are as basic as an Augustinian "do good and avoid evil." One or two points appear to urge change for its own sake, such as phasing out the traditional system of monthly measurement payments or providing "incentives for exceptional performance."[8]

An obvious unawareness of legal implications is, however, evidenced by other parts of the Report. In the discussion of specialist contractors and design, for example, Sir Michael speaks of the joint venture route where general contractor and specialist contractor "work together as a single corporate entity during the project".[9] In discussing contract provisions, as a further example, the Report says that "Guidance Notes" should be attached.[10] With what contractual effect?

One feature of the Latham Report is its endorsement of the New Engineering Contract. Sir Michael advances alterations to that new form to provide a secure trust fund into which client payments will be made before each period of work, a statement that owner and contractor affirm that they intend to establish a fair and reasonable

---

[6] *Ibid*, p.63.
[7] *Ibid*, § 5.18.
[8] This latter is suggestive of an award fee approach, with all of its subjectivity and complications. What about "value engineering" or contractor method innovation, within contract specifications, stimulated by the profit motive, or bonuses for early completion—all being approaches which are more objectively administered?
[9] *Constructing the Team, op cit*, p.29.
[10] *Ibid*, p.37.

agreement and mutual trust and make clear that "win-win" solutions to problems will be devised "in a spirit of partnership," and a provision in the main contract that only the NEC subcontract will be used.[11] This limitation on freedom of contract should also apply to restrict subcontractors "in their contractual dealings with sub-subcontractors." In North America the notion of the trust fund has been around for a long while and is fraught with legal and practical complexities. Sir Michael makes no indication as to how he considers this 'trust fund' is to operate as a discrete legal entity, when it is to come into force, what controls are to be incorporated and who is to decide how much is due if sums are disputed.

Dispute resolution

This is one area which Sir Michael deals with at length. It is particularly apposite that exactly one year after the Centre of Construction Law's conference in 1994, organised in response to the Latham Report,[12] that the subject of its 1995 conference addresses the fundamental needs of the industry: Commercial Dispute Resolution. Sir Michael recommended that all construction contracts should contain an adjucation provision as the first tier for resolution of disputes. Whether this is a realistic goal remains to be seen, but it is notable that few standard contract drafting bodies have arrived at a clause that is universally acceptable and enforceable.

I now turn to the main subject of this paper, the development of Alternative Dispute Resolution as it relates to the American construction market.

---

[11] Since this paper was written, the majority of these recommendations have been taken into account in the second edition of the NEC. It is notable that the name has also been changed to 'The Engineering and Construction Contract'. For a more detailed analysis of the changes see Cornes, D.L., *The Second Edition of the New Engineering Contract* [1996] 13 ICLR 97.

[12] The papers of which have been revised, expanded and updated and appear as *Risk, Management and Procurement in Construction*, Uff, J & Odams, A.M. (Eds) published by and available from the Centre of Construction Law and Management, King's College London.

Alternative Dispute Resolution

There is a general feeling within the American construction market that litigation and arbitration are not the fora in which to resolve technical disputes. This concern is being met by an array of dispute resolving procedural efforts under the generic title, "Alternative Dispute Resolution" ("ADR"). This new term is imprecise. The "ADR" acronym is explained variously as standing for 'amicable dispute resolution', 'appropriate dispute resolution' and 'administrative dispute resolution'. The wags also suggest that, for the really difficult cases, ADR means "another drink required." On analysis, it is evident that these "new" techniques are not really new at all; they are largely procedural devices of different degrees of formality or informality which are aimed at bringing the parties together in an agreed settlement at the pre-litigation phase. It is common in ADR for the services of an independent person who is familiar with the nature of the problem in hand to be engaged, because insiders, those directly involved with the problem, may have become entrenched in their positions or may even have allowed personal animosity to become dominant. Thus, we see dispute review boards (bringing in technical outsiders), mediation (bringing in a mediator who may be technically or legally, or even psychologically, orientated), and mini-trials (bringing in the senior officials of the parties) amongst other ADR variants. Since ADR measures are undertaken consensually, they can proceed during litigation, all is not lost because the lawyers are in court pursuing a concurrent action.

Figure 1 compares in tabular format some of the more popular forms of ADR, with arbitration and litigation. There is a somewhat theoretical discussion, ongoing in the UK and the US, as to whether arbitration is to be considered a form of ADR. My preference, as the heavy line indicates, is for the view that arbitration, like mediation, *et al.*, can only take place if the parties consent to it. While arbitration may sometimes take on some of the aspects of formal civil litigation, it is flexible enough and final enough to serve as a sensible middle ground between the rigidity of the court system on one side of the spectrum and the informality and sometimes non-final or unsuccessful conclusion of the other forms of ADR.

DISPUTE RESOLUTION				
Alternative Dispute Resolution ("ADR")				**Court**
Dispute Review Board	**Mini-Trial**	**Mediatio n**	**Arbitration**	**Litigation**
Private			Private	Matter of Public Record
Flexible Techniques			Flexible	Rigid Rules
Non-Aversarial, "amicable"			Adversarial	Adversarial
Expertise			Expertise	No Expertise
Non-Judgmental			Judgmental	Judgmental
(Fails if no agreement)				
_____			_____	_____
Agreed Settlement			Final Award	Final Decision
_____			_____	_____
			Very Limited Grounds of Appeal	Appeal as of right

An interesting example of ADR procedures in action is the method deployed by the US Army Corps of Engineers. This ADR method involves a non-binding hearing, in which within a fixed time frame the parties present their "best case" on entitlement and quantum in summary fashion to their "principal representatives" and a neutral advisory panel. Each party designates a neutral representative and the panel chairman is selected by the two neutrals; it may also be specified in the ADR agreement that the chairman is to be experienced in the particular disciplines involved in the claim. In this format, the party-designated neutral is conceivably more truly a neutral than a party-designated arbitrator because the agreement will typically require that the resumés of the prospective neutrals are provided to the parties as well as a disclosure of any circumstances likely to create a presumption of bias followed by a period within which objection can be made.[13] Prior to the hearing, the parties may submit 'position papers' to the principal representatives of the opposing side, as well as to the neutral advisors, and this may then be followed by rebuttal information. The hearing presentations are informal, rules of evidence do not apply and witnesses may be asked questions by the panel or by the principal representatives. In one format, the hearing may allow for a half day for each side followed by a period of deliberation among the panel members only. The neutral panel members then make a recommendation to the principal representatives who then negotiate. If the process fails to result in settlement, no information prepared is usable subsequently as evidence for the purpose of impeachment but evidence otherwise admissible continues to be admissible.

What is particularly valuable in this effort to reach settlement is that the claimant contractor under a Corps of Engineers construction contract would normally have to present his claim, after receiving a "Contracting Officer's" decision, to a Board of Contract Appeals within the Army Corps of Engineers. The serious problem with the Board procedure for some years has not been the perception that objectivity is unobtainable in an "in house" proceeding, as an outside observer might expect, but rather that the process usually takes years before a Board hearing is held and a decision reached.[14] As can be seen below, the process described is a variant of the mini-trial.

Dispute Review Boards

This mechanism is deployed on large projects only because of its cost. DRBs enjoy popularity with engineers but not particularly with lawyers. A DRB consists of a panel, constituted of no particular number of members, which meets periodically to review potential disputes on a jobsite as and when they arise. The decisions can be binding or non-binding and the method is generally regarded as a technical advisory board. A distinct advantage of this method is that

---

[13] Like a peremptory challenge, no reason for objection need be given.

[14] This is in some measure attributable to the fact that the Board process itself, built into the Corps' contracts, which decades ago intended quick administrative review on behalf of the Chief of Engineers, became encrusted with all of the rules and procedural paraphernalia of full-blown, adversarial, court proceedings.

potential disputes are addressed before they arise. We have, therefore, at least moved substantially from the old notion of avoiding jobsite unpleasantness by postponing claim submissions until after contract completion.[15] The principal enthusiasts of the DRB approach are found in the engineering profession and in the US the lead in promoting the concept has been taken by the American Society of Civil Engineers (ASCE).[16]

Early recognition of a potential dispute can sometimes lead to a technical solution, rather than a legal or financial one, a possibility indeed contemplated by the often-criticised notice provisions with respect to claims. Internationally, of course, the form of conditions of contract for civil works of FIDIC has moved from the intent of postponing claims to the end of the project[17] to the earlier addressing of claims as indicated by its current edition.[18] In the current edition, not only is it contemplated that arbitration may be under way while work continues, it is required that timely notice is given and that the Engineer may direct the keeping of appropriate contemporary records with respect to the claim.[19] On the other hand it has been suggested that the ready availability of the dispute review board panel makes its use more inevitable.

Currently, in the US dispute review boards function on a wide variety of projects, especially in the West where the concept received its original impetus.[20] There are also boards in operation in Boston, in connection with the contracts of the Central Artery/Tunnel project and

---

[15] Cynics have commented variously on the old approach but the conclusion is inescapable that fairness demands that disputes be addressed while records and witnesses are available.

[16] See Denning, "More Than an Underground Success"*Civil Engineering,* December 1993. It should be recalled here, of course, that the Channel Tunnel contract provided a dispute resolution process similar to that urged by ASCE and that most of the 16 recommendations, in disputes with an asserted total value of $3 billion, were accepted, and on this point see the interesting comment by former counsel involved in the project, Jeffery Roehl, in Odams, A.M. (Ed), *Comparative Studies in Construction Law: The Sweet Lectures,* p. 231.

[17] As indicated in the First Edition of the "Red Book," 1957.

[18] Fédération Internationale des Ingénieurs Conseils, Conditions of Contract for Works of Civil Engineering Construction, Fourth Edition, 1987.

[19] *Ibid,* clause 53.

[20] This is particularly so in Colorado and Washington state.

also in connection with contracts for the cleanup of Boston Harbour,[21] and in Baltimore, with respect to tunnel work. These boards are not identical in operation. While the strong suggestion of the ASCE is that the board is constituted to serve as a sort of rapid deployment force, available to make early, non-binding recommendations on a job with which the board members have become familiar, in some cases the boards have been constituted to serve in a review function, after an engineer's decision has been made, and the parties have become entrenched in their positions.

The American idea of the dispute review board, or of an "adjudicator," to act before formal arbitration is under way, has been embraced by the International Bank for Reconstruction and Development (the "World Bank") in its Standard Bidding Document for Procurement of Works (Smaller Contracts). In that form of conditions of contractm the adjudicator proposed to be appointed is named in the Bidding Data at the outset but can be rejeted by the Bidder; thereafter, either as the joint appointee of the Employer and the Contractor or as the appointee of the designated Appointing Authority, the Adjudicator attempts to resolve disputes within a 28-day period after notice of a dispute and before recourse to arbitration.

Mini-Trial

This method aims to facilitate resolution of the dispute before arbitration or litigation has commenced. A mini-trial is not really a trial, but is usually set up as a tightly scheduled presentation of the issues before senior officers of the disputing parties followed by a settlement effort. Variations on the theme may include a neutral facilitator, a neutral advisor or even a sort of "focus group" panel or simulated jury. Typically, it is agreed that the presentations are informal, that the strict rules of evidence do not apply and that the witnesses may simply provide narrative testimony. The key is the conciseness of the format and its confidentiality. If the effort fails to be concluded in a settlement by a fixed time, the process terminates. At that point, the usual remedies of arbitration and perhaps litigation are available. It may be that a report will issue from the mini-trial panel, if

---

[21] There is no discernible connection between the need for the Harbor cleanup perceived in the twentieth century and the eighteenth century "Boston Tea Party", although it is accepted that government programs move glacially in Massachusetts.

this forms part of the reference. That report would probably not be agreed to be admissible in a subsequent proceeding (whereas, in the dispute review board format, the recommendation of the board might be agreed between the parties to be allowable in evidence). It would likely also be agreed in this format that the use of certain evidence in the mini-trial hearing would not render it inadmissible, if it is otherwise admissible, in any subsequent litigation or arbitration.

Mediation

This method is primarily directed to reaching a rapid financial settlement, rather than focusing on technical solutions. In contrast with arbitration and litigation (which are essentially judgmental and conducted in an adversarial manner) mediation attempts to move the parties toward settlement by the use of an intermediary, usually from the construction industry. Typically the mediator will carry on "shuttle diplomacy" or a series of *ex parte* meeting with the parties, a procedure unthinkable in arbitration. The intermediary might be either an engineer or a lawyer, or even dual qualified, working over the parties in tandem or sequentially, and coaxing or bludgeoning them into settlement.[22]

Partnering

Mention may also be made of another new and sometimes equally imprecise term: partnering. Partnering (nothing to do with 'partnership') is often discussed in the context of dispute resolution, but is actually directed to dispute prevention.[23] Partnering is linked with ADR, in the sense that it is a concept which seeks to avoid litigation; the partnering effort could be combined with a relatively amicable form of ADR such as a dispute review board or a mediation process. A basic tenet of partnering is the establishment of a teamwork relationship and open communications at the outset of a project,

---

[22] See Molineux, "Mediating the Multi-Party Mélange,"*DART Newsletter* (Construction Industry Dispute Avoidance and Resolution Task Force), Washington, D.C., Fall 1 995

[23] See Edelman, "Partnering: The Foundation for Performance"1994 (Attachment to FIDIC *Dispute Resolution Task Committee Report);* Johnson, "'Partnering' in Government Contracts: The Ultimate in Dispute Resolution?" *World Arbitration and Mediation Report* (WAMR) 1 WAMR 141 (1990); Molineaux, "Is 'Partnering' an ADR Reality or Merely Cozy Atmosphere?," 2 WAMR 138 (1991).

usually between owner and contractor. This often takes the form of a 'retreat' or casual discussion between the parties and 'on-the-job' representatives about the project and the parties' goals. The personnel of the contractor may need to learn that the specifications are to be adhered to, even if they think they are unnecessarily and brutally excessive in light of vast past experience; and on the other hand the personnel of the owner, particularly the public owner, may need to learn that 'profit' is not an obscene concept. The teamwork understandings and trust reached during this retreat, sometimes aided by an enthusiastic 'facilitator', are frequently written into a partnering 'charter'. The use of the word charter is intentional, that is to say that the partnership does not arise from contract or within an agreement and does not affect the parties' contract obligations. In short, partnering does not relax contract terms or increase specification tolerances. Partnering can encourage the parties to be mutually helpful, within the contract.

There are, nevertheless, potential pitfalls implicit to partnering. It cannot be assumed that partnering will make easy the obstacles of a tough project. Nor can it be assumed, as is often suggested, that the atmosphere encouraged by parnering will inevitably lead to a better quality project. What needs to be considered is that the partnering concept, which comes from the private sector, will always be somewhat less effective in public work when public moneys are involved, and regulations and accountability demands are more strict.

Construction Arbitration

The American Arbitration Arbitration (AAA) has been and still is the dominant force in private industry in the US in promoting and administering the arbitration process. Construction arbitration is also under heavy fire in the United States; construction executives are impatient with the delay in a process advertised as faster than litigation, irritated by the costs, dubious as to the quality of the arbitrators and, at the end of the process, frustrated when receiving an award without reasons being stated. The AAA Rules do not now provide for reasoned awards and, unless jointly requested, are not normally prepared in the US, except in maritime and labour cases. Responding to the challenges of these criticisms, and also in response to the growth of some competitor organisations, such as ENDISPUTE and JAMS[24], the AAA established a task force in June 1994 to effect improvement.

Changing the rules

Specific changes have been recommended by that task force starting with distinct treatment for different sizes of cases in construction, that is; 'fast track' for cases involving claims of less than $50,000, 'standard track' for cases involving claims between $50,000 and $1 million, and a 'large, complex case' track for use in those cases where claims of $1 million are exceeded. The Task Force recommends sweeping changes in the AAA's arbitration rules and procedures, aimed at radically speeding up the process and giving more authority to arbitrators. The recommended changes break out into three distinct areas:

a) Fast Track

The Task Force recommends that the AAA establish a fast track arbitration system including:

- a 60-day 'time standard' for case completion;
- a upper limit on time required to hear a case;
- the hearing to be concluded within thirty days of the arbitrator's appointment;
- a single day of hearing in most cases;
- establishment of a special pool of arbitrators who are pre-qualified to serve on an expedited basis;
- an expedited arbitrator appointment process, with party input;
- a mandatory 'preliminary telephone conference' with the arbitrator;
- no discovery, "except in extraordinary cases where the demands of justice require it";
- a presumption that cases involving less than $10,000 will be heard on documents only;
- an award in no more than 7 days after the hearing; and
- compensation for arbitrator service, at a standard rate to be established by the local regional construction advisory committee.

---

[24] The acronym for Judicial Arbitration and Mediation Scheme

b) Standard Track

The Task Force recommends a broad array of changes to the standard track, including:
- more party input into the AAA's preparation of lists of proposed arbitrators;
- free amendment of claims and counterclaims;
- express arbitrator authority to control the discovery process;
- an authority for the arbitrator to deny postponement requests if not for good cause;
- broad arbitrator authority to control the hearing, including express power to entertain dispositive motions (i.e., motions that can dispose of all or part of a case);
- greater arbitrator authority to limit cumulative or irrelevant evidence;
- simplification of post-award briefing process;
- written opinions upon the timely request of a party;
- arbitrator authority to correct technical errors in the award;
- arbitrator compensation starting with the first day of service—with AAA to provide the arbitrator's compensation policy with the biographical information sent to the parties; and
- a revised demand form and a new answer form, both of which seek more information from the parties to assist the AAA in better serving the parties.

c) Large Complex Case Track

The Task Force recommends the adoption of the Supplementary Procedures for Large, Complex Commercial Disputes. Key features of this system embody:
- mandatory use of the procedures in cases involving claims of more than $1 million;
- early administrative conference with the AAA and an elite panel, compensated at their customary rate;
- three arbitrators, at least one of which shall be an attorney with knowledge and experience in construction matters;
- a mandatory preliminary hearing with the arbitrators, which may be conducted by teleconference;

- broad arbitrator authority to order and control discovery, including depositions;
- a presumption that hearings will proceed on a consecutive or block basis; and
- arbitrator authority to direct the recording of hearings.

Discovery

Discovery is a perennial bugbear for arbitration. This is particularly so with construction arbitration, whether a claim in a particular case is by a contractor against an owner or by a subcontractor against the general (or prime) contractor. One of the criticisms of arbitration which is lately often heard is that it is becoming "like litigation". Discovery in litigation is regarded as a device to obtain facts and documents and other information necessary to a party's case and to prevent surprise or prejudice. In theory, for construction disputes, the adversarial system and the confrontational approach of cross-examination would seem to be of less importance than in other kinds of disputes, construction projects generate plenty of records, even with all the projections as to the "paperless office," the use of e-mail, and so forth. In this respect, arbitration is still very different from litigation, although there are those who would say that arbitration, as discussed above, is so like litigation that it should not be included within the term ADR. Somehow, a key feature of arbitration, which is speed, is inconsistent with discovery of construction records. Thus we often speak of discovery with an automatic verbal coupling: 'protracted discovery'.

Generally in the US the overloaded courts, formerly jealous of arbitration, are happy to support arbitration and will defer to the arbitrator or tribunal to manage a fair and effective information exchange. The courts vary somewhat in their attitude toward arbitration, because, for a starter, the state laws which touch on arbitration differ widely across the fifty jurisdictions. The courts recognise the principle *pacta sunt servanda* and as there is widespread reference in the standard forms[25] to the Rules of the American Arbitration Association, arbitration impinges on a high percentage of

---

[25] See for example those published by the American Institute of Architects and the Associated General Contractors of America.

disputes arising from commercial contracts. The AAA Construction Industry Rules, referred to by those documents, provide, at Section 31, as follows:

> " 31. *Evidence - The parties may offer such evidence as is pertinent and material to the controversy and shall produce such additional evidence as the arbitrator may deem necessary to an understanding and determination of the controversy. An arbitrator* **authorized by law** *to subpoena witnesses or documents may do so upon the request of any party, or independently ....*" (Emphasis added.)

One will note that the Rules written for national use are thus cautiously aware of the differences in state law and sufficiently generalised to accommodate the particular situation without attempting to give a right to discovery. In other words, all that the rule does is to allow the arbitrator to subpoena witnesses and documents if the local law already allows it. What happens in practice is rather different. Exceptionally, there may have been an extended arbitration clause which provided for discovery, but what happens in practice is that counsel voluntarily co-operate and agree on a reasonable exchange of document. There is, of course, the additional incentive of not wanting to appear recalcitrant or evasive before the arbitrator. Section 10 of the AAA Construction Rules provides:

10. Administrative Conference, Preliminary Hearing, and Mediation Conference

"At the request of any party or at the discretion of the AAA, an administrative conference with the AAA and the parties and/or their representatives will be scheduled in appropriate cases to expedite the arbitration proceedings. There is no administrative fee for this service.

In large or complex cases, at the request of any party or at the discretion of the arbitrator or the AAA, a preliminary hearing with the parties and/or their representatives and the arbitrator may be scheduled by the arbitrator to specify the issues to be resolved, to stipulate to uncontested facts, and to consider any other matters that will expedite the arbitration proceedings.

Consistent with the expedited nature of arbitration, the arbitrator may, at the preliminary hearing, establish (i) the extent of and schedule for the production of relevant documents and other information, (ii) the identification of any witnesses to be called, and (iii) a schedule for further hearings to resolve the dispute. There is no administrative fee for the first preliminary hearing...."

At that juncture, if the discovery question has been raised, counsel may have to make an assessment more psychological than legal: If the production of a key document is resisted, counsel perhaps wins the immediate battle but the risk is of antagonising the arbitrators by appearing less than candid, especially if it appears that a document, or a deposition for that matter, is important to unravelling the case. Many states in the US have enacted arbitration statutes which are modelled after an American Uniform Arbitration Act. That Act provides that arbitrators may issue subpoenas "for the production of books, records, and other evidence, and shall have the power to administer oaths." But this is generally for use at hearing, not in the pre-hearing context, and a showing of necessity is normally required.

Apart from state law, it should be noted that the Federal Arbitration Act[26] provides that arbitrators may issue subpoenas and that a court order may be obtained to enforce subpoenas issued. In the new AAA International Rules, which are close to the UNCITRAL Rules, there is provision for the arbitrators' discretion to include the authority to order document production. It has been suggested that in the international context a civil law lawyer-arbitrator is less likely than a common law arbitrator to make a direct order for the production of documents. Without making the discretionary aspect sound too controlling, it should also be appreciated that a common law lawyer with a litigation background, sitting as or on an arbitral tribunal, is considered more disposed to grant or urge discovery than either a non-lawyer arbitrator or a non-litigator lawyer arbitrator.

---

[26] 9 U.S.C. § 1 *et seq.*; and see the expansive work (5 volumes) of Macneil, I.R., Speidel, R.E. & Stipanowich, T.J. *Federal Arbitration Law: Agreements, Awards and Remedies under the Federal Arbitration Act*, Little, Brown and Company, Boston, 1995.

Conclusion

As has been examined above, there is a basic dissatisfaction with the process and procedure of dispute resolution in the United States. Presently there are other varieties of ADR being tried, sometimes tailored to fit a particular dispute in much the same way that the expertise of an arbitration panel might be selected to fit the nature of a claim, for example, in soils, scheduling, and in accounting. However, the terminology is imprecise; what one person regards to be a "mini-trial" another might very well call a "neutral advisory panel hearing." This lead to confusion and can undermine the entirely valid attempts to expedite dispute settlement.

One initiative which warrants close scrutiny is termed 'Med-Arb'. This method contemplates that a mediator, familiar with both sides of a case, can convert his role into that of an arbitrator if the mediation fails to result in a settlement. The obvious object is to save time and money. It is difficult to see this approach working in practice for two reasons: the candour necessary for mediation to work would hardly be forthcoming if counsel suspect that the case may not settle; secondly, the mediator-*qua* arbitrator would have to 'blank out' everything contentious or admitted against interest that he had heard in the *ex parte* caucuses during the failed mediation.

It may, however, be purely coincidental that the AAA states in its rules that:

> "*With the consent of the parties, the AAA at any stage of the proceeding may arrange a mediation conference under the Construction Industry Mediation Rules, in order to facilitate settlement. The mediator shall not be an arbitrator appointed to the case.*"[27]

---

[27] Section 10

15. ADR and Lawyer Negotiations

Simon Roberts

Synopsis

This paper examines Lord Woolf's Interim Report *Access to Justice*[1] in the context of whether litigation is fundamentally suitable as a vehicle for settlement of disputes or represents the only method to achieve the end result.

Introduction

Over generations a particular culture of disputing has grown up in England, with parties resorting early, almost as a matter of course, to lawyers. So a single professional group has come to secure a virtual monopoly of control over dispute processes, managing them in accordance with their norms and understandings. At the same time, they have successfully projected a privileged association between their professional activities and the potent abstract conception of "justice". All this places formidable difficulties in the way of effective external criticism of "the public justice system", and makes it seem normal and right for a fundamental review of the system to be conducted from the inside, as has been the case with Lord Woolf's recent Interim Report .

Lawyers have generally approached disputes in a distinctive way, setting out on the path towards the court at an early stage, hence conceptualising all of this part of their work as "litigation". They have nonetheless aimed to "settle" disputes through bilateral exchanges with the other side ("lawyer negotiations"), typically a very long way along the avenue to trial, rather than allow them to go all the way to judgement. So a particular syndrome has developed under which "late" settlement is achieved by using the procedural framework prescribed for bringing a dispute to trial and judgment: litigation has come to be the chosen vehicle for settlement-directed negotiations. Thus in litigation two conceptually distinct goals have become entwined with each other, resolution through

---

1 *Access to Justice: Interim Report to the Lord Chancellor on the Civil Justice System in England and Wales*, June 1995.

settlement and resolution through authoritative third-party determination, sharing a common procedural route. One result of this entanglement, of course, is that there is no mystery over the present growing interest in settlement and the concurrent increasing load upon the courts.

The "duality" of litigation, this entrenched habit of approaching settlement by setting off towards the judge, has long been recognised, and been subject to extensive scholarly discussion, notably in North America.[2] But while aspects of this link have received critical examination, and the value of "settlement" itself placed in question, the notion that the path to adjudication is an appropriate arena for negotiation has not been seriously challenged. This position is maintained in Lord Woolf's Interim Report. While radical changes in the management of litigation are proposed, its fundamental suitability as a vehicle for achieving settlement is taken for granted. I argue here that the failure to criticise this use of civil procedure represents a central weakness of Lord Woolf's report.

The Woolf Report—Access to Justice

Lord Woolf's current commission takes place against a long history of uneasiness with the civil justice system. All over the common law world, civil justice arrangements had been under sustained critical examination for much of the period following the Second World War. A broad 'access to justice' movement had registered very general concern about the costs, delays and general inaccessibility of adjudication,[3] while a parallel discussion had critisised adjudication itself, pointing to the advantages of 'settlement'.[4] In the mid-1970's, a third discussion began to develop under the label of 'Alternative Dispute Resolution' and its universal acronym 'ADR'. This looked beyond the renovation of adjudication and arguments about the merit of settlement through lawyer negotiations to the possibilities of complementary and alternative forms. Under the

---

2   See particularly Galanter, M., *World of deals: using negotiation to teach legal process* (1984) 34 Journal of Legal Education 268; Galanter, M. & Cahill, M., *'Most Cases Settle': judicial promotion and regulation of settlements*, (1994) 46 Stan L R, 1339.

3   Cappelletti, M. & Garth, B. (Eds) *Access to Justice*, Vol.1 (1978).

4   Burger, W., *Agenda for 2000 AD: a need for systematic anticipation* (1976) 70 Federal Rules Decisions 83; Bok, D., *A flawed system of law and practice training* (1983) 33 Journal of Legal Education 530.

stimulus of these conversations, civil justice became subject to sporadic official scrutiny, culminating in the protracted Civil Justice Review, concluded in 1988.

The Civil Justice Review resulted in some limited but important procedural revisions.[5] But during the 1980s more general changes became noticeable. Any attempt to categorise these changes must involve over-simplification, but in the broadest terms three things seem to have been happening simultaneously in this jurisdiction. First, some new professional groups had begun to emerge, offering institutionalised support for party negotiations away from the surveillance of the legal profession. Second, in response to these developments, lawyers had initiated a counter-movement of recovery, becoming much more self-conscious about their negotiation procedures and re-modelling certain areas of litigation practice. Third, the courts were beginning to show increasing interest and involvement in preparations for trial, revealing a new determination to regulate the terms of access to the courts. Proponents of all these developments sought to co-opt the 'ADR' label.[6]

ADR Prior to Woolf

So three distinct developments, the embryonic growth of a new cadre of professionals in dispute resolution in competition with lawyers; the responsive adjustments undertaken by the legal profession; and the growth of novel threshold procedures in front of the courts, have become identified with "ADR". ADR is thus a fugitive label, claimed by diverse interests rather than a coherent set of institutions and practices. Nor is it something growing up primarily outside the legal sphere. While one strand of ADR can be seen as a precarious movement of escape and resistance, ADR is centrally something which lawyers do, its scope increasingly carefully marked out in practitioners texts.[7] In England, lawyers may at first have been cautious about, even uninterested, in ADR. But over the last five years they have moved rapidly to coopt it. The gracious but patronising tone of the Bar Council Report on

---

5   See Zuckerman, A.A.S., *A reform of civil procedure: rationing procedure rather than access to justice* (1995) 22 Journal of Law and Society 155.

6   Roberts, S., *Re-Exploring the Pathways to Decision-making* (1994) 12 Law in Context 9.

7   The arrival of ADR as part of the English lawyer's repertoire is underlined by Sweet & Maxwell's publication of texts on the subject in successive years: Bevan, A., *Alternative Dispute Resolution*, 1992; Brown, H. & Marriott, A.L., *ADR Principles and Practice* 1993.

Alternative Dispute Resolution, concluding 'that the case was made out for the courts themselves to embrace the systems of alternative dispute resolution'[8], perfectly captures the flavour of what has taken place.

The present, tentative steps towards the institutionalisation of 'mediation' and the emergence of a new professional grouping, the 'mediators', dependent as they are upon an apparently growing fashion for party negotiations remains precarious. This development is directly challenged by the counter-claim by lawyers that they are going to be mediators and that mediation is an established part of legal practice. If mediation is to develop in the context of established legal practice, it is hard to see it emerging as a narrow, facilitatory form of intervention, concentrated around the support of communications between the parties. It will emerge as an 'evaluative' intervention, and lawyers are already using this term, not readily distinguishable from counselling, advisory and consultative processes. Similarly, it will only be through the survival of the 'mediator' as an autonomous professional that distinctive practice standards and institutions of quality assurance will crystallise.

The emergent 'professionals in dispute resolution' are threatened from another quarter. In a number of jurisdictions, mediators are being drawn into the public justice system, notably in the context of family disputes. This is already the case in Australia, and in England is directly proposed in the Government White Paper on divorce reform.[9] The offer of 'partnership' poses a serious dilemma. Precarious independence is traded for economic security in any move closer to government and the courts. The potential consequences of such a move, in terms of co-option and regulation, are well documented.[10]

From the standpoint of the lawyer, the developments outlined above represent a dual threat to their previously unchallenged control of the conduct of dispute processes. This threat has prompted two principal reactions. First, the arrival of other professionals in dispute resolution and the entrenchment of new threshold procedures in the courts have converged, forcing lawyers to give much more attention to their practices in pursuit of settlement. The lawyer's control over client and settlement

---

8 Report of the Committee on Alternative Dispute Resolution (General Council of the Bar, October 1991).

9 *Looking to the Future*

10 Abel, R., *The Politics of Informal Justice*, 1982; Auerbach, J., *Justice Without Law*, 1983.

process is threatened at crucial moments, forcing reconsideration of the established habit of late-stage negotiations. One move to recover the situation lies in resort to the technical procedures of the mini-trial and early neutral evaluation, measures best understood as devices to head off consumer revolt by implicating the client in the settlement process and thus sharing control over it with him.

More generally this enforced concern with lawyer negotiations brings to the centre of attention a very important, hitherto largely uncharted area of legal practice. But while it would be going too far to say that both practitioners and academic lawyers have thought about negotiation only in the context of 'litigation', this is not far from the mark. The overriding presence of the court still informs the way in which lawyers write about negotiations. An immediately noticeable feature of this literature is its almost exclusive focus on 'strategic' issues; it is taken for granted that 'litigation' with its attendant procedures furnishes the overall processual framework. Even the most sophisticated work within this impoverished genre devotes marginal attention to larger questions about the nature and processual shape of negotiations.[11]

The second general reaction on the part of lawyers has been to present themselves in neutral advisory and consultancy roles and to attempt the co-option of 'mediation' as part of legal practice. The novel pretention to neutrality which these moves involve represents a step with far reaching and so far little considered consequences.[12]

Looking towards the court, the novel threshold procedures now in place and being advocated, represent an enormous shift when thought about in the context of existing understandings of what courts are and what they do. Reaching out as some of them do into the period before the trial, they considerably extend the involvement of the court in a domain hitherto occupied by the parties and their professional representatives alone. So far it is uncertain how we should characterise these changes. Perhaps at present it is possible to view them simply as the beginnings of a new, relatively discrete procedural phase interposed between lawyer-

---

11 See e.g. Fisher, R. & Ury, W., *Getting to Yes*, 1981; Goldberg, S., Sander, F. & Rogers, N., *Dispute Resolution*, 1992; Murray, J., Rau, A. & Sherman, E., *Processes of Dispute Resolution: The Role of Lawyers*, 1988; the Negotiation Journal, passim.

12 Roberts, S., *Alternative Dispute Resolution and Civil Justice: an unresolved relationship* (1993) 56 MLR 452.

negotiations and the trial, during which an institutionalised search for a settlement takes place. But the growing readiness among some members of the judiciary themselves to attempt 'mediation' takes these changes further than that, towards a fundamental transformation of the judicial role, as does the increased propensity of judges to assume a diagnostic function.

The Interim Report and its Background

The disposition of the courts to intervene in the litigation process prior to trial developed far earlier in the United States than it did in this jurisdiction.[13] But in England it has now assumed a rapidly increasing momentum. In some areas this intervention has come to extend far beyond facilitating the excavation and exchange of information and ensuring that the landscape does not change too much before a court can act. It has come to involve the active sponsorship of settlement and the postponement of adjudication while that objective is pursued. This new managerial approach became visible first in the Divorce County Courts, but is already recognisable across a much wider field. It is exemplified in the amendment of the Guide to Commercial Court Practice "to ensure that legal advisers in all cases consider with their clients and the other parties concerned the possibility of attempting to resolve the particular dispute or particular issues by mediation, conciliation or otherwise."[14] The present stance of the judiciary was confirmed in a general Practice Direction of 24 January, 1995, from the Lord Chief Justice and the Vice-Chancellor, setting out new requirements in the preparation and control of cases.[15] Announcing the Direction, the Lord Chief Justice said:

> *"The aim is to try and change the whole culture, the ethos, applying in the field of civil litigation. We have over the years been too ready to allow those who are litigating to dictate the pace at which cases proceed."*

Against this background, Lord Woolf has produced an Interim Report which shares Lord Taylor's perspective and ambitions, going on to make

---

13 The American history is discussed in Galanter, M., *The emergence of judge as mediator in civil cases* (1986) 69 **Judicature** 256.

14 Practice Statement of 10 December 1993.

15 [1995] 1 WLR 262.

a diagnosis of surprising bluntness. Contemporary problems are attributed to the 'unrestrained adversarial culture of the present system'.[16] Responsibility for this malaise, with its results in delay and excessive economic costs, is laid unequivocally at the door of the profession: 'The problem of cost is fuelled by the excessively combative environment in which so much litigation is now conducted'.[17] With regard to delay: 'Judicial experience is that it is for the advisers' convenience that many adjournments are agreed'.[18] Again: 'In the majority of cases the reasons for delay arise from failure to progress the case efficiently ... wasting time on procedural skirmishing to wear down an opponent'.[19] In the result, 'settlement too often occurs at too late a stage in the proceedings' .... involving 'the parties in substantial additional costs'.[20]

Overall, Lord Woolf sketches with astonishing candour a picture of lawyers abusing the litigation process by using it as an arena for settlement strategies which suit them, but involve unnecessary costs and delays for their clients. Having identified the central problem in 'the uncontrolled nature of the litigation process'[21] under which 'the conduct, pace and extent of litigation are left almost completely to the parties',[22] the Report proposes one way to retrieve the situation: 'a fundamental shift in the responsibility for the management of civil litigation from litigants and their legal advisers to the courts'.[23]

Case management is openly seen as having a dual objective:

> *"Its overall purpose is to encourage settlement of disputes at the earliest appropriate stage; and, where trial is unavoidable, to ensure that cases proceed as quickly as possible to a final hearing which is itself of strictly limited duration."*[24]

In the jargon of post-modernism, there is something of a 'paradox' here. The judge, the archetype of authoritative third-party decision-making, is to assume responsibility for active supervision of the procedural path

---

16 *Access to Justice, op cit,* § I.4.1
17 *Ibid,* § I.3.12
18 *Ibid,* § I.3.31
19 *Ibid,* § I.3.36
20 *Ibid,* § I.3.37;38
21 *Ibid,* § I.3.1
22 *Ibid,* § I.3.5
23 *Ibid,* § I.4.2
24 *Ibid,* § II.5.16

which, in the vast majority of cases, will lead to settlement—the antithesis of judgment.

This proposal represents an enormous change in the historic role of the English judge, who has traditionally remained a potent but immobile backdrop to the preparations for trial. Even though Lord Woolf might argue that in instituting case management across the board of civil litigation he is doing no more than accelerate and rationalise a movement already in train, this radical shift in responsibility perhaps requires more careful justification than it receives in the Interim Report. If the primary objective is promoting 'settlement of disputes at the earliest appropriate stage', do we want to encourage lawyer negotiations for which the court assumes responsibility, in the immediate run up to the trial? On another level, this new, wide-ranging involvement might adversely affect the court's primary role of authoritative third-party decision-making?

The central difficulty with the Interim Report is that the procedural implications of the dual objectives of case management (trying to sponsor early settlement and getting appropriate cases speedily in front of the judge) are not fully thought through. He does not propose the establishment of a new, relatively discrete, procedural phase in which court sponsorship of 'settlement' is in temporal terms the primary objective, to be followed by a clear run through to judgment if settlement attempts fail. Rather, we are offered a 'mixed' process in which both objectives are taken forward concurrently within a single procedural framework. While a lot of thought has been given to delineating 'fast-track' and 'multi-track' routes to trial and judgment, the framework envisaged for settlement seeking remains hazy.

This problem is linked to one very conservative feature of the Interim Report. While case management can be seen as a radical prescription, Lord Woolf has perhaps been unimaginative in going along with the assumption that litigation must be the shared vehicle for lawyer negotiations and adjudication. In endorsing the position of the Heilbron/Hodge Working Party,[25] Lord Woolf recognises that 'the philosophy of litigation should be primarily to encourage early settlement of disputes',[26] but at the same time in much of the language and assumptions of the Report clings to the idea that litigation is really about

---

25 *Civil Justice on Trial—The Case for Change* (1993).
26 *Access to Justice, op cit*, § I.2.7

getting in front of the judge. The Report shrinks from the more radical solution of trying to disentangle settlement attempts from resort to adjudication.

At this point another structural weakness of the Report is highlighted. Given the central place accorded to the achievement of settlement, and the open recognition that litigation is a vehicle for this, it is puzzling that very little is said directly about lawyer negotiations. If we are to persist, as Woolf evidently concedes, in allowing civil procedure to provide the framework for lawyer negotiations, we need to theorise these representative negotiations in a way which reveals their processual shape, enabling a procedural environment to be developed appropriately around them.

ADR in the Woolf Report

A polite but cautious chapter on "Alternative Approaches to Dispensing Justice" recognises that 'litigation is not the only means of achieving '...the fair, appropriate and effective resolution of civil disputes',[27] and that it may under some circumstances be beneficial for parties 'to choose a form of dispute resolution that will enable them to work out a mutually acceptable solution rather than submit to legally correct adjudication'.[28] But Lord Woolf does not 'propose that ADR should be compulsory either as an alternative or as a preliminary to litigation'[29] or consider the time right 'to introduce a new system of court-annexed ADR'.[30]

Instead, Woolf proposes that ADR should be brought into the frame in two ways, both building on the Practice Direction of 24 January 1995. First, responsibility for drawing ADR to the attention of disputants is laid upon lawyers in general terms: 'It is to be hoped that most lawyers will regard it as their responsibility to be able fully to acquaint their clients with the options ...'.[31] Second, the Report proposes that judges should, as a matter of routine, discuss the use of ADR with the parties, rather than their legal representatives, at case management conferences and pre-trial

---

27 *Ibid*, § IV.18.1
28 *Ibid*, § IV.18.2
29 *Ibid*, § IV.18.3
30 *Ibid*, § IV.18.30
31 *Ibid*, § IV.18.32

reviews.[32] The outcome of this discussion would assist the judge to plan the future procedural route of the case, enabling him to take into account 'any unreasonable refusal to attempt ADR ' in doing so.[33]

While these proposals sound sensible at first sight, it is surely unrealistic to place upon lawyers the burden of publicising those parts of ADR which lie outside the scope of legal practice. We are already seeing, in the family sphere, a growing reluctance on the part of solicitors to refer disputes to voluntary sector mediators. Who is really going to risk placing valuable work in the hands of a threatening competitor? If there is a real intent to loosen the primary hold of lawyers over disputing, the pressure to do this will have to come from outside the profession, as the recent Government White Paper on the reform of divorce recognises.

So far as general judicial sponsorship of ADR is concerned, the proposed 'case management' procedures offer the obvious occasion for this. Careful use of this tool could become a significant means of bringing about earlier settlement. Woolf's strategy of insisting upon the lay parties' presence at case management conferences and the pre-trial reviews[34] and then discussing ADR directly with them, in effect co-opts the support of the client against the professional adviser. Judging by earlier experience, for example, the use of Directions Appointments in the Divorce County Courts under s.8 of the Children Act to discuss settlement, lawyers will react to this threat to their control over the client by seeking to bring forward their own settlement attempts to a time before the case management conference, ensuring discussion of 'settlement' on their terms.

Lord Woolf's way of handling ADR, as a discrete topic discussed in a separate chapter, in itself prevents him thinking about it in the most productive way. As the Report makes clear, 'ADR' is a label covering a wide variety of different interventions, from processes of third party determination (tribunals and arbitration) to specialised client-management devices developed by lawyers (the 'mini-trial') to facilitate party negotiations (mediation). These interventions are potentially appropriate at very different moments in the life-cycle of disputes, and need to be related in different ways to the conventional path marked out

---

32 *Ibid*, § IV.18.33
33 *Ibid*, § IV,18.34
34 "The lay client, or someone fully authorised to act on his behalf, will be required to attend both hearings." (II.8.8.).

by civil procedure. They cannot sensibly be discussed all of a piece in the way Woolf attempts.

Take the treatment of mediation. The Report states hesitantly, but accurately, that mediation 'is perhaps best described as a form of facilitated negotiation where a neutral third party guides the parties to their own solution'.[35] Two roles are identified for mediation: the first as an early stage procedure, 'preventing disputes entering the court system at all' (and here disputes between neighbours are singled out as being particularly appropriate); the second, as a means of facilitating settlement without the need for a trial at some stage 'after proceedings have been commenced'.[36]

But all this is left very vague. While mediation has obvious applications in facilitating party negotiations, by providing a means of communication between parties at a stage before a dispute has passed into the sphere of professional management, it is not clear how it might be used beyond that. The implication is that mediation might have a role as a bridging intervention between two legal teams. If there is such a role, it needs to be delineated much more precisely.

The Report also remains vague as to whether mediation is seen as an autonomous professional intervention, or as a novel facet of legal and other professional practices. At one point the idea is floated that distinguished retired professionals, solicitors, surveyors, engineers and patent agents are specified, might mediate in their retirement as 'civil magistrates'.[37] This bizarre montage, suggesting the same ignorance of the specialist nature of mediation as revealed in the earlier Beldham Report, can hardly represent Lord Woolf's considered view and deserves to be reconsidered before the final report.

In the same way, the Interim Report offers enthusiastic support for 'mini-trials', which are 'presided over by a judicial figure or neutral adviser, and involve the abbreviated presentation of evidence by representatives of the parties who have authority to settle the dispute'.[38] But there is no serious effort to explore the nature of this institution, or the conditions under which it might appropriately be used. The device, otherwise known

---

35 *Access to Justice, op cit*, § IV.18.11
36 *Ibid*, § IV.18.24-25
37 *Ibid*, § IV.18.37
38 *Access to Justice, op cit*, § IV.18.9

as the 'modified settlement conference' or 'executive tribunal' and closely related to 'early neutral evaluation' (ENE)—is one of a family of procedures developed in North America in the handling of complex commercial disputes. These were first used at a pre-trial stage, but have subsequently been adapted by the judiciary as tools for sponsoring settlement.

The mini-trial is essentially a predictive, forecasting device, invoked for the purposes of client management where legal teams find it difficult to bring clients round to the idea of settlement. The procedure followed is for the teams to present their respective cases to the lay parties themselves, who are assisted in evaluating their positions by a 'neutral adviser'. In this way clients gain directly their own understanding of the strengths and weaknesses of their respective cases and are provided with an indication of the likely outcome of adjudication.

Lawyers who advocate and use these devices say that one of the greatest obstacles to settlement is the stressed, impassioned corporate executive who will not listen to sensible professional advice in cases where a negotiated outcome is in the client's best interests. They claim that these procedures are often successful in bring clients 'back to reality', making them agree to settle. It is hard to know what to make of these procedures, or of the justification for them offered by those who use them. They seem to imply a huge lack of confidence in traditional lawyering practises; and necessarily involve an unwelcome loss of control on the part of the lawyer. I have argued before[39] that these devices have their most immediate application as means of damping down unrealistic expectations which the legal teams may themselves have recklessly nourished, even created, at an earlier stage in the dispute process. They are the product of, and only made necessary in, a culture where the habit of late settlement, advantageous only to the profession, has left the client with insufficient information and advice in the early phases of a dispute. Arguably, their encouragement merely sustains existing habits which it is Lord Woolf's stated objective to get away from. More thought needs to be given to these procedures before they are endorsed in a final report.

---

39 Roberts, S., *Alternative Dispute Resolution and Civil Justice: an unresolved relationship* (1993) 56 MLR 452.

Conclusion

Woolf's recognition of, and concurrence in, a dual nature for litigation leaves the divergent objectives of settlement and judgment sadly entangled. His central project of judicial case management consequently implicates the courts in the management of negotiations as well as the achievement of adjudication. This is an inherently problematic approach which in the last resort leaves the very nature of 'the court' uncertain, as the early critics of 'informal justice' insisted. If fresh energy is to be directed towards early settlement (and that seems right) the path to judgment must be preserved uncluttered where that first objective fails.

An alternative platform for modernisation would be to prize settlement and the pursuit of adjudication apart, providing one pathway for settlement-directed negotiation, and another leading to trial and judgment. Obviously, these two paths may sometimes have to be travelled sequentially, where settlement fails. But once disentangled, the path to settlement can be properly constructed around the natural processual phases of negotiation, and the one towards the trial around the imperatives of judgment. Once that blueprint is secure, the signposts indicating complementary and alternative forms will fall into place along the route. None of this is to deny that where adjudication is available, bilateral negotiations and third party determinations are inevitably to some extent entwined. Parties will negotiate with their own perceptions of "what legal rules are" in mind, with an eye to what the judge might do in their case if they were subsequently to resort to adjudication. But it does not follow, as is presently the case in this culture, that negotiation must follow the route of civil process. Nor need there be active involvement of the court in sponsoring settlement. Careful thought should precede further institutionalisation of judicial case management with settlement as a primary objective.

Part IV

The Role of the Court

16. Making the Best Use of Courts

Richard Fernyhough

Synopsis

This paper examines how procedure can be deployed to promote litigation as a cost-effective, user-friendly and expedient method to resolve commercial disputes.

Introduction

It is widely accepted that any system of civil justice should ensure the speedy, economic and just disposal of disputes between citizens. But this laudable aim is generally not desired by at least one party to the dispute. In the commercial context, the resolution of the great majority of disputes will involve the passing of sums of money, often very significant sums, from one party to the other. The party who considers that he will ultimately be the paying party generally has no desire to see that evil day come too soon. It is thus the common experience of litigators that defendants to commercial disputes will often deploy every means, frequently with the encouragement of their lawyers, to put off the evil day as long as possible. Such delaying tactics, not only delay the proceedings considerably but also add to their cost. It is thus in the area of procedure that considerable injustice can arise. But such injustices cannot be cured unless the procedural rules which control the resolution of the dispute are capable of effective deployment and the Tribunal which operates those rules is prepared to do so effectively and forcefully. In this respect the situation obtaining in arbitration in England and Wales needs to be contrasted with the situation in litigation.

Procedural Controls in Arbitration and Litigation

It is often said that the arbitrator is "the master of his own procedure".[1] But what does this lofty phrase mean in reality? Firstly the procedural rules which the arbitrator must apply are those which the parties have agreed shall apply to that particular Arbitration. There are very many different sets of Arbitration Rules some more effective than others. Frequently the parties do not expressly agree any particular procedural rules. What then is the arbitrator to do? Before he can become master of his procedure he must know what that procedure is. If the parties do not agree on a procedure, what is he to do? Here the experience and personality of the arbitrator is critical. If he is a lawyer with lengthy High Court experience in litigation, he is very likely to turn to the Rules of the Supreme Court as a guide to the procedure which he will adopt. By contrast if the arbitrator is an engineer or an architect he is likely to turn for guidance to the Arbitration Rules promulgated by the ICE or the RIBA. But once he has decided which procedural rules to apply, is he really master of his own procedure? What if the parties agree on a certain procedure, for example an oral hearing lasting twelve weeks, when the arbitrator considers that the issues in dispute can satisfactorily be resolved partly by written submissions and partly by an oral hearing lasting three weeks? The answer to this question is far from certain. Some commentators take the view that if the arbitrator is truly master of his own procedure he must be able to decide how the hearing is to be conducted even against the wishes of both parties. The more traditional view favoured by other commentators is that, since Arbitration is fundamentally a consensual process, the arbitrator is bound by any procedure agreed between the parties. The new Arbitration Act comes down in favour of "party autonomy" on this issue. Section 34 provides as follows:

"34(1)   The parties are free to agree on all matters of procedure and evidence arising in connection with the arbitral proceedings.

(2) If or to the extent that there is no agreement, it shall be for the Tribunal to determine all procedural and evidential matters."

---

[1] See for example Lord Diplock in the *Bremer-Vulkan Schiffbau und Maschinenfabrik v South India Shipping Corporation Ltd* [1981] AC 909 and Goff J. in *Carlisle Place Investments Limited v. Wimpey Construction (UK) Limited* (1980) 15 BLR 109.

Again section 38 provides as follows:

> *"38(1) The parties are free to agree on the powers exercisable by the arbitral tribunal for the purposes of and in relation to the proceedings."*

The new Act which generally makes party autonomy its paramount criterion, if enacted, will make the arbitrator subservient to the agreement of the parties on all matters of procedure. He will certainly not be "master of his own procedure" under such a regime. Of course, even under the new Act, where the parties do not agree upon the procedure to be adopted, the arbitrator has full power and authority to impose his own will in all procedural matters.

The position of a judge sitting in Court is quite different. All judges of the High Court of Justice are subject to and must comply with the Rules of the Supreme Court enshrined in the Supreme Court Practice 1995 ("the White Book"). These procedural rules are highly detailed and give the judge absolute control over the proceedings in his Court. In particular and by contrast with the position of the arbitrator, he may make whatever procedural directions or orders he thinks fit, provided they comply with the Rules of the Supreme Court, regardless of the wishes of the parties. In other words the judge is not bound by any agreement which the parties make as to matters of procedure and may even refuse to make a "Consent Order" an Order of the Court. Thus it can truly be said that the judge is "master of his own procedure". But the critical question remains, namely "How will the judge exercise the wide powers given to him by the Rules of the Supreme Court?"

In recent years there has been a tendency for judges trying weighty cases, especially commercial litigation, to allow the cases to be run very much by the parties. Under the adversarial system which obtains in this jurisdiction, the judges have largely been content to allow the parties to run the procedural side of actions, only intervening where they were invited to do so. Thus judges have been "re-active" rather than "pro-active". But during this period it has been observed that the costs of commercial litigation have got completely out of control and the trials of such cases have got longer and longer.[2] Reacting to user disquiet at these developments both the legal profession and the judges have taken steps

---

[2] This is also the experience of non-commercial litigation.

to reverse this trend and to bring commercial litigation under much closer judicial control.

In January 1995 the Official Referee's Barristers Association and the Official Referee's Solicitors Association published a Joint Report on Official Referee's Practice and Procedure.[3] That Report made a number of detailed proposals as to how the resolution of construction disputes in Court could be made quicker and cheaper. The principal thrust of the Report was that the judges should exert greater and more direct control over actions from beginning to end. In particular it was suggested that the judges should exert their powers to limit the extent of the discovery of documents in cases and should control the length of the hearing by laying down and adhering to a timetable for every phase of the trial.

At about the same time, the Lord Chief Justice and the Vice Chancellor issued a Joint Practice Direction entitled *Civil Litigation: Case Management*.[4] This Practice Direction, if implemented in full by the judges, will revolutionise High Court litigation. It marks a complete break with the past and heralds in a new era of pro-active judges who manage the cases from start to finish and dictate to the parties how the case will be conducted. Paragraph 1 of the Practice Direction sets the scene as follows:

> "*1. The paramount importance of reducing the cost and delay of civil litigation makes it necessary for judges sitting at first instance to assert greater control over the preparation for and conduct of hearings than has hitherto been customary. Failure by practitioners to conduct cases economically will be visited by appropriate orders for costs, including wasted costs orders.*
>
> *2. The Court will accordingly exercise its discretion to limit (a) discovery; (b) the length of oral submissions; (c) the time allowed for the examination and cross examination of witnesses; (d) the issues on which it wishes to be addressed; (e) reading aloud from documents and authorities.*"

---

[3] The "Official Referees" are full High Court judges in all but name and have very wide experience in all manner of construction disputes. There are eight full time Official Referees sitting in London in St. Dunstans House, Fetter Lane, London. In the provinces there are many other Circuit judges who act as Official Referees when required

[4] [1995] 1 WLR 262

It remains to be seen how this important Practice Direction will operate in practice. But if the judges use the powers given to them to the full, there is no doubt that the whole face of civil litigation in this country will change. Equally there is little doubt that the result will be that disputes will be resolved more quickly and at a lesser cost than has hitherto been the case. Whether the quality of the decision will be impaired remains to be seen but even if this were so in certain cases it is considered that this is easily the lesser of two evils.

Court Procedure in Action

I will now turn to consider some of the powers which the judge trying construction disputes can exercise in order to reduce the complexity of the legal proceedings, speed up the process and arrive at a just decision at a reasonable cost. In this section I shall be describing the procedure operating in the Official Referee's Courts since, as I have said, that is where the great majority of the larger construction disputes, which are not arbitrated, are resolved. Some of the procedures which I shall describe are already in use: others, it is hoped, will be tried in the future.

Pleadings

It is generally agreed that, certainly in construction disputes, many pleadings are too long, and yet, paradoxically, not sufficiently informative. Voluminous Further and Better Particulars of uninformative pleadings can serve to obscure rather than reveal the real issues in dispute. By analogy with Order 72 of the Rules of the Supreme Court— which applies to the Commercial Court—it is suggested that judges should in particular ensure that:

- Pleadings only contain matters of fact; evidence should not be pleaded.
- Pleadings should be as brief as possible.
- Further and Better Particulars should only be required where absolutely essential.
- All parties should be required to plead their case positively; a mere denial or non-admission of the other party's case should no longer be regarded as an acceptable pleading. Even a Defendant should be required to state positively what his case is.

- At the close of the pleadings in any complex case, Counsel for the parties should be required to agree a Statement of the Issues remaining which arise from the pleadings. This statement will then become the "Agenda for the trial". Thereafter reference back to the main body of the pleadings should only infrequently be necessary.

Discovery of Documents

The Court should exercise its powers rigorously to limit the ambit of the discovery of documents. In construction disputes the present position is little short of scandalous. In many disputes literally tens of thousands of documents are discovered and copied many times which have no conceivable relevance to the issues in dispute. The waste of time, energy and money, to say nothing of the appalling toll taken on trees, is breathtaking. The parties do not seem to be able to control this process themselves. The Court has power to do so.

Preliminary Issues

Once the judge has become familiar with the issues in a particular case (usually only after the pleadings are closed) then consideration will be given to the identification of any issues which can usefully be extracted from the case and tried first. The Official Referees are particularly adept at identifying and isolating important issues which, once decided, might well allow the parties to resolve the remaining issues by agreement. Typical preliminary issues are: whether the action is statute barred; or whether a Final Certificate provides a complete defence to the action. Such issues can be ordered to be tried first even against the wishes of the parties. A particularly pro-active judge may even decide to try certain preliminary issues in a particular order or sequence before embarking upon the remainder of the trial. Experience shows that this course does not always save costs and sometimes it even increases them. But the judicious identification and trial of a preliminary issue is a very useful tool in the reduction of the length and costs of litigation in complex actions.

Bundles

To the non-cognoscenti the term "bundles" is a term of art which means the files of documents prepared for the trial. In a large, complicated construction case there may easily be one hundred files of such documents prepared for the trial. Each file may contain three or four hundred pages. If there are four parties to the dispute, each file will probably be copied at least fourteen times (two Counsel and one Solicitor for each party, the witnesses and the judge). Simple mathematics will tell you that the total number of documents copied for the trial will be something of the order of 500,000 pages. Yet during the course of the hearing experience shows that often only 5% or, at most, 15% of the documents in the trial bundles are ever referred to. But nothing is done about this appalling waste of resources. In future it is hoped that, where judges are confronted with this situation, they will enquire into who was responsible for insisting that so many documents found their way into the trial bundles. If the judge, after enquiry, is satisfied that there was no reasonable prospect that certain categories of documents would be needed at the trial, he should be prepared to make a Costs Order which will discourage this type of behaviour.

Written Submissions

In all but the shortest cases, written submissions, both in opening and in closing, will be required from all parties to the action. On this topic the 1995 Practice Direction provides as follows:

> *No.8 Not less than three clear days before the hearing of an action or application each party should lodge with the Court (with copies to other parties) a Skeleton Argument concisely summarising that partys' submissions in relation to each of the issues, and citing the main authorities relied upon which may be attached. Skeleton Arguments should be as brief as the nature of the issues allows, and should not without leave of the Court exceed twenty pages of double spaced A4 paper.*

> *No.9 The opening speech should be succinct. At its conclusion other parties may be invited briefly to amplify their Skeleton Argument. In a heavy case the Court may in conjunction with final speeches require written submissions, including the findings of fact which each party contends.*

Thus the current movement from oral to written advocacy continues and judges will increasingly expect that a party's submissions be reduced to writing. This is not the place to debate the merits of this development which, in any event, is probably inevitable and irreversible. Suffice to say that the additional burden which detailed written submissions place upon the Court is considerable and judges are going to have to spend far more time reading in their Chambers than hitherto. Thus judges who try commercial disputes will find themselves spending less time in open Court.

The Trial

In all but the shortest cases the judge will hold a Pre-Trial Review (PTR) well before the hearing date. In order to be effective the PTR should take place at least six weeks before the trial and longer if possible. At the PTR the judge will run through a checklist to ensure that the case will truly be ready for trial. Such a checklist will include any amendments to the pleadings, any outstanding interrogatories, disputes over the discovery of documents etc. But most importantly of all, at the PTR, after hearing submissions from Counsel for the parties who will actually conduct the action, the judge will lay down the timetable for the hearing. This will include details of which witnesses are to be called, in what order and how long their cross-examination is to last. In a recent case an Official Referee reduced the estimated length of the cross-examination of a key witness from many weeks to ten days, much to the surprise and outrage of the Counsel who was bent on an exhaustive "old-style" cross-examination. Every phase of the trial is capable of being time-tabled. The judge is quite entitled to direct that the hearing will be concluded in, say, 12 days even if both parties estimate that double that period will be required. At the hearing itself the judge will expect the timetable to be adhered to unless good cause can be shown to deviate from it. The unexpected is the norm in civil litigation and the judge will retain full discretion to modify or extend or even to curtail the timetable as circumstances require.

Conclusion

If parties to construction disputes wish to have them resolved by the Courts, then, as I have shown, the structures are in place to ensure that those disputes are determined quickly, economically and justly. Further the judges are likely to be astute to use their very considerable powers to achieve these ends. The profligate Plaintiff and his counter-part, the dilatory Defendant, will no longer be tolerated. Any unnecessary expenditure of costs is likely to be visited with an unpleasant Costs Order. By these means public justice should offer an attractive alternative to dispute resolution in the private sector. In particular and, by contrast with the philosophy behind the new Arbitration Act, the concept of "party autonomy" has no place in the modern conduct of commercial litigation. Commercial actions will now be "managed" by the judges and the wishes of the parties will, if necessary, be subordinated to the three-legged goal of speed, economy and justice.

17. The Role of the French court in International Arbitration Proceedings

Carole Malinvaud

Synopsis

This paper examines briefly the role of the French courts at the outset of international arbitration proceedings arising from construction disputes. Consideration is given to the role of the courts in the mustering of evidence as well as in granting interim or conservatory measures before the filing of the request for arbitration, and in the appointment of arbitrators.

Introduction

Arbitration is a fairly common procedure in France to resolve construction disputes either between contractors and clients or between main contractors and sub-contractors. The role of the French court is aimed at helping and co-operating with the Arbitral Tribunal,[1] its powers derive from either statute[2] or case law. The court aims to facilitate arbitration at the outset of proceedings, when one party commonly uses its best endeavours to delay the appointment of the tribunal, when a debtor tries to organise its insolvency, or when urgency requires that interim measures be ordered to protect factual evidence for use later in the proceedings.

Two points must, however, be stressed:

- as extensive as the powers granted to the French court may appear from an outside point of view, their goal is to ease the role of the tribunal and never to allow a domestic court to trespass on the jurisdiction of the tribunal; and

---

[1] The Arbitral Tribunal (hereafter tribunal) consists of two party-appointed arbitrators and a third arbitrator, who receives his appointment from the other two by agreement.

[2] Now incorporated in the Nouveau Code de Procédure Civile (NCPC), Articles 1492 to 1497.

- as their name suggests, provisional measures are provisional, therefore any provisional measure can be appealed to the court of Appeal, and the tribunal having jurisdiction over the merits of the case is not bound by any provisional measures ordered by a court when rendering its final award.

This paper focuses on the role of the court at the outset of arbitral proceedings. Issues relating to the enforcement of the award as well as the possible interim measures that may be taken after the filing of the Request for Arbitration are excluded from this study.

Appointment of Arbitrators

In order to facilitate the constitution of the arbitral tribunal, and with proper regard to the will of the parties, the President of the Tribunal de Grande Instance of Paris[3] may in certain circumstances appoint one or more arbitrators. The following rules will only apply if the place of arbitration is in France, and if the parties have not provided for the application of other specific rules of arbitration, such as the International Chamber of Commerce (ICC) rules, or if there is an express provision to the effect that French procedural law applies.

Conditions for an Application

The application to the President of the TGI of Paris is governed by Article 1493 of the NCPC, al. 2 which states as follows:

> "*Either directly or by reference to rules of arbitration, the arbitral agreement may designate the arbitrator or arbitrators or prescribe the method for their appointment.*
>
> *In arbitrations which take place in France or those for which the parties have provided for the application of French procedural law, if the constitution of the Arbitral Tribunal is impeded, the more diligent party may, in the absence of any clause to the*

---

[3] The Tribunal de Grande Instance (TGI) is the common law court of first instance, unless otherwise provided. The TGI in Paris is the only court with jurisdiction to hear cases arising from international commercial arbitrations. The President is therefore familiar with arbitration and the requirements of the parties.

contrary, make an application to the President of the Tribunal de Grande Instance of Paris in accordance with Article 1457."

In order to apply to the President of the TGI, it is necessary that the procedure for the appointment of the tribunal be blocked or impeded in some way. The applicant would need to show, for example, that the respondent party has refused to appoint its arbitrator, therefore bringing the arbitration procedure to a standstill, or that the two arbitrators appointed by each party have been unable to agree on the name of the third arbitrator, or that the appointment of an arbitrator should be objected to.

For the sake of efficiency, the procedural rules engender speed and simplicity. The application is made by either party serving notice on the other and filing the application with the court seized as an urgent matter. The relevant rules are found in article 1457 of the NCPC:

> *"In the cases mentioned in article 1444, 1454, 1456 and 1463, the President of the Tribunal seized as an urgent matter* (matière de référé) *by a party or by the Arbitral Tribunal shall issue a decision in the form of an order not subject to review* (recours).
>
> *However, this order may be appealed if the President declares that there was no occasion for such a designation on one of the grounds mentioned in article 1444 alinea 3; this appeal is brought, tried and judged as a jurisdictional objection* (contredit de compétence)."

As the purpose of this procedure is to allow the arbitration to continue, the judicial order is subject to this limit on review. However, in practice, the President of the TGI of Paris is mindful of the will of the parties when dealing with the appointment of arbitrators and pragmatic in finding a solution.

Practical Significance of the President's Powers

There is no indication whatsoever in the statutes as to the way in which the President should grant orders appointing arbitrators in international proceedings. Nevertheless since 1980, orders rendered have proved to be, on the one hand, very respectful of the will of the parties, and on the other hand, very aware of the fact that it is an urgent matter which must not be delayed as a tactic by either party.

In cases where the respondent's arbitrator is to be appointed, the President usually gives the party a time limit to appoint an arbitrator himself, in which case he will simply confirm the appointment made. Alternatively, he may, for example, ask the respondent to propose various names, and make his decision on the basis of the list. The consideration given to co-operation with the parties is particularly relevant in international construction matters as one party may well need to appoint an arbitrator with expertise in construction law and/or speaking various languages.

A further example is where the President is asked to appoint the third arbitrator. There is often an unofficial exchange of views between the parties, and the President before deciding on the name of the third arbitrator may allow the parties a period of time for them to try and reach an agreement as to the appointment of the third arbitrator. The court is aware of the range of delaying tactics frequently employed by parties. Accordingly, the periods granted by the President for the parties to reach an agreement on the name of an arbitrator, or in order for a party to appoint its own arbitrator are usually limited to a few days to two or three weeks.

The President is also aware of, and sympathetic to, circumstances affecting particular types of case. In construction, multi-party contracts giving rise to multi-party disputes are common, and, in such cases, it is often particularly difficult to reach an agreement on the names of the three arbitrators. The President can be of great assistance to the parties by making his appointment after an informal exchange of views with the parties and possibly after inviting the parties to propose names themselves. An advantage of the possibility of intervention by the President is that the reluctant party often decides that it could be better to go ahead and designate its own arbitrator rather than to suffer the consequences of the summary order of the court.

Interim or Conservatory Measures

There is no Statute regulating the power of the courts[4] to grant interim or conservatory measures; the power is derived mainly from case law. Consistent support is given to the principle that a request to the court for interim or conservatory measures does not constitute a waiver of the arbitration provision. This serves to support and reinforce the effectiveness of international arbitration while respecting the will of the parties.

The wide ranging nature of those measures could seemingly lead to interference by the judicial legal system in the arbitration proceedings, but intervention by the court is mostly justified by the urgency of the situation in any given case. The measures are not only conservatory, they are also temporary and therefore the tribunal, on hearing the merits of the case, retains full jurisdiction and is not bound by the order issued by the court. Unlike appointment of arbitrators, interim or conservatory measures are always susceptible to review by appellate courts.

Interim and conservatory measures are particularly useful in construction cases as they permit orders to preserve factual evidence, provide an interim payment pending the final award, or even to obtain the payment of a provisional sum ("référé provision"). These measures generally do not encroach upon the merits of the case. The only exception is the "référé-provision", and this is considered separately below.

Interim Measures

French courts have held consistently: that an application by a party to the court for investigative or conservatory measures does not constitute

---

[4]   Jurisdiction for interim and conservatory measures is enjoyed by either the President of the TGI or the President of the Commercial court (*Tribunal de Commerce*), depending on the nature of the measure requested.

a breach of the contractual agreement to arbitrate;[5] as a matter of fact, summary orders can be granted by a French court after the filing of the request for arbitration;[6] and parties can make provision to waive their right to seek a grant of conservatory measures.[7]

Measures for future investigations

When one party needs to protect factual evidence for use later on in the proceedings, for example where a technical expert will be required to report on the state of work already performed by the Contractor, the party can therefore apply to the French court pursuant to Article 145 of the NCPC which provides that:

> "*If there exists a legitimate reason to preserve or to establish, prior to any proceeding, proof of the fact upon which the resolution of a litigation may depend, legally admissible measures of proof-taking may be ordered upon demand of any interested person, on motion or in a summary proceeding* (sur requête ou en référé)".

The only conditions for a request for such a measure are that there is "legitimate reason" to preserve or to establish a fact, and that it takes place prior to any proceedings. In case of arbitration, this means that this measure can therefore only be ordered before the filing of the request for Arbitration. There is no requirement for urgency and usually the judicial proceedings take the form of summary *interpartes* proceedings even though in certain circumstances, such a measure can also be ordered on motion. This measure is very useful in construction cases, even though the tribunal is not bound by the expert's report and can later appoint another expert.

---

[5] Cass. Com. 3 juil 1951, Dalloz 1951, p. 701 ; Cass. Civ. 2e, 4 déc. 1953, Dalloz 1954, p. 108 ; Cass. Com. 4 nov. 1959, Gaz. Pal. 1960, 1, p. 191.

[6] Cass. Civ. 3e., 7 juin et 9 juil. 1979, Société d'Exploitation du Cinéma Rex c/ société Rex et SCI La Lagune et autres c/ SARL Sercif, Rev. Arb. 1980, p. 78.

[7] Cour Cass. 1ère 18 nov. 1986, société Atlantic Triton / République Populaire Révolutionnaire de Guinée, Droit Pratique du Commerce International 1988, p. 275 ; Cass. Civ. 2e , 20 mars 1989, société F.T.Danel c/ Sotiaf Informatique, Rev. Arb. 1989, p. 494, Note Couchez.

Conservatory measures

Such measures are particularly helpful in order to preserve a state of fact and prevent imminent damage. For example, the court can grant a conservatory seizure of assets, or an attachment or a deposit in an escrow account, when there is a risk that the debtor might become insolvent before the end of the arbitration procedure. There is no encroachment on the merits of the case, and, therefore, no encroachment on the jurisdiction of the tribunal, as the requirement to obtain a conservatory measure is that the claim is justified in principle without any investigation into the merits of the case.

Conservatory measures are granted by summary *interpartes* proceedings pursuant to Article 808 and 809 of the NCPC which states as follows:

Article 808

"In all cases of urgency, the President of the Tribunal de Grande Instance may order summarily any measures which will not prejudice any serious adversary proceeding (contestation sérieuse) *or which is required by the existence of a dispute."*

Article 809 al 1

"The President may always, even in the case of a serious dispute, summarily prescribe measures of a conservatory nature or of restoration which are required either to prevent imminent damage or to terminate a manifestly unlawful disturbance."

The temporary nature of such a decision allows the tribunal, which subsequently hears the case, to have full jurisdiction and freedom to rule upon the merits. A comfortable balance now exists between the power of the tribunal and the intervention of the court to grant necessary provisional and conservatory measures.[8]

---

[8] Cour Cass. 1ère., 28 juin 1989, *Eurodif* c/ *République islamique d'Iran*, Rev Arb 1989 p.653, note Ph. Fouchard.

The Institution of 'Référé Provision'

This is a specific procedure under French law which allows the creditor to obtain a summary order from the French court granting him an interim payment which may even amount to the entire claim. This order may be granted if there is no defence to the claim. In principle, there is no requirement for urgency as the debt is indisputable. However, in international arbitration the applicant must demonstrate urgency in the matter,[9] and that there is no real defence to the claim.

As an example of the operation of "référé-provision", I cite the Channel Tunnel case.[10] Prior to filing of the arbitration, TML requested the Commercial Court to grant a order for an interim payment of approximately £60,000,000. Within a couple of days the President held that as the claim was not seriously challenged, and that the sum was due, an order would be made accordingly. Thus, even though there was a legitimate arbitration clause, the court held that there was no legitimate reason for the claim for non-payment and, as the arbitration had not yet been filed, was able to order payment, which was enforced immediately.

Article 809 al. 2 of the NCPC provides that :

> *"Where the obligation is not seriously in dispute, he* (the President) *may grant an advance to the creditor or order performance of the obligation even if it is an obligation to do* (obligation de faire)."

Such an order can be granted even though the parties have provided for an arbitration clause in their contract, mainly because it is only a provisional measure and therefore the tribunal is not bound by the court's decision.[11]

---

9   Urgency is not normally required for Article 809 al. 2 of the NCPC but has been introduced in the case of international arbitrations: Cour Cass. 6 mars 1990, *Horeva c/ Citas*, Rev. Arb. 1990, p. 633 ; Cour d'Appel de Paris, 30 juin 1992, Euralair, Rev. Arb. 1992, p. 666 ; Cour d'Appel de Versailles, 22 mai 1992, Dunes, Rev. Arb. 1992, p. 666.

10 Unpublished, Tri. com, Nanterre 16 février 1990.

11 Cour Cass. 1ère. 20 mars 1989. *Société The Authority for Supply Commodities Cairo-Estram c/ Société Ipitiade International*, Rev Arb 1989, p. 494, note N.Couchez.

This position has been criticised to some extent, because in order to verify that the obligation is *"not seriously in dispute"* the court has to pay heed to the merits of the case, and therefore one could argue that the court is encroaching on the jurisdiction of the tribunal. Nevertheless, reported cases show that the intervention of the court has a generally beneficial impact,[12] and is very effective in accelerating the resolution of disputes where the claim is not seriously challenged, bearing in mind that requirements for obtaining such an order are strictly defined.

As a fail-safe device, such a "référé-provision" order can only be granted if the entire tribunal has not yet been appointed; the filing of the request for arbitration does not of itself prevent an application. However, once the tribunal is appointed, it has sole jurisdiction to make such an order, as an interim award.

The measure of "référé provision" might at first sight appear dangerous and speculative. In fact it is a very useful tool when the claim is not seriously challenged, because the creditor can obtain an order within two or three weeks and enforce it immediately. This order is subject to review, does not bind the tribunal, and is strictly limited within specific requirements. As such, it is considered to be very useful, provided it does not constitute a trespass on the tribunal's jurisdiction on the merits of the case.

Conclusion

Following the new arbitration regulations in 1981, the French courts have developed a balance between the aid and co-operation they may provide, and the necessary fundamental respect of the exclusive jurisdiction of the tribunal over the merits. On the one hand, the court is capable of assisting the parties and the arbitral tribunal in a number of ways when needed throughout the proceedings. On the other hand once the arbitral award has been rendered, the Court of Appeal (*"Cour d'Appel"*) exercises only very limited control over the validity and the enforcement of the award. The requirements for *"exequatur"*

---

[12] Cour d'Appel, Paris 30 janvier 1992, *Société Air Charter* c/ *Euralair et autres*, Rev Arb 1992, p.666, note J.H.Moitry.

(registration of the award) are very easy to satisfy, and the circumstances in which an international award may be challenged is restricted only to five hypotheses such as the absence of arbitration provision or if the enforcement of the award is contrary to international public order. [13]

---

[13] NCPC Article 1502

18. Civil Law-style Procedure: A Comparative Outlook

Claude Reymond

Synopsis

This paper examines and compares the essential differences between arbitral tribunals conducted according to civil and common law procedure.

Introduction

By contrast with Common Law procedure, there is no uniform procedure in Civil law countries. There is as much difference in the procedure practised, say, in the Spanish Courts and in the German Courts than between the practice of a French avocat and that of an English barrister. By contrast with England (until recently), arbitrators sitting in Civil law countries are not bound to adopt more or less strictly the pattern of procedure practised in the State Courts. Indeed the trend in the recent arbitration statutes (Belgium, 1972; France, 1981; Netherlands, 1985; Switzerland, 1987; Italy, 1992; etc.) has been to give to the parties and to the arbitrators complete freedom in the organisation of the arbitral procedure, subject only to the basic requirements of natural justice.

Thus, when participating in and organising arbitrations, Civil lawyers do not feel bound to follow the rules of procedure practised in the Courts. But it is clear that they tend to organise the arbitration by following the general pattern of litigation in their Courts, that they tend to consider as reflecting universally accepted principles.

Some essential features of Civil law procedure

Perhaps one should insist, in a comparative perspective, on underlining the two major differences between our systems:
* Writing v. orality; and
* Control of the proceedings by the arbitrator v. waiting for the trial.

There are many historical reasons for these differences. The major one, from a comparative point of view, is that in civil jurisdictions there was never a jury. Indeed, the jury system was borrowed from England for criminal matters only, and it is now disappearing.

Importance of writing

At the beginning of the arbitration, the parties are expected to present their entire case in detailed memorials, both on the facts and on the law, and to communicate forthwith their written evidence (documents, experts' reports, etc.) and the legal authorities on which they rely. The purpose of this initial phase of the arbitration is to identify the issues, so as to concentrate the evidence and the arguments on those that remain in dispute. This implies a great amount of preparation from the lawyers and from the arbitrators since the initial stage of the arbitration.

Control of the proceedings by the arbitrator

At this stage, the participation of the arbitrator consists mostly in the administrative direction of the proceedings:

- establishment of a calendar, settling difficulties on production of evidence plus, if required by either side, interlocutory matters:
  - interim injunctions,
  - appointment of an expert,
  - security for costs, etc.

From the beginning of the arbitration, the arbitrator is very much in command of the proceedings. But, contrary to a widespread belief in Common law countries, he does not interfere with the substance of the parties' presentations, which remain their responsibility. They have both the burden of allegation (of going forward) and the burden of proof.

Conferences

In many Civil law systems, there is a system of conferences between the judge in charge of the proceedings (by contrast with the Court which will decide the case, ordinarily a panel of three to five judges) and counsel. The purpose of these conferences is to settle procedural difficulties, to organise evidentiary orders, such as evidence by witnesses, appointment of experts, interim measures, etc., and to determine the issues of fact to be decided by the Court. This method is increasingly adopted in international arbitration, at various stages.

The evidentiary stage of the proceedings

Turning now to the evidentiary stage of the proceedings, the first basic difference with Common law practice is that the arbitrator already knows the story, through its study of the parties' detailed memorials and of the documentary evidence. There is therefore no need for opening speeches, nor for reading aloud documents. Second, the production and discussion of evidence is made in stages, through successive hearings; there is no trial. Third, the evidentiary stage does not retell the whole story ; it is limited to the disputed issues on which the arbitrator receives the evidence of witnesses, discusses the opinion of the expert(s), whose written reports have been submitted long before, and hears Counsel's last oral submissions.

The same applies to the discussion of the issues of law. If he does his homework correctly, the judge in charge is already familiar with the main contention of the parties, and with the authorities (cases, opinions of legal writers) on which they rely. There is no need, therefore, to read them aloud in Court. This method is usually followed in arbitrations Civil law style.

I owe an illuminating comparison to two lawyers who practice in Geneva, Louis Gaillard and Ian Meakin: civil proceedings unfold like a film with several intervals ; at the end of the last episode, the film is finished, and the arbitrator considers the whole for his award. Common law procedure is the (lengthy) preparation and performance of a theatre production which tells the whole story.

The award

Civilian arbitrators are under a duty to issue a reasoned award, both on facts and on law, which tends to be a rather lengthy and complete document.

Inquisitorial v. Accusatorial procedure ?

One common misconception on your side of the Channel is that Civil law style procedure is inquisitorial.

In Civil law countries, inquisitorial procedure applies possibly in criminal matters. As you have already noticed, there is very little room for inquisition by the civilian arbitrator. His overall control of the proceedings is more of a managerial nature. On merits, the arbitrator's duty is to assess the evidence offered by the parties in support of their case. He may possibly express the wish to see a document referred to in another document before him (e.g. the Main Contract in a dispute on a Sub-Contract, the letter to which a document on file purported to answer) or to hear as a witness an individual who appears from the evidence to have played a key role. But he does not go very much further. I suspect English arbitrators do the same.

The arbitrator's inquisitorial role is perhaps more evident with regard to <u>experts</u>. In the civilian tradition, the expert is appointed by the arbitrator, who establishes his terms of reference. Thus the expert <u>advises</u> the arbitrator. At this point, one should underline the difference in the <u>profile of the arbitrator</u>. In Civil law countries he is nearly always a lawyer (an *avocat*, a Judge or a law lecturer). Hence the necessity to resort to experts in all technical matters. This is possibly one of the weaknesses of the system, as was underlined by Lord Mustill a few years ago.

The civilian tradition is also of a <u>tribunal of three</u>, rather than of a single arbitrator.

The problem of the production of documents

The concept of <u>discovery</u> (within the meaning of English or American Court procedure) is alien to the Civil law tradition. Indeed, it is frowned upon by civilian lawyers as a typical example of inquisitorial procedure in the worst sense of the word.

Apart from its historical origin (discovery is a product of Equity, and Civil law countries ignore the Law/Equity dichotomy), this attitude is

the effect of the strict adherence to the principle of burden of proof—
Onus probandi incumbat alleganti.

The maximum that a Civil law Court or arbitrator may (or will accept
to) do is to order the production, at the request of one party, of
specifically identified documents held by the other, to the extent he
considers them necessary for the clarification of a particular issue. In
certain systems, the Court does not even have such power ; it may
simply infer from the refusal of the party to produce a document that
this document contains evidence detrimental to its case. In any event,
there is no possibility of launching a fishing expedition in the files of
the other side.

In view of its limited extent with regard to the production of evidence, I
do not think the "inquisitorial" power of the civilian arbitrator corrects
the gap (if any) created by the absence of the duty of discovery. But as
to whether discovery really has a place in arbitration, civilian lawyers
note with interest that the power of the English Courts to order
discovery in arbitration was abolished in 1990, and that there was no
question of restoring it in the new Arbitration Act.

The role of the Courts

My generation has witnessed, on the Continent as in England, a
fundamental change in the attitude of the Courts vis-à-vis arbitration.
From a traditionally reserved and often critical attitude against what
they resented as a wish to oust their jurisdiction, the Courts have
moved to a definitively supportive, sometimes enthusiastic position.
This has been particularly significant with the French Courts, who
have, in a series of landmark judgments, actually modified or at least
limited the effect of statutory provisions in the field of international
arbitration. Law reform by case law is not reserved to Common law
countries.

In the Continental countries which are usually preferred as venues for
international arbitration (France, the Netherlands, Belgium,
Switzerland, to name four of them), the arbitration community and the
Courts were able to convince Parliament to reflect this change in the
arbitration statutes. Thus the legislations enacted in the eighties are
marked by two fundamental options:

- first, the Courts are here to support arbitration since the beginning of the proceedings : appointment and replacement of arbitrators, enforcement of injunctions, etc.; and
- secondly, review of arbitral awards is only possible for major violations of natural justice in the proceedings, and, on merits, on awards that contradict public policy, as distinct from a mere error of law, which remains the position in English law under section 69 of the Arbitration Act 1996.

There are traditionally less instances of Court assistance in Civil law countries than in English arbitration law, as exemplified by the list at section 12 of the Arbitration Act, 1950. In the Civil law legislations, the major instances of the supporting role of the Courts concern the appointment, replacement (or destitution) of arbitrators. Indeed French Courts (in fact the President of the Tribunal of First Instance of Paris, whose role is similar to that of the Commercial Court in London) refrain from taking any decision beyond these matters. In other countries, recent enactments have granted to the Courts additional supporting powers in such fields as confirmation of injunctions or subpoenaing of witnesses.

By contrast, Civil law systems never knew anything like to power of the English Courts to decide issues of law in the course of an arbitration, be it in the ancient form of the special case or in the present form of the determination of a preliminary point of law (as taken over at section 43 of the Draft Arbitration Bill). Thus, if there is very little if no interference of the Courts, their supporting powers are definitely less developed in Civil law countries than in England. Indeed, it is for us one of the characteristics of English arbitration law that there is a sort of continuous exchange between arbitrators and the Courts.

The power of the arbitrator and its limits

It would be wrong to think that the Continental arbitrator is some sort of *despote éclairé* of the Enlightenment.

His authority is first limited by the agreement of the parties, which remains overriding, were it only for article V(1)(d) of the New York Convention. The parties are free to adopt any set of procedural rules, ad hoc or pre-existing (UNCITRAL Rules are becoming increasingly popular, and quite rightly so). They may choose a purely Common law procedure, as I have experienced over the last five years in an arbitration conducted on both sides by American lawyers.

On the question of parties' autonomy, I would like to underline here that one of the major problems of contemporary arbitration is to find an acceptable equilibrium between the autonomy of the parties and the power of the arbitrator to conduct the arbitration. In this connection, I would like to mention two questions. The first concerns the agreement of the parties on procedure: What constitutes such an agreement? If it is contained in the original arbitration clause or in *ad hoc* submission, the situation is clear. But what about later understandings on individual issues of procedure, such as joint applications of the parties? In my view they are not more than common proposals; therefore they do not bind the arbitrator.

From the point of view of the arbitrator, it is important that if there is an agreement on procedure, it should be communicated no later than at the time of his designation and acceptance. Otherwise, he could be caught in an arbitration he would not have accepted or for which he would not be equipped.

The second question is even more delicate: are there limits to the autonomy of the parties as to procedure? Is the arbitrator bound to accept and follow any agreement, even if it is detrimental to a proper conduct of the arbitration?

Twenty years ago, most Courts considered that arbitration had to follow the pattern of procedure practised before them, and this is reflected at article V(1)(d) of the New York Convention. In certain countries, arbitration statutes contained a chapter on procedure; this is still the case with the Model Law. The efforts of the arbitration community over the last twenty years have now obtained that most modern statutes provide that the parties, and failing them, the arbitrator, enjoy full autonomy in the shaping and conduct of the procedure. Is there a limit to this autonomy? I tend to think that is the case. The nature of arbitration as a decisional process requires that the arbitrator should be empowered to conduct the proceedings to their end with acceptable speed and reasonable efficiency; if I may borrow a concept, an *inherent power*, to conduct the proceedings, derived from the scope of the arbitration agreement and from his character as a decision maker. I accept that it is a bold proposition, but I think it deserves discussion.

The second limitation of the arbitrator's authority was best expressed by Giorgio Bernini, ICCA's previous president, when he said: *'The arbitrator holds the scale of Justice, but not its sword.'* The Civil law arbitrator is not very well equipped against the delays and failures of the parties. What can he do if a party submits a memorial after the expiration of the time limit for so doing or when a party produces a memorial or a set of documents without authorisation, on the eve of a major hearing? If he accepts them, the other side will complain of inequality of treatment. If he rejects them, the party will complain of an excessive procedural outlook. The English system, which allows the arbitrator to seek for a Court order (as reflected at section 42 of the Arbitration Act 1996), is probably better. Further thinking on the inherent powers of the arbitrator may help to solve these difficulties.

Concluding remarks

The participation of lawyers of different backgrounds in international arbitration has certainly enriched and enlarged their intellectual horizon. Civil law has benefited from and indeed borrowed certain Common law features, such as the submission of affidavits by witnesses in advance of their hearing, which is now regularly practised in Civil law arbitration. The common law may possibly have borrowed some of the features of civilian systems. Obvious examples may be found in recent changes in the procedure before the Court of Appeal, such as skeleton arguments or reconciliation of experts' findings. I think there is no doubt that the present trend towards substantial changes in common law Court procedure is due, to some extent at least, to the experience gathered by English lawyers when engaged in arbitration with natives of Civil law countries. When I hear that Lord Woolf is enquiring on other systems of procedures, as Solon did when preparing the constitution of Athens, I feel that something has changed since the time of Lord Justice Scrutton. If I may say so, English lawyers have been in this more perceptive than their American colleagues, who still believe that international arbitration may be conducted as an ordinary case before a more or less 'illiterate' jury.

My second remark is an appeal to the imagination of the arbitration community in the shaping of its procedure. As noted earlier, most arbitration statutes give a wide freedom to the parties and to the arbitrators, now adopted in England by virtue of the Arbitration Act 1996. Indeed, there have been, over the last few years, major pronouncements from prominent members of the judiciary stating that it is already the case under English law as it stands. Arbitrators and Counsel (the latter being regularly criticised in each issue of the Journal of the Chartered Institute for insisting for Court procedure) are therefore free to borrow procedural devices from other legal traditions. But they can (and should) also be inventive, in developing procedural solutions shaped for the particularities of each individual case.

That is, in my view, the best method for keeping to international arbitration its present liberal character. I am worried by the present trend towards the establishment of uniform rules of procedure for international arbitration, such as the recent UNCITRAL Guidelines launched by Mr Howard Holtzman, or the proposal for the establishment of an International Arbitration Court, recently supported by Judge Stephen Schwebel. If this tendency were allowed to prevail, international arbitration would be no different from proceedings in Court, and we should have to develop something new to escape it.

Appendix

American Arbitration Association Construction Industry Arbitration Rules

Construction Industry Arbitration Rules of the American Arbitration Association

Applicable Procedures

Fast Track Unless the AAA in its discretion determines otherwise, the Fast Track Procedures shall be applied in any case where no party's disclosed claim or counterclaim exceeds $50,000, exclusive of claimed interest, arbitration fees and costs. Parties are encouraged to agree to the Fast Track Procedures in cases involving more than $50,000. The Procedures will not be applied, absent agreement by the parties, in cases in which there is no disclosed monetary claim, or in any multi-party case.

The Fast Track Procedures shall be applied as described in Sections F-1 through F-13 of these rules, in addition to any other portion of these rules that is not in conflict with the Fast Track Procedures.

Large, Complex Case Track Unless all parties agree otherwise, the Procedures for Large, Complex Construction Cases set forth in Sections L-1 through L-6 of these rules shall apply to all cases administered by the American Arbitration Association under these rules in which the claim or counterclaim of any party is at least $1,000,000 exclusive of claimed interest and arbitration costs and fees. Parties may also agree to use the Procedures in cases involving claims under $1,000,000, or in cases with undetermined or non-monetary claims. The Large, Complex Construction Case Procedures shall be applied as described in Sections L-1 through L-6 of these Rules, in addition

to any other portion of these rules that are not in conflict with the Large, Complex Construction Case Procedures.

Regular Track Cases All other cases shall be administered in accordance with Sections R-1 through R-53 of these rules.

Fast Track

F-1. Applicability
Unless the parties or the AAA determine otherwise, these procedures shall apply in any case in which no party's total disclosed claim or counterclaim exceeds $50,000, exclusive of claimed interest, and arbitration fees and costs. Parties are encouraged to agree to use these procedures in cases involving more than $50,000. The procedures will not be applied, absent agreement by the parties, in cases in which there is no disclosed monetary claim or in any multi-party case. The fast track rules shall be applied as described herein, in addition to any other portion of the "regular track" rules that are not in conflict.

F-2. Limitation on Extensions
In the absence of extraordinary circumstances, the AAA may grant a party no more than one seven-day extension of the time in which to respond to the demand for arbitration or counterclaim as provided in Section F-5. In extraordinary instances, the AAA or the arbitrator may grant an additional extension.

F-3. Changes of Claim or Counterclaim
A claim or counterclaim may be increased in amount upon the agreement of the other party, or the consent of the arbitrator. No new or different claim

may be submitted, however, once the time for filing an answer has expired.

If an increased claim or counterclaim exceeds $50,000, the case will be transferred to the Regular Track unless: 1) the party with the claim or counter-claim exceeding $50,000 agrees to waive any award exceeding that amount; or 2) all parties and the arbitrator agree that the case may remain in the Fast Track.

F 4. Communication of Notices

The parties shall accept all notices from the AAA by mail, overnight delivery, telephone or electronic facsimile ("fax"). Such notices by the AAA shall subsequently be confirmed in writing to the parties. Should there be a failure to confirm in writing any notice hereunder, the proceeding shall nonetheless be valid if notice has, in fact, been given by telephone. Where all parties and the arbitrator agree, notices may be transmitted by electronic mail ("Email"), or other method of communication.

F-5. Appointment and Qualification of Arbitrator

Immediately after the filing of (a) the submission or (b) the answering statement or the expiration of the time within which the answering statement is to be filed, the AAA will transmit to the parties a listing and biographical information from its roster of arbitrators knowledgeable in construction who are available for service in Fast Track cases. The parties are encouraged to agree to an arbitrator from this roster, and to advise the Association of their agreement, or any factual objections to any of the listed arbitrators, within seven (7) days of the AAA's transmission of the roster. The AAA will appoint the agreed-upon arbitrator, or in the event the parties cannot agree on an arbitrator, will designate the arbitrator from among those names not stricken for factual objections.

The parties will be given notice by the AAA of the appointment of the arbitrator, who shall be subject to disqualification for the reasons specified in Section R-19 of the Regular Track portion of these rules. Within the time period established by the AAA, the parties shall notify the AAA of any objection to the arbitrator appointed. Any objection by a party to the arbitrator shall be for cause and shall be confirmed in writing to the AAA with a copy to the other party or parties.

F-6. Preliminary Telephone Conference

Unless otherwise agreed by the parties and the arbitrator, as promptly as practicable after the appointment of the arbitrator, a preliminary telephone conference shall be held among the parties or their attorneys or representatives, and the arbitrator.

F-7. Exchange of Exhibits

At least two business days prior to the hearing, the parties shall exchange copies of all exhibits they intend to submit at the hearing. The arbitrator is authorized to resolve any disputes concerning the exchange of exhibits.

F-8. Discovery

There shall be no discovery, except as provided in Section F-7 or as ordered by the arbitrator in extraordinary cases when the demands of justice require it.

F-9. Date, Time, and Place of Hearing

Where no party's claim exceeds $10,000, exclusive of claimed interest and arbitration fees and costs, the dispute shall be resolved by submission of documents, unless any party requests an oral hearing, or the arbitrator determines that an oral hearing is necessary. The arbitrator shall establish a fair and equitable procedure for the submission of documents.

In all other cases, unless the parties agree otherwise, there shall be a hearing. The arbitrator shall set the date, time, and place of the hearing, which shall be scheduled to take place within thirty days of confirmation of the arbitrator's appointment. The AAA will notify the parties in advance of the hearing date. A formal notice of hearing will also be sent by the AAA to the parties.

F-10. The Hearing

Generally, the hearing shall not exceed one day. Unless the arbitrator determines otherwise, each party shall have equal opportunity to submit its proofs and complete its case. The arbitrator shall determine the order of the hearing, and may require further submission of documents within two days after the hearing. For good cause shown, the arbitrator may schedule one additional hearing day within seven business days after the initial day of hearing.

Generally, there will be no stenographic record. Any party desiring a stenographic record shall make arrangements directly with a stenographer, and shall notify the other party of these arrangements in advance of the hearing. A copy shall be made available for inspection by the other party and the arbitrator, at the expense of the ordering party

F-11. Time of Award

Unless otherwise agreed by the parties, the award shall be rendered not later than seven calendar days from the date of the closing of the hearing.

F-12. Time Standards

The arbitration shall be completed by settlement or award within sixty (60) days of confirmation of the arbitrator's appointment, unless all parties and the arbitrator agree otherwise or the arbitrator extends this time in extraordinary cases when the demands of justice require it. The Association may relax these time standards in the event the parties submit their dispute to mediation.

F-13. Arbitrator's Compensation

Arbitrators will receive compensation at a per case rate to be suggested by the AAA regional office administering the case, except for cases in which no party's disclosed claim exceeds $10,000. In such cases, arbitrators will customarily serve for one day of hearing without such compensation.

Regular Track

R-1. Agreement of Parties

The parties shall be deemed to have made these rules a part of their arbitration agreement whenever they have provided for arbitration by the American Arbitration Association (hereinafter AAA) or under its construction Industry Arbitration Rules. These rules and any amendment of them shall apply in the form obtaining at the time the demand for arbitration or submission agreement is received by the AAA. The parties, by written agreement, may vary the procedures set forth in these rules.

R-2. Name of Tribunal

Any tribunal constituted by the parties for the settlement of their dispute under these rules shall be called the Construction Industry Arbitration Tribunal.

R-3. Administrator and Delegation of Duties

When parties agree to arbitrate under these rules, or when they provide for arbitration by the AAA and an arbitration is initiated under these rules, they thereby authorize the AAA to administer the arbitration. The authority and duties of the AAA are prescribed in the agreement of the parties and in these rules, and may be carried out through such of the AAA's representatives as it may direct.

R-4. National Roster of Neutrals

In cooperation with the National Construction Industry Dispute Resolution Committee, the AAA shall establish and maintain a National Roster of Construction Industry Neutrals and shall appoint arbitrators as provided in these rules.

R-5. Regional Offices

The ASWA may, in its discretion, assign the administration of an arbitration to any of its regional offices.

R-6. Initiation under an Arbitration Provision in a Contract

Arbitration under an arbitration provision in a contract shall be initiated in the following manner.

(a) The initiating party (hereinafter claimant) shall, within the time period, if any, specified in the contract(s), give written notice to the other party (hereinafter respondent) of its intention to arbitrate (demand), which notice shall contain a statement setting forth the nature of the dispute, the amount involved, if any, the remedy sought, and the hearing locale requested, and

(b) shall file at any regional office of the AAA two copies of the notice and two copies of the arbitration provisions of the contract, together with the appropriate filing fee as provided in the schedule of administrative fees.

The AAA shall give notice of such filing to the respondent or respondents. A respondent may file an answering statement in duplicate with the AAA within ten days after notice from the AAA, in which event the respondent shall at the same time send a copy of the answering statement to the claimant. If a counterclaim is asserted, it shall contain a statement setting forth the nature of the counterclaim, the amount involved, if any, and the remedy sought. If a counterclaim is made, the appropriate fee shall be forwarded to the AAA with the answering statement. If no answering statement is filed within the stated time, it will be treated as a denial of the claim. Failure to file an answering statement shall not operate to delay the arbitration.

R-7. Initiation under a Submission

Parties to any existing dispute may commence an arbitration under these rules by filing at any regional office of the AAA two copies of a written submission to arbitrate under these rules, signed by the parties. It shall contain a statement of the matter in dispute, the amount involved, if any, the remedy sought, and the hearing locale requested, together with the appropriate filing fee as provided in the schedule of administrative fees.

R-8. Changes of Claim

A party may at any time prior to the close of the hearing increase or decrease the amount of its claim or counterclaim. Any new or different claim or counterclaim, as opposed to an increase or decrease in the amount of a pending claim or counterclaim, shall be made in writing and filed with the AAA, and a copy shall be mailed to the other party, who shall have a period of ten days from the date of such mailing within which to file an answer with the AAA. After the arbitrator is appointed no new or different claim or counterclaim may be submitted to that arbitrator except with the arbitrator's consent.

R-9. Administrative Conference, Preliminary Hearing, and Mediation Conference

At the request of any party or at the discretion of the AAA, an administrative conference with the AAA and the parties and/or their representatives will be scheduled in appropriate cases to expedite the arbitration proceedings.

At the request of any party or at the discretion of the arbitrator or the AAA, a preliminary hearing with the parties and/or their representatives and the arbitrator may be scheduled by the arbitrator to specify the issues to be resolved, to stipulate to uncontested facts, to establish a schedule for hearings to resolve the dispute, and to consider any other matters that will expedite the arbitration proceedings.

With the consent of the parties, the AAA at any stage of the proceeding may arrange a mediation conference under the Construction Industry Mediation Rules, in order to facilitate settlement. The mediator shall not be an arbitrator appointed to the case. Where the parties to a pending arbitration agree to mediate under the AAA's rules, no additional administrative fee is required to initiate the mediation.

R-10. Exchange of Information

Consistent with the expedited nature of arbitration, the arbitrator may direct (i) the production of documents and other information, and (ii) the identification of any witnesses to be called. At least two business days prior to the hearing, the parties shall exchange copies of all exhibits they intend to submit at the hearing. The arbitrator is authorized to resolve any disputes concerning the exchange of information.

R-11. Fixing of Locale

The parties may mutually agree on the locale where the arbitration is to be held. If any party requests that the hearing be held in a specific locale and the other party files no objection thereto within ten days after notice of the request has been sent to it by the AAA, the locale shall be the one requested. If a party objects to the locale requested by the other party, the AAA shall have the power to determine the locale and its decision shall be final and binding.

R-12. Qualifications of an Arbitrator

Any neutral arbitrator appointed pursuant to Section R-13, R-14, R-15, F-5, or L-3, or selected by mutual choice of the parties or their appointees, shall be subject to disqualification for the reasons specified in Section R-19. If the parties' specifically so agree in writing, the arbitrator shall not be subject to disqualification for those reasons.

Unless the parties agree otherwise, an arbitrator selected unilaterally by one party is a party-appointed arbitrator and is not subject to disqualification pursuant to Section R-19.

The term "arbitrator" in these rules refers to the arbitration Roster of Neutrals, whether composed of one or more arbitrators and whether the arbitrators are neutral or party appointed.

R-13. Appointment from Roster

If the parties have not appointed an arbitrator and have not provided any other method of appointment, the arbitrator shall be appointed in the following manner: immediately after the filing of (a) the submission or (b) the answering statement or the expiration of the time within which the answering statement is to be filed, the AAA shall send simultaneously to each party to t]he dispute an identical list of names of persons chosen from the Roster of Neutrals.

Each party to the dispute shall have ten days from the transmittal date in which to strike names objected to, number the remaining names in order of preference, and return the list to the AAA. In a single-arbitrator case, each party may strike three names on a peremptory basis. In a multi-arbitrator case, each party may strike five names on a per-emptory basis. If a party does not return the list within the time specified, all persons named therein shall be deemed acceptable. From among the persons who have been approved on both lists, and in accordance with the designated order of mutual preference, the AAA shall invite the acceptance of an arbitrator to serve. If the parties fail to agree on any of the persons named, or if acceptable arbitrators are unable to act, or if for any other reason the appointment cannot be made from the submitted lists, the AAA shall have the power to make the appointment from among other members of the Roster of Neutrals without the submission of additional lists.

R-14. Direct Appointment by a Party

If the agreement of the parties names an arbitrator or specifies a method of appointing an arbitrator, that designation or method shall be followed. The notice of appointment, with the name and address of the arbitrator, shall be filed with the AAA by the appointing party. Upon the request of any appointing party, the AAA shall submit a list of members of the Roster of Neutrals from which the party may, if it so desires, make the appointment.

If the agreement specifies a period of time within which an arbitrator shall be appointed and any party fails to make the appointment within that period, the AAA shall make the appointment.

If no period of time is specified in the agreement, the AAA shall notify the party to make the appointment. If within ten days thereafter an arbitrator has not been appointed by a party, the AAA shall make the appointment.

R-15. Appointment of Neutral Arbitrator by Party-Appointed Arbitrators or Parties

If the parties have selected party-appointed arbitrators, or if such arbitrators have been appointed as provided in Section R-14, and the parties have authorized them to appoint a neutral arbitrator within a specified time and no appointment is made within that time or any agreed extension, the AAA may appoint a neutral arbitrator, who shall act as chairperson.

If no period of time is specified for appointment of the neutral arbitrator and the party-appointed arbitrators or the parties do not make the appointment within ten days from the date of the appointment of the last party-appointed arbitrator, the AAA may appoint the neutral arbitrator, who shall act as chairperson.

If the parties have agreed that their party-appointed arbitrators shall appoint the neutral arbitrator from the roster, the AAA shall furnish to the party-appointed arbitrators, in the manner provided in Section R-13, a list selected from the roster, and the appointment of the neutral arbitrator shall be made as provided in that section.

R-16. Nationality of Arbitrator in International Arbitration

Where the parties are nationals or residents of different countries, any neutral arbitrator shall, upon the request of either party, be appointed from among the nationals of a country other than that of any of the parties. The request must be made prior to the time set for the appointment of the arbitrator as agreed by the parties or set by these rules.

R-17. Number of Arbitrators

If the arbitration agreement does not specify the number of arbitrators, the dispute shall be heard and determined by one arbitrator, unless the AAA, in its discretion, directs that a greater number of arbitrators be appointed.

R-18. Notice to Arbitrator of Appointment

Notice of the appointment of the neutral arbitrator, whether appointed mutually by the parties or by the AAA, shall be sent to the arbitrator by the AAA, together with a copy of these rules, and the signed acceptance of the arbitrator shall be filed with the AAA prior to the opening of the first hearing.

R-19. Disclosure and Challenge Procedure

Any person appointed as neutral arbitrator shall disclose to the AAA any circumstance likely to affect impartiality, including any bias or any financial or personal interest in the result of the arbitration or any past or present relationship with the parties or their representatives. Upon receipt of such information from the arbitrator or another source, the AAA shall communicate the information to the parties and, if it deems it appropriate to do so, to the arbitrator and others. Upon objection of a party to the continued service of a neutral arbitrator, the AAA shall determine whether the arbitrator should be disqualified and shall inform the parties of its decision, which shall be conclusive.

R-20. Vacancies

If for any reason an arbitrator is unable to perform the duties of the office, the AAA may, on proof satisfactory to it, declare the office vacant. Vacancies shall be filled in accordance with the applicable provisions of these rules.

In the event of a vacancy in a roster of neutral arbitrators after the hearings have commenced, the remaining arbitrator or arbitrators may continue with the hearing and determination of the controversy, unless the parties agree otherwise.

R-21. Date, Time, and Place of Hearing

The arbitrator shall set the date time, and place for each hearing. The AAA shall send a notice of hearing to the parties at least ten days in advance of the hearing date, unless otherwise agreed by the parties.

R-22. Representation

Any party may be represented by counsel or other authorized representative. A party intending to be so represented shall notify the other party and the AAA of the name and address of the representative at least three days prior to the date set for the hearing at which that person is first to appear. When such a representative initiates an arbitration or responds for a party, notice is deemed to have been given.

R-23. Stenographic Record

Any party desiring a stenographic record shall make arrangements directly with a stenographer and shall notify the other parties of these arrangements in advance of the hearing. The requesting party or parties shall pay the cost of the record. If the transcript is agreed by the parties to be or determined by the arbitrator to be, the official record of the proceeding, it must be made available to the arbitrator and to the other parties for inspection, at a date, time, and place determined by the arbitrator.

R-24. Interpreters

Any party wishing an interpreter shall make all arrangements directly with the interpreter and shall assume the costs of the service.

R-25. Attendance at Hearings

The arbitrator shall maintain the privacy of the hearings unless the law provides to the contrary. Any person having a direct interest in the arbitration is entitled to attend hearings. The arbitrator shall otherwise have the power to require the exclusion of any witness, other than a party or other essential person, during the testimony of any other witness. It shall be discretionary with the arbitrator to determine the propriety of the attendance of any other person.

R-26. Postponements

The arbitrator for good cause shown may postpone any hearing upon the request of a party or upon the agreement of all parties, or upon the arbitrator's own initiative.

R-27. Oaths

Before proceeding with the first hearing, each arbitrator may take an oath of office and, if required by law, shall do so. The arbitrator may require witnesses to testify under oath administered by any duly qualified person and, if it is required by law or requested by any party, shall do so.

R-28. Majority Decision

All decisions of the arbitrators must be by a majority. The award must also be made by a majority unless the concurrence of all is expressly required by the arbitration agreement or by law.

R-29. Order of Proceedings and Communication with Arbitrator

A hearing shall be opened by the filing of the oath of the arbitrator.

The Claimant shall then present evidence to support its claim. The Respondent party shall then present evidence supporting its defense. Witnesses for each party shall submit to questions or other examination. The arbitrator has the discretion to vary this procedure and shall afford a full and equal opportunity to all parties to be heard. Exhibits, when offered by either party, may be received in evidence by the arbitrator.

The arbitrator shall control the proceedings with a view to expediting the resolution of the dispute. In order to expedite the proceedings the arbitrator may control the order of proof, bifurcate proceedings, exclude cumulative or irrelevant testimony or evidence, and direct the parties to focus the presentation of evidence on decisive issues. The arbitrator shall entertain motions, including motions that dispose of all or part of a claim, or that may expedite the proceedings, and may also make preliminary rulings and enter interlocutory orders.

There shall be no direct communication between the parties and a neutral arbitrator other than at the hearing, unless the parties and the arbitrator agree otherwise. Any other oral or written communication from the parties to the neutral arbitrator shall be directed to the AAA for transmittal to the arbitrator.

R-30. Arbitration in the Absence of a Party or Representative

Unless the law provides to the contrary, the arbitration may proceed in the absence of any party or representative who, after due notice, fails to be present or fails to obtain a postponement. An award shall not be made solely on the default of a party. The arbitrator shall require the party who is present to submit such evidence as the arbitrator may require for the making of an award.

R-31. Evidence

The parties may offer such evidence as is relevant and material to the dispute and shall produce such evidence as the arbitrator may deem necessary to an understanding and determination of the dispute. An arbitrator or other person authorized by law to subpoena witnesses or documents may do so upon the request of any party or independently.

The arbitrator shall be the judge of the relevance and materiality of the evidence offered, and conformity to legal rules of evidence shall not be necessary. The arbitrator may request offers of proof, and may reject evidence deemed by the arbitrator to be cumulative, unreliable, unnecessary, or of slight value compared to the time and expense involved. All evidence shall be taken in the presence of all of the arbitrators and all of the parties, except where: 1) any of the parties is absent, in default, or has waived the right to be present, or 2) the parties and the arbitrators agree otherwise.

R-32. Evidence by Affidavit and Posthearing Filing of Documents or Other Evidence

The arbitrator may receive and consider the evidence of witnesses by affidavit, but shall give it only such weight as the arbitrator deems it entitled to after consideration of any objection made to its admission.

If the parties agree or the arbitrator directs that documents or other evidence be submitted to the arbitrator after the hearing, the documents or other evidence, unless otherwise agreed by the parties and the arbitrator, shall be filed with the AAA for transmission to the arbitrator. All parties shall be afforded an opportunity to examine and respond to such documents or other evidence.

R-33. Inspection or Investigation

An arbitrator finding it necessary to make an inspection or investigation in connection with the arbitration shall advise the parties by notice transmitted at the hearing or through the AAA of the date and time. Any party who so desires may be present at such an inspection or investigation.

R-34. Interim Measures of Protection

(a) At the request of any party, the tribunal may take whatever interim measures it deems necessary with respect to the dispute, including measures for the conservation of property.

(b) Such interim measures may be taken in the form of an interim award should the tribunal may require security for the costs of such measures.

R-35. Closing of Hearing

When satisfied that the presentation of the parties is complete, the arbitrator shall declare the hearing closed.

If documents or a response are to be filed as provided in Section R-32, or if briefs are to be filed, the hearing shall be declared closed as at the final date set by the arbitrator for the receipt of documents, response, or briefs. The time limit within which the arbitrator is required to make the award shall commence to run, in the absence of other agreements by the parties and the arbitrator, upon the closing of the hearing.

R-36. Reopening of Hearing

The hearing may be reopened on the arbitrator's initiative, or by direction of the arbitrator upon application of a party, at any time before the award is made. If reopening the hearing would prevent the making of the award within the specific time agreed to by the parties in the arbitration agreement, the matter may not be reopened unless the parties agree to an extension of time. When no specific date is fixed by agreement of the parties, the arbitrator shall have thirty days from the closing of the reopened hearing within which to make an award.

R-37. Waiver of Oral Hearing

The parties may provide, by written agreement, for the waiver of oral hearings. If the parties agree to waive oral hearings after the appointment of the arbitrator, the consent of the arbitrator must be obtained

R-38. Waiver of Rules

Any party who proceeds with the arbitration after knowledge that any provision or requirement of these rules has not been complied with and who fails to state an objection in writing shall be deemed to have waived the right to object.

R-39. Extensions of Time

The parties may modify any period of time by mutual agreement. The AAA or the arbitrator may for good cause extend any period of time established by these rules, except the time for making the award. The AAA shall notify the parties of any extension.

R-40. Serving of Notice

Each party shall be deemed to have consented that any papers, notices, or process necessary or proper for the initiation or continuation of an arbitration under these rules; for any court action in connection therewith; or for the entry of judgment on any award made under these rules, may be served on a party by mail addressed to the party or its representative at the last known address or by personal service, in or outside the state where the arbitration is to be held, provided that reasonable opportunity to be heard with regard thereto has been granted to the party.

The AAA and the parties may also use facsimile transmission, telex, telegram, or other written forms of electronic communication to give the notices required by these rules. Where all parties and the arbitrator agree, notices may be transmitted by electronic mail ("E-mail"), or other method of communication.

R-41. Time of Award

The award shall be made promptly by the arbitrator and, unless otherwise agreed by the parties or specified by law, no later than thirty days from the date of closing the hearing, or, if oral hearings have been waived, from the date of the AAA's transmittal of the final statements and proofs to the arbitrator

R 42. Form of Award

The award shall be in writing and shall be signed by a majority of the arbitrators. It shall be executed in the manner required by law. The arbitrator shall provide a concise, written breakdown of the award. If requested in writing by all parties prior to the appointment of the arbitrator, or if the arbitrator believes it is appropriate to do so, the arbitrator shall provide a written explanation of the award.

R-43. Scope of Award

The arbitrator may grant any remedy or relief, including equitable relief, that the arbitrator deems just and equitable and within the scope of the agreement of the parties. The arbitrator shall, in the award, assess arbitration fees, expenses, and compensation as provided in Sections R-49, R-50, and R-51 in favor of any party and, in the event that any administrative fees or expenses are due the AAA, in favor of the AAA.

R-44. Modification of Award

Within twenty (20) days after the transmittal of an award, any party, upon notice to the other parties, may request the arbitrator to correct any clerical, typographical, technical or computational errors in the award. The arbitrator is not empowered to redetermine the merits of any claim already decided.

The other parties shall be given ten (10) days to respond to the request. The arbitrator shall dispose of the request within twenty (20) days after transmittal by the AAA to the arbitrator of the request and any response thereto.

If applicable law provides a different procedural time frame, that procedure shall be followed.

R-45. Award upon Settlement

If the parties settle their dispute during the course of the arbitration, the arbitrator may set forth the terms of the agreed settlement in an award. Such an award is referred to as a consent award.

R-46. Delivery of Award to Parties

Parties shall accept as legal delivery of the award the placing of the award or a true copy thereof in the mail addressed to a party or its representative at the last known address, personal service of the award, or the filing of the award in any other manner that is permitted by law.

R-47. Release of Documents for Judicial Proceedings

The AAA shall, upon the written request of a party, furnish to the party, at its expense, certified copies of any papers in the AAA's possession that may be required in judicial proceedings relating to the arbitration.

R-48. Applications to Court and Exclusion of Liability

(a) No judicial proceeding by a party relating to the subject matter of the arbitration shall be deemed a waiver of the party's right to arbitrate.

(b) Neither the AAA nor any arbitrator in a proceeding under these rules is a necessary party in judicial proceedings relating to the arbitration.

(c) Parties to these rules shall be deemed to have consented that judgment upon the arbitration award may be entered in any federal or state court having jurisdiction thereof.

(d) Neither the AAA nor any arbitrator shall be liable to any party for any act or omission in connection with any arbitration conducted under these rules.

R-49. Administrative Fees

As a not-for-profit organization, the AAA shall prescribe filing and other administrative fees and service charges to compensate it for the cost of providing administrative services. The fees in effect when the fee or charge is incurred shall be applicable.

The filing fee shall be advanced by the initiating party or parties, subject to final apportionment by the arbitrator in the award.

The AAA may, in the event of extreme hardship on the part of any party, defer or reduce the administrative fees.

R-50. Expenses

The expenses of witnesses for either side shall be paid by the party producing such witnesses. All other expenses of the arbitration, including required travel and other expenses of the arbitrator, AAA representatives, and any witness and the cost of any proof produced at the direct request of the arbitrator, shall be borne equally by the parties, unless they agree otherwise or unless the arbitrator in the award assesses such expenses or any part thereof against any specified party or parties.

R-51. Neutral Arbitrator's Compensation

Arbitrators shall charge a rate consistent with the arbitrator's stated rate of compensation, beginning with the first day of hearing.

If there is disagreement concerning the terms of compensation, an appropriate rate shall be established with the arbitrator by the Association and confirmed to the parties.

Any arrangement for the compensation of a neutral arbitrator shall be made through the AAA and not directly between the parties and the arbitrator.

R-52. Deposits

The AAA may require the parties to deposit in advance of any hearings such sums of money as it deems necessary to cover the expense of the arbitration, including the arbitrator's fee, if any, and shall render an accounting to the parties and return any unexpended balance at the conclusion of the case.

R-53. Interpretation and Application of Rules

The arbitrator shall interpret and apply these rules insofar as they relate to the arbitrator's powers and duties. When there is more than one arbitrator and a difference arises among them concerning the meaning or application of these rules, it shall be decided by a majority vote. If that is not possible, either an arbitrator or a party may refer the question to the AAA for final decision. All other rules shall be interpreted and applied by the AAA.

Large, Complex Construction Case Track

L-1. Applicability

(a) Unless the parties agree otherwise, these Procedures for Large, Complex Construction Cases (hereinafter "Procedures") shall apply to all cases administered by the AAA under the Construction Industry Arbitration Rules in which the disclosed claim or counterclaim of any party is at least $1,000,000 exclusive of claimed interest, and arbitration fees and costs. Parties may also agree to using these Procedures in cases involving claims or counterclaims under $1,000,000, or in non-monetary cases or in cases involving claims of undetermined amount. These Procedures are designed to complement the "Regular Track" of these rules. To the extent that there is any variance between such rules and these Procedures, the Procedures shall control. Any such cases are herein referred to as "Large, Complex Construction Cases."

(b) The parties to any arbitration proceeding that is to be subject to the Procedures may, prior to the appointment of the arbitrator(s) and by consent of all parties, agree to eliminate, modify or alter any of these Procedures, and, in such case, these Procedures as so modified or altered shall apply to that particular case.

After appointment of the arbitrator(s), such modifications may be made only with the consent of the arbitrators.

L-2. Administrative Conference

Prior to the dissemination of a list of potential arbitrators, the AAA shall, unless it determines same to be unnecessary, conduct an administrative conference with the parties or their attorneys or other representatives, either in person or by conference call, at the discretion of the AAA. Such administrative conference shall be conducted for the following purposes and for such additional purposes as the parties or the AAA may deem appropriate:

(a) to obtain additional information about the nature and magnitude of the dispute and the anticipated length of hearing and scheduling;

(b) to discuss the views of the parties about the technical and other qualifications of the arbitrators;
(c) to obtain conflicts statements from the parties; and

(d) to consider, with the parties, whether mediation or other non-adjudicative methods of dispute resolution might be appropriate.

L-3. Arbitrators

(a) Large, Complex Construction Cases shall be heard and determined by either one or three arbitrators, as may be agreed upon by the parties. If the parties are unable to agree upon the number of arbitrators, then three arbitrators shall hear and determine the case.

(b) The AAA shall appoint arbitrators as agreed by the parties. If they are unable to agree on a method of appointment, the AAA shall appoint arbitrators from the Large, Complex Construction Case Roster, in the manner provided in the Regular Track portion of these rules.

L-4. Preliminary Hearing

As promptly as practicable after the selection of the arbitrators, a preliminary hearing shall be held among the parties or their attorneys or other representatives and the arbitrator(s). With the consent of the arbitrator(s) and the parties, the preliminary hearing may: (a)

be conducted by the Chair of the roster rather than all the arbitrators; (b) be conducted by telephone conference call rather than in person; or (c) be omitted.

At the preliminary hearing the matters to be considered shall include, without limitation: (a) service of a detailed statement of claims, damages; and defenses, a statement of the issues asserted by each party and positions with respect thereto, and any legal authorities the parties may wish to bring to the attention of the arbitrators; (b) stipulations to uncontested facts; (c) the extent to which discovery shall be conducted; (d) exchange and pre-marking of those documents which each party believes may be offered at the hearing; (e) the identification and availability of witnesses, including experts, and such matters with respect to witnesses including their biographies and expected testimony as may be appropriate; (f) whether, and the extent to which, any sworn statements and/or depositions may be introduced; (g) the extent to which hearings will proceed on consecutive days; (h) whether a stenographic or other official record of the proceedings shall be maintained; and (i) the possibility of utilizing mediation or other nonadjudicative methods of dispute resolution.

L-5. Management of Proceedings

(a) Arbitrators shall take such steps as they may deem necessary or desirable to avoid delay and to achieve a just, speedy and cost-effective resolution of Large, Complex Construction Cases.

(b) Parties shall cooperate in the exchange of documents, exhibits and information within such party's control if the arbitrators consider such production to be consistent with the goal of achieving a just, speedy and cost-effective resolution of a Large, Complex

Construction Case. The parties may conduct such document discovery as may be agreed to by all the parties provided, however, that the arbitrators may place such limitations on the conduct of such discovery as the arbitrators shall deem appropriate. If the parties cannot agree on document discovery, the arbitrators, for good cause shown and consistent with the expedited nature of arbitration. may establish the extent of same.

(c) The arbitrators upon good cause shown may order the conduct of the deposition of, or the propounding of interrogatories to, such persons who may possess information determined by the arbitrators to be necessary to a determination of a Large, Complex Construction Case.

(d) Generally, hearings will be scheduled on consecutive days or in blocks of consecutive days in order to maximize efficiency and minimize costs.

(e) The arbitrators may direct the recording of the hearings, the cost of which shall be borne equally by the parties.

L-6. Interest, Fees and Costs

The award of the arbitrators may include: (a) interest at such rate and from such date as the arbitrators may deem appropriate; (b) an apportionment between the parties of all or part of the fees and expenses of the AAA and the compensation and expenses of the arbitrators; and (c) an award of attorneys' fees if all parties have requested such an award or it is authorized by law or their arbitration agreement.

Select Bibliography

Select Bibliography

Brown, H.J., & Marriott, A.L. *ADR Principles and Practice* Sweet & Maxwell, London, 1993.

Craig, W.L., Park, W.W. & Paulsson, J. *International Chamber of Commerce Arbitration 2nd Edition*, Oceana, New York, 1990.

Hunter, M., Marriott, A.L. & Veeder, V.V. (Eds.) *The Internationalistaion of International Arbitration* The LCIA Centenary Conference, Graham & Trotman/Martinus Nijhoff, London, 1995.

Mcneil, I.R. *American Arbitration Law*, Oxford 1992.

Macneil, I.R., Speidel, R.E. & Stipanowich, T.J. *Federal Arbitration Law: Agreements, Awards and Remedies under the Federal Arbitration Act*, Little, Brown and Company, Boston, 1995.

Mustill, M.J. & Boyd, S. *Commercial Arbitration 2nd Edition*, Butterworths, London 1989.

Odams, A.M.(Ed.) *Comparative Studies in Construction Law: The Sweet Lectures*, Construction Law Press, London, 1995.

Redfern, A. & Hunter, M. *Law and Practice of International Commercial Arbitration 2nd Edition*, Sweet & Maxwell, London, 1991.

Rose, F.D. (Ed.) *International Commercial and Maritime Arbitration*, Sweet & Maxwell, London, 19 .

Sanders, P. (Ed.) *International Arbitration: Liber Amicorum for Martin Domke*, Martinus Nijhoff, The Hague, 1967.

Uff, J. & Jones, E. (Eds)   *International and ICC Arbitration,* Centre of Construction Law & Management, King's College London, 1990.

Uff, J. & Odams, A.M. (Eds)   *Risk, Management and Procurement in Construction,* Centre of Construction Law & Management, King's College London, 1995.

Index

Index

A

B

C

F

G

L

M

N

P

R